LEFT

INTELLECTUALS

AND

POPULAR CULTURE

IN

TWENTIETH-CENTURY

AMERICA

The
University
of North
Carolina
Press
Chapel Hill
&
London

Left INTELLECTUALS

&Popular CULTURE

in Twentieth-Century America

PAUL R. GORMAN

© 1996
The University of
North Carolina Press
All rights reserved
Manufactured in
the United States
of America

The paper in
this book meets the
guidelines for perma-
nence and durability
of the Committee on
Production Guidelines
for Book Longevity of
the Council on Library
Resources.

Library of Congress
Cataloging-in-Publication Data
Gorman, Paul R.
Left intellectuals and popular culture in
twentieth-century America / by Paul R.
Gorman.
p.   cm.
Includes bibliographical references and
index.
ISBN 0-8078-2248-5 (cloth : alk. paper).
— ISBN 0-8078-4556-6 (pbk. : alk. paper)
1. United States—Intellectual life—20th
century.   2. Popular culture—United
States—History—20th century.
3. Intellectuals—United States—
History—20th century.
4. Radicalism—United States—
History—20th century.
5. Liberalism—United States—
History—20th century.   6. Criticism—
United States—History—20th century.
I. Title.
E169.I.G677   1996
973.9—dc20   95-14387
                          CIP

00   99   98   97   96   5   4   3   2   1

For my parents, BOB & ELLEN GORMAN

CONTENTS

Acknowledgments, *xi*

Introduction: The Specter of Mass Culture, *1*

1 Defending the Old Order, *13*

2 Healthy Recreation versus "Exploiting Pleasure"

   in the Progressive Era, *34*

3 Modernism, Cultural Radicals, and Mass Entertainments, *53*

4 Social Scientists and "Deviant" Entertainments, *83*

5 American Communism and Popular Entertainments, *108*

6 The Cosmopolitan Intellectual Critique: *Partisan Review*, *137*

7 Dwight Macdonald and the Culmination of the

   Mass Culture Critique, *158*

Epilogue: The Critique under Fire, *186*

Notes, *193*

Select Bibliography, *225*

Index, *235*

ILLUSTRATIONS

"Pulp" magazine covers, 1954, *3*

New York City newsstand, 1903, *16*

Title page of Rollin Hartt's *The People at Play*, 1909, *18*

Cartoon attacking the sensationalism of popular

   "yellow" journalism, 1898, *27*

Stimulating city life, Buffalo, New York, 1905, *46*

Title page of the *Little Review*, 1917, *66*

Illustration from *The Seven Lively Arts*, depicting

   the popular artists Seldes championed, 1924, *79*

Popular motion picture theater, Chicago, 1927, *92*

The ubiquitous American automobile, Omaha, Nebraska, 1938, *100*

Communist Party headquarters, New York City, ca. 1934, *111*

Omaha, Nebraska, newsstand, 1938, *127*

Norman Rockwell, "New Television Antenna," 1949, *155*

Dwight Macdonald, 1940s, *160*

Drive-in movie audience, 1950s, *175*

ACKNOWLEDGMENTS

I owe many debts of thanks, some long overdue, to those who have lent help and support to this project. My study began as a doctoral dissertation at the University of California, Berkeley, under Lawrence W. Levine. Larry, in his wisdom, gave me the freedom to struggle through my early, muddled ideas and then sharpened my emerging interpretation with his unmatched perspective on American culture. James N. Gregory offered excellent editorial suggestions and much-needed moral support, and Michael P. Rogin was both a font of fascinating ideas and a model of tolerance for views he does not share. A special thanks is due for Larry and Cornelia Levine's gracious hospitality in hosting our dissertation group at Berkeley. The group provided the ideal environment for a first-time author: sympathetic readers, searching critics, and fun-loving friends.

I am grateful to those who read and helped me improve my final draft. Daniel Horowitz and Roland Marchand offered many important suggestions, and Professor Horowitz's generous, careful attention to the manuscript especially honed my argument. I owe particular thanks to my friends and University of Alabama colleagues Lawrence F. Kohl and Richard B. Megraw. Larry and Rich did double duty: reading the work and providing important criticisms, and enduring the effects of the project on me (with much less criticism). Larry Kohl's artful prodding revived this project when it had begun to gather dust at Alabama, and, ultimately, his foresight helped keep me employed. Such great friends made the book possible.

I am indebted to the staff at The University of North Carolina Press for its efficiency and courtesy. I need especially to thank Executive Editor Lew Bateman for his care and attention to my work. Librarians Judith A. Schiff of Yale University and Eileen Flanagan of the Chicago Historical Society were helpful in my search for illustrations, as was the staff at the Robert F. Wagner Labor Archives, New York University.

Kathie became my wife during the last revisions of this manuscript and selflessly joined in its labor. She gave me invaluable practical help, but, most important, her caring and good humor saw the project through. I thank all my family for their patience and encouragement. My greatest debt is to my parents, Bob and Ellen Gorman, for their love, support, and wisdom. I dedicate the book to them.

LEFT

INTELLECTUALS

AND

POPULAR CULTURE

IN

TWENTIETH-CENTURY

AMERICA

In 1988, the federal Department of Education published a study designed to reach a definitive judgment about whether television watching was harmful to children. The investigators sorted through scores of analyses that had been produced over decades to try to determine what findings about the medium were most reliable. Once the survey was complete, however, they were no closer to a clear answer. What they found instead was that this body of research revealed more about the analysts of television than about their subject. The authors of the study were less convinced of the noxious effects of television claimed by many of the researchers than that there was an obvious bias in their work. Flawed or sloppy methods and unreliable evidence marred a number of the analyses. More important, the study found that most of the research had been designed to support the foreordained conclusion that television was necessarily dangerous.

Such an insistent indictment of the nation's most popular entertainment betrays an assumption about the mass arts that has prevailed among America's intellectuals over the past century. As one author of the report put it, beliefs about the harmfulness of television "seem to satisfy some kind of need among educated people." He described this practice of ascribing malign effects, based on scant evidence, as "almost an American mythology." Negative preconceptions about the medium became more accepted the more times they were repeated.[1]

This kind of prejudice has extended well beyond television. TV bashing is only the most recent expression of a general bias against mass entertainments that has been held by American intellectuals in the modern era. The nature and sources of that bias are the subject of this book.

Since the late nineteenth century, intellectuals in the United States have mounted a consistent criticism of the mass arts. The critics have included purveyors of ideas from academia, politics, and the arts and letters. They have charged that entertainments ranging from popular theater, motion pictures, and dance halls to hit records, romance novels, and television are harmful to the public. This criticism has often overlapped with an older distrust of local ethnic or working-class amusements and with religious proscriptions against certain recreations. But the blanket condemnations of mainstream, broadly popular entertainments by twentieth-century critics mark the beginning of a significantly different body of thought. The full flower of the attacks came in the decade and a half after World War II, when hostility toward the entertainments became, in the words of one scholar, "de rigeur" for intellectuals.[2] The historian Ronald Edsforth has described how, during the early Cold War, "becoming a professor included learning how to dismiss popular culture, and how to discourage students from taking it seriously." English instructors in the late 1950s established a new section of the Modern Language Association to study mass culture and, in the words of their policy statement, "to learn what clearly separates the best-seller from the work of distinction, and . . . offer our students the necessary exercises in discrimination." The negative focus on the popular arts continued to grow among cultural critics in this period until the most influential group, the New York literary community, talked "obsessively" about mass culture, as Irving Howe has recalled. The criticisms became something of a national crusade in 1954 when the psychiatrist Fredric Wertham published *The Seduction of the Innocent*, linking the prevailing concerns about juvenile delinquency and disorder to the influence of comic books. For the next two years, the Senate Subcommittee to Investigate Juvenile Delinquency in the United States focused on mass-media entertainments as the primary cause of the nation's supposed plague of deranged youth.[3]

Another measure of the growing pervasiveness of popular arts criticism in America is the way it changed our vocabulary. Until the 1930s, there were few instances where the words "mass" and "culture" were used together in English. The phrase "mass culture" became part of common parlance only after World War II, and then, chiefly with a negative connotation. In such a brief span, "mass culture" had come to designate a system of popular leisure practices and arts that were considered wholly new to urban and industrial society. And the system was believed to be almost synonymous with social corruption and decay.[4]

The mass culture critique is still relevant today, as evidenced by condemnations of certain television programs and movies and increasing fears about the purported effects of rap or hip-hop music. Yet in recent decades there has also been a growing acceptance and even appreciation of popular culture in some American intellectual circles. Led especially by younger scholars who have matured in the age of mass entertainments, many cultural analysts have turned from simply condemning the mass arts to reading them as legiti-

"Pulp" magazine covers from 1954 show the depictions of sex, violence, and horror that captured American audiences in the postwar years and brought mass culture critics to predict moral cataclysm. (Wide World Photo, Library of Congress, LC-US262-90898)

mate expressions of Americans' tastes and values. The mass culture critique remains important even in these new sympathetic understandings, though. Because the critique has wielded such influence, many students of the popular arts feel the need to refute its charges directly. Efforts to establish a more positive view of mass entertainments also continue to clash with the critique as academics debate their curricula. On one hand, when educators choose which of the expressions of the diverse cultures of America, or the world, to study, many find the most commonly shared forms—mass culture—are increasingly difficult to exclude. On the other, the critique encourages all who are concerned with the matter of values to dismiss popular forms.

That mass culture criticisms should exist in modern society is certainly not surprising. Condemnations of the popular arts and entertainments in Western culture date from at least ancient Greece and Rome. In those classical civilizations the provision of "bread and circuses" was cited, much like modern entertainments, both as a cause of social decline and evidence of its advance. The historian Patrick Brantlinger has shown that mass culture, defined broadly as the cultural effects of democracy and economic advance, has been equated with social decay through the centuries based on two related themes. The first criticizes popular culture by drawing parallels between the experiences of contemporary societies and the decline of imperial Rome. The second looks to classical societies for an ideal of social order and finds the subsequent growth of popular culture to be evidence of modern decadence.[5]

Brantlinger's analysis of these distinctly antimodern prophecies of decline raises a central question about the criticisms made by many modern American intellectuals. Even a casual survey of the general entertainment critique over the first sixty years of the twentieth century shows that a majority of the critics came from the left and liberal side of the political-philosophical spectrum. This is readily understood considering the weakness of the political Right in the early twentieth century. But in this era of increasing democracy, how did these leftist critics who so often pronounced their allegiance to the "common" men and women reconcile that position with these notions of decadence?

Considering the philosophical outlook of most left-liberal thinkers, it again seems anomalous that they would be the leading proponents of mass culture criticism. With a few important exceptions, they have been the most optimistic of twentieth-century intellectuals. They would seem the least inclined to follow the theories of social decay or the collapse of civilization that Brantlinger has described. Few leftist American critics ever adopted the outlook of despair that affected many fin de siècle European writers and artists, for example. Even amid the tragedy of economic collapse in the 1930s, all but the fiercest of the critics maintained a faith in America's ability to right itself and create a desirable society. At the most elemental level of their social outlook, left-liberal intellectuals had been the most consistently optimistic about the character and abilities of the public in the twentieth century. Their general faith in the goodness of human nature and the citizens' potential to improve, if not perfect, their society stands out as seemingly inimical to the pessimism of the tradition of mass entertainment criticisms.[6]

The specific concern of this book, therefore, is to suggest why the intellectuals who would appear to be most empathetic to the experiences of the broad American public became the most consistent critics of the people's favorite arts, and how they handled these seemingly contradictory sympathies.

Some of the groundwork for this analysis has already been laid. Recent historical literature about popular culture, as well as studies of the critics themselves, has offered astute insights into the strictures against entertainments. Most of the work has centered on two periods. For the first, from the 1890s to the 1920s, scholars have detailed the growth of entertainments such as amusement parks, motion pictures, dance halls, popular music, and other urban nightlife and have explained their role in breaking up the Victorian moral and cultural synthesis. Though only a few of these studies have been expressly concerned with understanding the criticism of mass culture, many have provided glimpses into its sources as they explain the social effects of the amusements. They have clearly established that popular culture forms drew opprobrium from a variety of defenders of older standards of behavior and art and from reformers interested in controlling or mediating the influence of the new cultural communications.[7]

The work on the second era that has received particular attention—the latter 1930s through the 1950s—has focused more on the sources of mass culture criticism. It has traced the range of intellectuals' concerns about the mass arts through the dramatic changes that occurred from the Great Depression to the Cold War era and postwar prosperity. Entertainment condemnations have been explained as reactions to a number of circumstances or forces: the influential Communist line in the arts and letters of the 1930s, the rise of totalitarian systems, the emergence of an independent youth culture after the Second World War, and the effects of new mass media on cultural expression. One well-defined tack in several interpretations attributes left and liberal critics' contempt for entertainments to their desire to maintain an adversarial relationship with American society. They merely substituted cultural for political targets in these more dangerous times, the analysts contend. The sociologist Paul Lazarsfeld, in another explanation, attributes the criticism to liberal intellectuals' feeling that they had been "gypped" in their efforts at social betterment in the early century. All their struggles simply had not improved the masses' cultural tastes.[8]

These studies have been indispensable in forming our sense of modern cultural change. Yet, even taken together, they cannot explain the whole of the hostilities toward the popular arts. This inability results from most of the literature being focused on particular eras that have been singled out for their conspicuous evidence of changing values. When the mass culture charges are placed on a broader chronological scale, as part of the intellectual history of the whole twentieth century, for example, the cumulative impression is of a sporadic or episodic critique. The studies tend to portray the entertainment worries only as reactions to certain major social shifts or crises. The criticism has no doubt been more frequent or prominent in these periods. But because these studies ignore the interim eras, the episodic model misses the degree of consistency in the criticisms over the first half of the century. These chronic charges leveled against the mass arts likely reflect the core values of modern intellectuals as accurately as do their writings in the midst of particular crises.

Recent analysts of cultural thought have shown the value of this longer perspective on intellectuals' condemnations of the popular arts. Lawrence Levine and Paul Dimaggio have documented elitist efforts in the late nineteenth and early twentieth centuries to establish a hierarchy of expressive forms and regiment the presentation of the arts to the public. Their conception of the Gilded Age as a watershed in ideas about culture raises the idea that a set of common, evolved understandings shaped intellectuals' views of the popular arts throughout the first half of the twentieth century. My investigation begins with the turn of the century, when capitalism in its advanced stages produced a class of professional "brainworkers," and when the term "intellectual" began to be used to denote their self-conscious difference from the majority. It explores the intellectuals' criticism with an eye to the continuities in attitudes toward the mass entertainments, as well as attention to the innovations that were established in that thinking.[9]

While a longer view of the mass culture critique is necessary, it is also important that the complaints voiced in that critique be taken as serious ideas. The color, and even outrageousness, of many of the mass culture charges tempts analysts to dismiss them as showy poses of ill humor, snobbery, or intellectual elitism. But while these sentiments may play some role in the criticism, they cannot fully explain it. Why have the mass arts, of all the trappings of democratic society, been so consistently singled out for this bad feeling? And why should thinkers seeking to show their superiority turn to bashing media that make few claims to status or intellectual challenge? To get to the more complex motivations that shaped the critique, it must be considered as a discrete system of ideas, with its own internal logic.

I approach the mass culture criticism as a set of interrelated understandings that have evolved since the early twentieth century. Intellectuals most often made their criticisms in public forums, intending to convince their colleagues. Therefore, the primary evidence for this study is published material. The criticisms are surveyed in literary magazines, political and professional journals, monographs, textbooks, and newspapers.

As for definitions, I use the terms "popular arts" and "popular culture" in their literal sense, to refer to forms of expression that attract the largest audiences. "Mass culture" is used as a more technical description, referring specifically to expression created for transmission through the mass media. These "mass" forms may or may not prove to be "popular." I have limited my survey to intellectuals' reactions to modern entertainments designed to reach beyond local or class-specific audiences. Rather than offering an encyclopedic account of all critics, I have tried to identify each new theme in the criticism, define its major proponents, and locate the sources of their ideas. The survey proceeds chronologically, each chapter treating a succeeding stage of the critique.

The first chapter considers the central criticisms of the mass entertainments made by conservative writers in the first two decades of the twentieth century. It sketches objections to the popular arts based on concerns about public morality and the efficacy of elevating arts, concerns that were dominant through much of the nineteenth century. The conservatives' practice of blaming offensive entertainments on the moral failings they perceived in the lower classes provides a contrast to emerging left and liberal explanations.

Chapter 2 begins consideration of the modern liberal critique with the ideas of progressive reformers. The progressives shared many of the conservatives' moral objections to mass entertainments, as well as their social prejudices, but had a greater faith in human nature and greater appreciation of modern social ills. They ascribed mass culture problems to harsh work and living conditions and to unscrupulous entrepreneurs who exploited the public's natural desire for recreation. Mass culture patrons were reconceived as victims of their circumstances.

Chapter 3 looks at the self-described cultural radicals of the 1920s, whose dedication to overthrowing the stodgy, elitist Victorian standards for the arts produced a new aesthetic appreciation for some of the entertainments, but also a renewed disdain for many forms as socially regressive. Randolph Bourne's new conception of the entertainments as threats to cultural pluralism is discussed, as is the selective championing of the popular arts practiced by Gilbert Seldes.

Chapter 4 investigates the concerns about mass entertainments expressed by professional social scientists in the interwar era. Sociologists accepted mass entertainments as natural products of modern urban life but so lamented the social and psychological costs of that life that the entertainments appeared to be vehicles of disintegration. The models of modernization created by anthropologists and sociologists were used in social science texts to equate mass culture with damaged psyches and the destruction of community.

The fifth and sixth chapters treat the censure of mass culture by the influential American leftists of the twentieth century, Communists in the late 1920s and 1930s and the "New York Intellectuals" from the Great Depression through the 1950s. The Communists resurrected the progressives' thesis of popular victimization at the hands of entertainments, melding it with the social scientists' diagnosis of a fundamentally hollow modern civilization to condemn American capitalist society as a whole as the source of entertainment ills. The New York Intellectuals brought together socialist understandings and a revamped cultural radicalism rooted in the most challenging modernist letters and criticism. By the beginning of World War II, these critics had begun to see the proletariat both as helpless victims of capitalism and as a hindrance to revolutionary change. They resurrected the conservative crusade to protect the "high" arts from the pressures of popular taste.

Chapter 7 traces the ideas of America's most influential mass culture critic, Dwight Macdonald, and shows how the different threads of the critique over the first half of the century came together in his writings in the 1940s and 1950s. Macdonald drew upon victimization models, the concern for the elite arts, and sociological judgments about the fragility of mass society and helped bring the critique to its greatest prominence after World War II. He also represents the exhaustion of the critique by the middle of the century. Macdonald ultimately surrendered all hope of changing America's culture in the face of the immense powers he ascribed to mass entertainments and the reluctance of the public to choose better forms. His decision to give up on the masses brought the left and liberal criticism back to the conservatives' position: intellectuals were portrayed as being fundamentally at odds with the mass of debauched citizens and their debased entertainments.

An epilogue examines how the culmination of the critique with Macdonald effectively cleared the field for new ideas about the entertainments. Since the 1960s, investigators have focused more on the nature of the entertainments and the way audiences use them. The mass culture public was reconceived as more active and resourceful. The public's discrimination in making some forms popular and discarding others alerted analysts to the way the popular imagination shapes entertainments. Audiences began to be treated as groups of responsible individuals who derived their own meanings from the products of the entertainment industries.

Several overlapping themes emerge from this analysis. My main contention is that the mass culture critique was shaped more by the social concerns of intellectuals than by their observations of entertainments. Left and liberal thinkers were an intellectual cadre in the making in the early twentieth century, at the same time that the mass entertainments were being established. The intellectuals developed the mass culture critique as an ideology to guide them in understanding the explosive growth of entertainments and in working out their own roles in the emerging mass democratic society. They read their concerns about modernity into their conclusions about the public's use of the popular arts. Thus, entertainments became centrally important in shaping their views on the nature of the public, the role of the arts and letters, and the responsibilities of an educated elite in the modern era.

While I do not deny the critics' contention that mass entertainments were capable of creating or exacerbating social problems, I find that the prominent critics rarely studied the effects of entertainments closely or with enough objectivity to make fair judgments about their possible harm. Their considerations of mass culture typically started from preconceptions about the public's passivity, suggestibility, or lack of imagination that made its interactions with entertainments seem dangerous by definition. The most consistent feature of the critique stems from this view of the public. Intellectuals assumed that entertainments were literal embodiments of particular values and that they produced direct and immediate effects on their audiences.

By recognizing the mass culture critique as an ideology shared by left and liberal thinkers rather than a scientific diagnosis, its sources and sustained appeal become more understandable. Intellectuals created the general critique out of a genuine humanitarian concern for the effects of America's new culture of mass entertainments. The particular charges that made up the critique were formed as left and liberal intellectuals pursued this concern amid the other, broader problems that they faced in trying to define their place in the modern society. Specifically, the mass culture critique helped sensitive, socially concerned intellectuals solve two difficult problems.

The first was the proper relationship of intellectuals or "privileged intelligence" to the larger public in a society that so venerated democracy. Were highly educated brainworkers to serve as "lawgivers," sternly dispensing their expertise to the public from above, enjoying their superior status but risking condescension? Or should they answer egalitarian urges and work in close contact with the masses, sympathetic to their concerns and open to their influence? These are obviously the extreme possibilities, yet they serve to show that the mass culture critique presented intellectuals the chance to do both simultaneously. Beginning with the progressives, the attack on entertainments allowed individuals to be concerned for the state of the lower classes and to defend them actively while still maintaining the superiority and universality of their own standards for the arts. The mass culture concerns thus encouraged the intellectuals' paternalism and hastened the formation of what might be called a "democratic clerisy," an intelligentsia that justified its superior standing by its devotion to protecting democracy.

The second problem was how intellectuals could interact reasonably and responsibly with the public when most differed in ethnic, class, and educational background from the masses. The critique finessed this division by presenting entertainments as a common threat that cut across social lines and required a common defense. In its early stages, it cast the entertainments as powerful invasive forces whose values were alien to American communities. Critics presented patrons from all groups as similarly harmed, and thus their inherent differences became secondary. In this process, I show, the critics ignored the desires of the groups that differed from their own, and they did not confront their own social prejudices. Intellectuals could legitimately speak for the people, in other words, because the critique artificially recast the people as being all of one interest.

Implicit in my evaluation of the mass culture critique is a set of understandings about popular culture that differs from the critics'. My approach is derived from contemporary studies of entertainments and is rooted in the understanding that one of the most basic human desires is for meaning and order in life and that our popular culture is one source of these. We create meaning for and give order to our experiences through our minds' structuring of the world, on the one hand, and our social institutions' (family, community, society) structuring of us, on the other. A thorough analysis of the functioning of twentieth-century popular culture therefore involves considering the public as active agents creating understandings from their media and as social beings whose engagements with those media may be encouraged or constrained by their environments.

The most accurate analyses of popular culture must, then, encompass both the production and reception of these entertainments. This involves accounting for at least three major aspects of cultural communication. First, the analysis should spell out the purposes and controls that underlie the communications media and divine how these influences affect the cultural products. Second, it should investigate the products or "texts" themselves to identify what raw materials they offer audiences for making their interpretations, what larger social meanings might be encoded in these forms. Third, the analysis should consider how a popular culture text is received or "read" by the audience and evaluate its subsequent social impact.[10]

My conclusion is that modern left critics of the entertainments have, in the main, presumed the social effects of entertainments or extrapolated the effects from the behaviors of audiences, slighting audiences' roles in receiving and interpreting the forms. They have consequently been prone to overestimate the entertainments' role in controlling ideas and behavior.

This book is therefore both an analysis and a criticism. The latter needs a word of explanation. I consider many of the mass culture critics treated here to be among the more thoughtful, compassionate, fair-minded intellectuals of our century. Because I share most of their sympathies, my objections to their views on the popular arts are intended as a criticism from within their own tradition. These critics raised important questions about mass entertainments' potential to influence the public and their effects on culture as a whole, questions that still perplex us today. And while I contend that they were often wrong in their answers, I believe that their critique emerged from a sincere dedication to improving America and helping the less powerful that nonetheless secures their honor.

I

DEFENDING THE OLD ORDER

The strongest criticism of the popular arts in the United States in the early twentieth century came from conservative intellectuals. The chief criticisms of popular theater, novels, magazines, and the new motion pictures appeared in the nation's most prestigious journals of literature and opinion and built upon arguments already decades old. Critics attacked mass entertainments for pandering to base passions, interfering with social discipline and disrupting the institutional bulwarks that stabilized society. The lasting result of their criticism and their program to remediate American culture was the sanctioning of a facile stratification of the arts and their respective publics, a hierarchy that would last for generations.

The ill will of the genteel intellectuals toward popular culture stemmed from both contemporary conditions and longstanding ideas. Their discomfort with the values of the emerging urban, corporate-industrial, immigrant society and its cultural forms exacerbated the more immediate class and ethnic prejudices many felt toward newcomers in their cities. These complaints in turn reinforced ideas inherited from Western intellectual tradition that defamed the popular arts as misguided interpretations of modern life. Ultimately, the scorn of the genteel intellectuals for the nation's most popular entertainments also reflected their larger, more fundamental problem: finding a suitable role for intellectuals and "privileged intelligence" in modern democratic society.

Mass entertainments were, of course, just one of the pressing problems for genteel intellectuals in the early twentieth century. The world in which they had held cultural sway was threatened on several fronts. The enormous transformations wrought by rapid and largely unregulated industrial growth, mass immigration, and the emerging patterns of life in the metropolises disrupted intellectual endeavor and profoundly unsettled them. Genteel writers continued to offer cultural prescriptions for the nation, believing that their intellectual and moral judgments accorded them status as leaders. But their influence was fast dwindling, and more powerful forces were quickly overwhelming them. The economic order was largely beyond their influence, with the ruthlessness of corporate capitalism, the rise of working-class protest, and the growth of socialism in America. The emergence of the "new woman," dissatisfied with the nineteenth century's version of domestic virtue and intent on changing social patterns, challenged their basic beliefs about the roles of the sexes. Millions of new arrivals from southern and eastern Europe made genteel intellects keenly aware that the unified American culture they so desired was becoming anachronistic. National consensus on values and behavior seemed ever more remote as differences of all types multiplied. Even in the sphere of intellectual opinion, which the conservatives policed so carefully, powerful changes were challenging their hegemony. "Questioners," "liberators," "scoffers," "amoralists" and other cultural revolutionaries whom the historian Henry May has described as the initiators of the modern era in America were undermining many of the values and standards espoused in literary journals in the first decades of the twentieth century. Together, these challenges to the older order left many of the conservative writers despairing for the future. As one impeccably genteel commentator concluded in 1911, the face of the nation as she knew it had almost completely changed since the 1870s. "Somewhere," wrote Cornelia Comer, "there was an awful break in the orderly evolution of American society."[1]

Historians in recent decades have chronicled the variety of approaches that intellectuals made to respond to these momentous social changes. Educators created the modern university to bring organization to knowledge; social scientists elevated their interests to an academic discipline and a profession with aspirations of providing newer sources of social authority and explaining the increasingly complex world; sensitive thinkers reacted against the spiritual and psychological challenges of modern culture by trying to recapture the satisfactions of premodern life and "folk" ways; the reform-minded pursued political and social programs to try to cope with the enormous forces altering Americans' lives. One response did not exclude others, and we know that many intellectuals became involved in several at once. For many genteel critics, cultural reform was more important than any intellectual programs because the arts and letters were the touchstones for society's moral and spiritual standards. Therefore, the cultural realm was the crucial ground for holding out against what they saw as modern vulgarity, indulgence, and materialism.[2]

Mass entertainments were becoming a crisis for conservative critics in the early century because of their sheer expansion. The new motion pictures, introduced in 1905, drew hundreds of thousands of patrons a week in major cities. Daily newspapers, increasingly written to entertain the public in the late nineteenth century, enjoyed vastly increased circulations in the twentieth century. By the time America entered into World War I, there were more than 2,500 daily papers in the United States, and circulation approached 29 million. Popular magazines experienced a similarly rapid growth: about 3,500 titles published in 1885, and by 1905 more than 6,000. Ten periodicals had circulations of 500,000 by 1905. Vaudeville shows, amusement parks, and dance halls all drew tens of thousands of patrons per week. And saloons, the workingman's chief recreation spots, may have drawn as many as half the residents of cities such as Boston or Chicago in a single day.[3]

Equally new were the social groups who produced some of the most prominent popular arts. Jewish immigrants from eastern Europe broke the middle-class, Anglo-Saxon control over motion pictures and revolutionized the industry in the second decade of the new century. African American

The abundant offerings at this New York City newsstand, 1903, show the growth of mass circulation magazines in the early twentieth century. (Library of Congress, LC-D401-16161)

composers and itinerant piano players made ragtime music a national obsession before World War I. European Jews who came to New York transformed their popular music into the national expression and big business in Tin Pan Alley. Jewish businessmen also dominated entertainment as agents, managers, and owners of theaters and vaudeville houses. Most of the major cabaret stars of the early century also had recent immigrant origins.[4]

The social sources, content, and spread of the entertainments made them unwelcome to America's older cultural elites. Editors for the nation's most prestigious journals responded by trying to quarantine them, as much as possible, from their pages. The *Atlantic Monthly*, the *Dial*, the *North American Review*, and similar magazines rarely considered the popular arts in their major articles. These journals, which the historian Henry May has aptly characterized as the twentieth century's remaining "fortresses" of the Victorian cultural order, also only occasionally gave popular culture any extended analysis or discussion in less prominent pieces devoted to other arts.[5]

The important exception was a series of articles written for the *Atlantic Monthly* in the early century. The articles, compiled under the title *The People at Play*, were written by journalist Rollin Lynde Hartt and published in 1909. Hartt had traveled across the United States surveying burlesque theaters, amusement parks, dime museums, motion pictures, the melodramatic stage, dance halls, popular literature, and professional baseball. The purpose of the book, he explained, was to defend the reputation of the public and its pastimes, to lead his readers "toward a more genial regard for their humble fellow creatures" through a sympathetic consideration of popular amusements. His analysis provides a useful key for interpreting the other, less-developed criticisms in the genteel journals.

Hartt's approach assumed the entertainments would be alien to most *Atlantic Monthly* readers. By virtue of his education and research, Hartt, son of a prominent scientist, graduate of Williams College and Andover Theological Seminary, and a former Congregational minister, considered himself a qualified interpreter. He wrote as if he were an expedition guide leading his middle- and upper-class audience through a mysterious, aboriginal culture. He described the urban recreations in detail. The Folly burlesque house, for example, was where "the thousand low-browed men and boys" crowded in to see tasteless shows that reflected their minds and morals "with pitiless accuracy." He stressed how different the atmosphere of these performances was from the fare of what he called "cultured folk." From the garish posters at the entrance to the ragged, dirty auditorium awash in a "very ancient sniffiness," to the whistling and stamping uproar of the impatient audience, this was clearly not "legitimate" theater. Nor was the burlesque audience competent to practice such refinement or to appreciate serious stage production. "Incapable of sustained attention, assertive memory, logical inference, or that range of consciousness which groups many incidents into a harmonious whole," Hartt wrote, "they abhor the drama and adore burlesque—for its very fault's sake."

Much the same combination of bewilderment and bemused contempt marked Hartt's treatment of other amusements. He explained the popularity of acrobatic acts as due to the masses' "worship" of muscle. "Reduce the whole race to the Underworld's level," he suggested, "and you would

The title page of Rollin Hartt's 1909 survey of popular amusements, *The People at Play*, as drawn by the author.

reinstate the heroic age when he of stoutest brawn became chieftain of his tribe." At the amusement park, the crowd's hunger for death-defying feats came from a "morbid" or "primitive" kind of "blind instinct" that spurred them to become "seekers after shudders." Even the deportment of the public at Coney Island needed interpretation, according to Hartt. "To the popular mind," he wrote, explaining the physical closeness fostered by many amusements, "the caress means no more than the mildly affectionate phrases with which we begin and end our letters." Hartt believed that a huge chasm existed between the qualities and capabilities of his readers and those of the lower classes. His patronizing defense of the theme music that opened the dime museum's stage show was a typical example. These compositions, which he described as typically "an overture consisting mainly of drum," had to be considered for their effectiveness with their particular listeners. "Music less barbaric," Hartt opined, "would fail to penetrate the proletarian consciousness."[6]

To most late-twentieth-century sensibilities, Hartt's judgments amount to patent bigotry or prejudice. The reactions of contemporary reviewers of *The People at Play*, however, suggest that Hartt's attitudes toward the popular arts and their audiences were accepted in educated circles. The *New York Times* offered a strong endorsement of the book, declaring in a subheadline, "Mr. Hartt Writes a Valuable and Entertaining Work of Sociology." The *Times* found Hartt to be a careful and trustworthy analyst of the entertainment scene, and cautioned potential readers only that "if at times his pictures seem sordid and unpleasant, they may be accepted as neither false nor unsympathetic." Remarkably, the critic for the *Nation* thought that the book was not critical enough, chiding Hartt for handling the material "with kid gloves." The *Dial* magazine of Chicago could find fault only in Hartt's journalistic style, which it said appealed to "a low standard of literary taste," while the American Library Association's *Booklist* concluded, "The author's thorough understanding of his subject gives the book a decided sociological value, and his humor and wholesome geniality make it good for general reading."[7]

That Hartt's unabashed attacks could prove congenial to these weighty organs of opinion suggests the consensus that existed about the popular arts in the early twentieth century. The central themes from Hartt's book and occasional articles in the genteel magazines reveal the social and intellectual roots of the conservative popular-culture criticism. Specifically, they show

how the critics' notions of proper social order, the function of the arts and letters, and their own responsibilities as intellectuals came together.

––––––

By far, the most common charge in the genteel criticisms early in the century was that popular recreations were pandering to the base, physical passions and primal emotions of the public. Objections to entertainments began with complaints of indelicacy and extended to condemnations of the sensational or shocking. Rollin Hartt cited, as we have seen, "primitivism" in explaining the popularity of the dime museum sideshows. Audiences for melodrama sought "thrills," he wrote, "because the very dull require powerful stimulants to stave off torpor," and "only the glaringly sensational gets through their armor of stupidity to leave a vivid impression."[8]

Similar criticisms of the overdrawn and overstimulating were common in literary journals. In the *American Magazine* in 1909, the critic Samuel Hopkins Adams estimated that 20 percent of New York's theater presentations qualified as evil, chiefly for their "sensuality." Adams condemned the plays for their "sheer physical brutishness; the appeal to the Yahoo that lurks within all of us, to the beast that we hold in leash, out of respect to ourselves and to our fellows." He referred to New York as a city of "abnormal and unhealthy nervous tension" that produced theater audiences with "jaded nerve centers" requiring "a mental cocktail." "Shock will do it," he explained, "the appeal to the sensual and the animal within him will do it." Frederick Winsor, a preparatory school headmaster, feared for children in this emotionally overheated environment. Writing in the *Atlantic Monthly*, he linked the "unhealthy appetite for artificiality and excitement" generated by theatrical performances to boys' failure to control their sexual appetites. Adams, meanwhile, urged parents to be far more discriminating in what they let their sons see, so that "the influence of the stage [may] help him so to live that his bride looking straight into his eyes may be content."[9]

Mass circulation books and magazines were strongly criticized for making base appeals. The *Dial*, in 1913 still a firm supporter of traditional aesthetics, quoted one clergyman on the "poisonous" effects of modern fiction. "The tyranny of the novel betokens that faith has given way to feeling," he said, "and that feeling is debauched by excitement following on the loss of long-cherished ideals." In 1917, the magazine endorsed another criticism of popular literature, chastising "periodicals that ought to know better" for "so much ignoble striving for 'snappy' stories, 'racy' or 'spicy' humor, and 'compromising' plots." The *North American Review* lambasted popular literature in a 1913 piece by R. A. Scott-James, a British critic. He contended that "just as a donkey with a hard mouth can only be guided by violent jerks upon the reins, so a dull sensibility can only be awakened by the harshest literary appeal." Echoing Rollin Hartt, he lamented that the "sensibility of the crudest and, it is to be feared, the (at present) largest strata of society can be touched by the sheer extravagance of the novel of incident." Scott-James condemned astonishing plots and other "violent assaults upon the reader calculated to arouse him like pistol-shots, since a more moderate appeal would escape his attention." [10]

Even Owen Wister, a writer who had achieved a certain popularity as author of *The Virginian*, seemed eager to distance his work from the best-sellers. Writing on "Quack-Novels and Democracy" in the *Atlantic Monthly* in 1915, Wister criticized appeals to baser instincts and added a slam at the public's desire for novelty. He told of a young person entering the Philadelphia Library, approaching the desk, and asking for 'something good.' The librarian handed her an acclaimed modern work and "She sought its title-page, and instantly thrust back the volume with almost a scream of reproach. 'Why, that's two years old! That ain't fresh!'" The "freshness" the reader had come to expect, according to Wister, involved scenes of sexual passion and luxurious living. Such works seemed to him the equivalent of patent medicines. Like the "quack-medicine," "the quack-novel is (mostly) harmful; not always because it is poisonous (though this occurs), but because it pretends to be literature and is taken for literature by the millions who swallow it year after year as their chief mental nourishment, and whose brains it saps and dilutes." The *Dial* heartily endorsed Wister's article in an editorial comment, contending that "laxative literature" fostered "slackness, heedlessness, happy-go-lucky muddle-headedness, addiction to cheap sensationalism, a bland content with sounding words and pretty phrases in place of disagreeable truths and stern realities, and a general condition of self-complacent sloppiness." [11]

Similarly, the new motion pictures of the early twentieth century frequently were charged with making base appeals. The *American Review of Reviews* in 1908 offered the opinion of the motion picture expert C. H. Claudy that films were promulgating evil with their portrayals of "the realism of bloodshed, crime, and brutality." The magazine concluded that there were many worthwhile motion pictures being produced, "but there are many more that pander to low passions and have nothing but the dollar in sight." A 1914 piece in the same journal conceded that censorship efforts had eliminated many of the worst class of subjects ("indecency, wanton libel, and morbid scenes of crime"), but maintained that "the overwhelming majority of such shows still depend for success upon an overemotional and sensational appeal, — pretty highly spiced food for those five million adolescent minds to make their favorite daily meals from." The *North American Review* believed that, with the movies replacing the wicked "ultra-sensational melodrama" in popular theaters, the scale of evil was actually increasing. "The illiterate playgoers who could find satisfaction in these arbitrarily concocted plots, wherein probability, plausibility and verisimilitude were continually sacrificed to unexpectedly startling effect," it explained, "had their callous nerves more effectively stimulated and their crude tastes more deeply gratified by the melodramatic tales which could be told on the screen with far greater effectiveness." The taste for these manipulations of passions had a long history, the *Review* writer contended, in such venal blood sports as bullfights in Spain and gladiator battles in ancient Rome. These evils were "deep rooted in the baser instincts of man."[12]

When conservative critics condemned the sensuality of the popular arts, many were clearly voicing their class and ethnic prejudices. The audiences for mass entertainments in the early twentieth century were composed mainly of the working classes, and, in the major cities especially, large numbers were new immigrants from southern and eastern Europe. Whereas most of America's cultural elite came from Anglo-Saxon backgrounds and practiced Protestantism, many of the newcomers came from different cultures, looked different in complexion and dress, were barely literate in any language, and were Jewish or Catholic. The dominant racial ideology of the turn of the century deemed non-Anglo-Saxons inferior and held that the national origins of the immigrants condemned them to coarseness and immorality. Rollin Hartt wrote of his "friends among the proletarians" in his preface, but his book displayed prejudices. The lower classes were described as "rat-eyed," "pitiful blockheads," "incredibly dull," "densely ignorant," and possessors of "Neolithic minds." The genteel critics' repeated descriptions of childlike intellects, brutish physical appetites, and lack of moral sense reflected these long-standing stereotypes.[13]

Bourgeois social views reinforced the class prejudices of the genteel critics. The bourgeois outlook evolved in the United States (and in other societies) in the nineteenth century as social leaders reacted to the market revolution transforming American life. One response was to prescribe clear guidelines for respectable behavior. The hegemony exercised by the growing middle class stressed personal habits that included compulsive behavior, self-control, and self-denial. All of these values involved an implicit subjugation of natural or visceral emotions and reactions. Reformers, educators, and other social leaders struggled mightily to instill these habits in the populace in hopes of creating reliable, virtuous citizens who were essential for a democratic republic.

An unstated understanding of the bourgeois worldview was that citizens unable to master these values and practices must be relegated to a separate, inferior social category. This sense of the American social geography is evident in the conservative critics' objections to the entertainments. Mistrustful of those who responded to such passions, the writers concluded that the lower classes were fundamentally different from the readers of literary journals. Hartt's comments about the crowds at the dime museum are suggestive. He surmised from their behavior that there were two castes in America, "twin streams of population," that were staunchly separate. Centuries-old "proletarian ignorance" was a chief characteristic of the lower stream and was readily evident in the amusement attractions. Hartt's explanation of the "Underworld's" attraction to acrobats and their muscular feats was that the lower classes had never achieved "that divorce betwixt flesh and spirit which is our Puritan heritage."[14]

But while contemporary class and ethnic prejudices shaped the genteel critique of popular culture, they did not fully define it. The critics' fears about passions or sensuality also drew from intellectual sources deep within Western culture. Plato perhaps best captured the division within human nature that has intrigued philosophers for centuries. In the *Phaedrus*, he offered the arresting image of the human soul as a chariot driver, reining two horses representing our divided nature. One was all animal impulses, the other, rationality and control. Similar concerns about our physical or primal nature were central to ancient Christian asceticism. And images of carnality have been associated with "barbarian" outsiders for centuries. The injunctions of Protestantism against emotional display and the call to resist one's passions almost certainly influenced genteel critics as well.[15]

Scientific thinking brought these social and intellectual influences together, predisposing conservative writers against the popular arts. Though science-based industrialism shook the core values of their culture, most nineteenth-century intellectuals adopted a rationalist, scientific outlook. Moral progress, they trusted, would keep pace with material change. In this rational world of natural laws and observable reality they valued art forms that spoke to the presumably objective higher faculties: intellectual truth, ideal patterns of life, universal aesthetic and moral standards. Yet they knew that this rationalist means of understanding was not practiced by all. In fact, the scientific approach first arose in ancient Greece as a reaction against mythology, another way of knowing that explained phenomena through belief and imagination. This conflict of cosmologies remained important, for while the genteel critics' rationalism told them that the mythological worldview was outmoded fable and superstition, it continued to thrive in many of the popular arts of their own era.

Mass entertainments rooted their appeals in the worldviews of their audiences, and not all of those views were strictly rational. The scientific approaches fit the intellectuals and their elite social positions because their society could be understood as the orderly product of natural laws. For the lower classes, by contrast, life seemed frequently a matter of luck, fate, and mystery. Because the world often appeared beyond their rational influence or control, natural laws seemed more arbitrary. Meaning, or "wisdom," was best created through the emotional or spiritual faculties in such circumstances. In addition to scientific explanations, then, the broader public sought understanding from myth and other statements of belief and attitude. The popular arts became particularly adept at offering such statements through drama and narrative. Entertainment entrepreneurs tried to divine the ideas and beliefs of their audiences and create forms that would tap into their worldviews. Those that consistently engaged these views and made sense of many people's experience became truly "popular" arts.

An example of this split between science- and myth-oriented cultural forms is the development of "story" and "information" newspapers in the nineteenth and early twentieth centuries. The "penny press" grew enormously in the 1830s, when papers began to be written primarily for the semiliterate common folk in major cities. This new approach to journalism continued to expand later in the century with the success of the *National Police Gazette*, Joseph Pulitzer's *New York World*, and the papers of William Randolph Hearst. These papers were designed around human-interest stories easily accessible to all and appealing to emotions rather than intellect. While such "story" journalism was increasingly capturing readers from all classes, by the turn of the century the more educated and wealthier were making the *New York Times* a great success. The *Times* prided itself on accurate information—facts segregated from subjective judgments.

Each kind of journal tried to satisfy the myth or science orientation of its readers. While we cannot be sure how the papers engaged individuals of different classes, genders, and backgrounds, and while many different readings were possible, the papers clearly differed in the way they approached their content.

Information papers such as the *Times* took for granted that the world had a certain order for its readers. They also assumed the world possessed a reality independent of its observers. Their reports were therefore designed to "mirror" reality and provide objective knowledge. Readers were responsible for taking this disparate knowledge and recognizing its connections to create meaning. In effect, the information papers treated their readers as scientists who were aware of the general laws of societies and could fit new facts into these conceptual schemes.

The story press was aimed at readers whose worlds were less ordered and controllable, but who nonetheless sought to understand. The historian William R. Taylor has described how the popular press and other commercial cultural forms helped the public "decode" a city by making the tumultuous social world intelligible. More specifically, several scholars have proposed that the story papers worked by dramatizing disturbing real-life situations and drawing forth readers' reactions. Their stories selected and framed experiences that conflicted with dominant middle-class values or the taboos of their particular social group and simultaneously called upon readers to use their own beliefs to understand the dissonance. Sensational reports of crime, sex, and adventure allowed readers to indulge their own socially unacceptable desires and anxieties and provided emotional pleasure for them in vicariously violating middle-class norms. While dramatizing this conflict of standards and feelings, however, the titillating stories did not directly affect the social conditions that produced these conflicts, so they offered no solutions. Ultimately, readers were left to adjust to their situations. They were "entertained" in the sense that the stories seemed to address their life situations, and they were treated to a safe emotional thrill.[16]

Intellectuals who were not attuned to the understandings of the lower classes condemned the story papers as models for immorality. Sensational accounts of social deviance "make a pure mind almost impossible," argued Anthony Comstock, the founder of the New York Society for the Suppression of Vice. "They open the way for the grossest evils."

As we can now see, though, the criticisms of Comstock and other genteel writers stemmed largely from their presumption that all audiences read popular culture in the same way. As the anthropologist Clifford Geertz has written, aesthetic sense, or the practice of attaching cultural significance to art objects, is determined by local conditions. The critics, however, believed their informational approach was the only valid system of reading and therefore applied it to myth-inspired stories. Their reading was not "wrong" per se, it simply differed from the understandings of the story producers and their central audience. The critics failed to see that, as Geertz puts it, "Art and the equipment to grasp it are made in the same shop." By treating the tales of immorality as literal realities to be analyzed and judged like a *New York Times* story rather than as narrative vehicles designed for making the world intelligible and providing emotional pleasures, they ignored the local or social context.

For example, violent crimes were a staple of the story papers in the Gilded Age. One regular column in the *National Police Gazette* was even titled "Murder and Suicide: A Gush of Gore and Shattering Brains All Around the Horizon." To most genteel critics, accounts of these crimes in such grotesque detail seemed an invitation to the lower classes for further depravity, or at least a sign of popular indifference to the sanctity of life. To readers approaching these stories as dramas rather than facts, though, murder tales offered a vicarious violation of the most central of taboos, the taking of life. The tales also let readers ponder the mystery of the fine human line between those who murder and those who do not. The physical descriptions satisfied the wonder people have about their own bodies and the mysteriousness of the life force within them. Readers may have received frissons from these stories as well when they realized their own potential to suffer or commit such acts in the violent American cities of the era.

The sexual scandals that were the bread and butter of the yellow press were also open to different readings. Violations of female virtue could be interpreted as sinful or perhaps criminal acts in a literal reading, or as a symbolic twitting of Victorian sexual codes in another. For male readers, the

The sensationalism of popular "yellow" journalism was flayed in the respectable press at the turn of the century, as in this 1898 cartoon in *Life* magazine.

women involved in the scandals may have been objects of fantasy for their apparent willingness to give and receive pleasure openly, as the historian Elliott Gorn proposes. For females, these and other popular accounts denied the cult of true womanhood and its image of women without sexual impulses. The stories therefore highlighted a contradiction many likely felt in their own lives and gave them a sense of pleasure at elaborating the conflict.

These different understandings of the stories suggest how the genteel critics may have misread the popular arts and misunderstood what made them popular. In the case of the sensational papers, the critics concluded that, if people bought these patently evil forms in such enormous numbers, they desired evil for its own sake. The readers had to be as depraved as the stories.[17]

Beset by the perceived evils of popular culture, genteel intellectuals set themselves to defending their valued institutions. Critics tried to rally the conscience of the middle class, warning about the effects of entertainments on religious faith, the sanctity of the home and family, women's virtue, the work ethic, intellectual discipline, and even the role of books as the carrier of society's norms and traditions.[18] The one concern that surpassed all others was the threat that popular culture presented to the future of the "elite" arts and letters in America. "Culture" was the central force the genteel writers counted on to improve the public and guide its behavior. The way they used "Culture" as a badge of moral fitness and a shield against the broader public presaged the difficulties intellectuals would have in finding a suitable role in democratic society in succeeding decades.

Writers in the genteel journals of the early 1900s denounced popular culture not only for its direct threats to the social order, but for the elevating effects it could not produce. Critics bemoaned the entertainments' failure to appeal to the soul or spirit and their reluctance to try to improve public character and morality. These complaints were rooted in the social worries of the conservative intellectuals and in their notions of the purpose and function of the expressive arts.

In simplest terms, the critics idealized the "high" arts for their ability to enlighten and uplift the populace, to transcend immediate realities or experiences. The popular arts, by contrast, seemed content to mirror the outlines of life. This dichotomy between art and entertainment was most pronounced in the rhetorical pairings that appeared in the literary magazines: "high ideals" versus "entertainment"; "aesthetic, mental, and moral instruction" compared to "amusement"; and expressions of "the deepest mind of man" against "tales and ditties by which the rank and file of men beguile their empty leisure."[19]

This view of two incompatible realms of the arts and letters had two sources. One was the particular way in which the arts gained esteem in America in the nineteenth century; the other was the changing philosophy of aesthetics in the Western world. In the era after the American Revolution, writers in the United States were generally skeptical, if not critical, of forms of aesthetic expression. The nation was involved in the sober-minded mission of building a republic, and the arts suggested luxury, decadence, and the aristocratic culture of the old regime. The process of legitimizing expressive forms took place gradually over the antebellum years. The key was in promoting aesthetic objects as expressions of the nation's normative religious and moral values. Fears of the sensuality of the arts or the mystery and possible heresy of purely philosophical rationalizations for their worth were overcome by tying the arts to matters divine and unquestionably moral. Aesthetic forms were increasingly presented by their proponents as means to transcend the material and physical realities of life and reach the ideal.[20]

Linking that realm of the ideal with God was necessary for satisfying America's cultural arbiters, who were religious men. This was accomplished chiefly through the influence of the English philosopher and critic John Ruskin. Ruskin's theories linked beauty as it was found in nature to the qualities of divinity, thereby establishing a standard for aesthetic appreciation that merged theology and aesthetics. Once the arts were safely harnessed for moral ends, they were widely embraced by cultural leaders. They were also increasingly entrusted to support the social order. As sectarianism and secularization grew in America in the midcentury and after the Civil War, critics and reform advocates increasingly looked to the arts for help in developing or steering public behavior and shaping culture and values.[21]

While the arts were being honed as instruments for reforming social character over the course of the nineteenth century, they were increasingly considered as collectible objects with intrinsic value, or even fetishes. The broader circumstances for the elevation of aesthetic objects to the status of "precious works" with both spiritual and monetary worth are fairly clear — increasing wealth, social differentiation or stratification, and the extension of market values into ever more facets of life. But the ideas that more immediately triggered this change remain murky.

The literary theorist and critic Murray Krieger has argued that the philosophy of Immanuel Kant was a necessary precursor for creating aesthetic fetishes. He explains that, until the late eighteenth century, theories of aesthetics were organized around mimesis, the goal of mimicry or imitation. In this view, the arts were considered to be integrated with human life and were conceived as reproducers of that reality. The arts were expected to bring out the universal rules or truths that guided life, but, in the process, artists were not to manipulate the realities they observed. Art forms themselves were therefore not considered valuable as objects or "works" because they did not create anything. They only assembled imitated objects.

Philosophical developments in the late eighteenth century, however, began to change the perceived goal of art. Kant's ideas of human reason posited the "disinterestedness" or self-sufficiency of aesthetics. He suggested that expressive objects achieved their effect not by satisfying the audience's need for elucidation, but by meeting the internal demands of their form. This approach gave artists' freer reign to manipulate their media. It also separated aesthetic objects from social responsibilities and prepared the way for valuing the arts solely for the way they exploited their particular forms. It took decades for this new thinking to develop, of course, but simply by making aesthetic fabrications valuable as self-contained, self-sufficient articles rather than as representations, it fundamentally altered their stature. If art forms were accepted as socially "disinterested," then the criteria for judging them became far more personal and subjective. Worth was left to be determined largely by the judgment of those with power or influence. With such arbitrary standards, then, the arts became elite objects. Elites maintained their aesthetic authority by bringing others to adopt their attachment to particular forms.[22]

The problem for intellectuals trying to bring order to cultural life was that these newly prescribed functions of the arts—as reform instruments and objects of reverence—conflicted. One envisioned a broad social purpose, engaging the whole public. The other served more private ends for the privileged ranks. The functions were interwoven only because of the social changes of the late nineteenth century. The old elite of the early republic, declining in influence and losing faith in reforming both the new rich and the working classes, increasingly embraced the arts as its symbols of order and value. Many among the newly wealthy simultaneously sought aesthetic cachet to establish their social legitimacy. Their overlapping efforts brought cultural ideas together in what Lawrence Levine has termed "the emergence of cultural hierarchy" in the Gilded Age. These two threads were central in the creation of a distinct order of "high culture" in America and in the division of the arts and their audiences into segregated enclaves.[23]

The nature of the new cultural hierarchy is best illustrated in the internally conflicting agendas of cultural philanthropists. Those who created and directed institutions such as art museums, libraries, and orchestra and opera companies appear to have been undecided, at least until the last decades of the century, about the proper function of the arts in America. Should these forms be used to educate and elevate the public? Or, in the chaotic conditions of urban and industrial civilization, was it more important that these facilities insulate the arts from the masses, with the risk of etherealizing those forms? The culture managers most often pronounced the former and practiced the latter. The reason seems to be that these aesthetic objects had become too valuable, too much a part of their self-image and prestige, to be shared. Fetishism, in effect, triumphed over idealism. Cultural facilities generally became much more temples of art, places to pay homage to pro-claimed totems, than workshops where people could learn about the forms and make personal assessments of their value.[24]

Genteel intellectuals supported efforts at cultural reform and thus joined in stratifying society, putting themselves in a station above the general public and offering elevation on their own terms. The intellectuals' conception of cultural forms on a vertical scale compounded their anxiety about the popu-lar audiences that came from their misreadings of the popular arts. Critics concluded from their literal readings of entertainments that these audiences were immoral. And when most refused to scale this ladder of "Culture" and accept elite standards, it seemed they might be irredeemable as well.

The crucial assumption genteel intellectuals made was that tastes for the arts were based on universal standards (rather than perceptions shaped by individual or social situations). Moreover, they believed these standards existed on a graded scale. All people advanced through the same levels of taste according to their ethical and intellectual development. According to the harshest critics, then, persistent differences from genteel taste were not the result of different experiences for social groups but of weaknesses in character. This hierarchical conception of society, with its implication that those considering themselves morally superior had evolved to their status, was common in Western social thought in the Victorian era. When writers applied it to the arts, they conditioned later generations of intellectuals to see cultural differences on a vertical plane and bogged them down in two modes of response. At one extreme, some intellectuals endlessly investigated and itemized their differences from their supposed lessers and policed the hierarchy. At the other, reformers designed program after program for ele-vating the people, but typically only lifting them up the steps defined by the hierarchy. More commonly in America, intellectuals merged the responses to create a third mode. They were keenly attuned to their social difference from lower groups, but open to reform efforts. Only a small number con-sidered the differing tastes for the arts as legitimate differences in perception and sought their source. For the growing numbers of brainworkers in the early twentieth century, the hierarchy of the arts provided both a framework for understanding social differences and a high status. It encouraged intellectuals to maintain their social distinction within the democratic society.

By the early twentieth century, the general pessimism of conservative critics about the state of society discouraged grand claims about the potential for aesthetic culture to reform America. And if improvement was unlikely, defending existing achievements was all the more important. Clearly defined boundaries were necessary to distinguish the desired from the degraded and maintain the cultural order. Lorin Deland, a manager of a "legitimate" theater in Boston, captured the sentiment for separation most colorfully.

> Are we going to do without cake because that great army headed by the butcher, the baker, and the candlestick-maker, prefers to eat bread? . . . Must we wait on their higher development before we can indulge the taste that is our heritage? Shall we have no food for our hungry aestheticism because they have indigestion? . . . If we are to have higher dramatic art in this country with all the advantages which the exposition of such art would bring, it must come through a plan of segregating the classes on the line of mental and aesthetic appreciation.

Keeping with his professed sympathy for the masses, Rollin Hartt's closing thoughts in *The People at Play* were not as exasperated as Deland's. Walking out of the burlesque hall, he recalled reveling in the "moral and spiritual rebound" and the "sense of escape from out of the realm of riot and unreason." But in the longer perspective, he saw only social good in the entertainments. The "survival of benightedness" they encouraged among the underclasses was central to the nation's health, he suggested, producing docility and staving off revolution. Between the typical dime museum patron and desperation, Hartt wrote, there was only "a vast and beneficent foolishness," and so he expressed his gratitude that "foolishness" was what the amusement best offered.[25]

Hartt and Deland both expressed the disdain for the entertainments and their audiences as well as the deep misunderstanding of these art forms that was at the center of genteel criticism of popular culture in the early twentieth century. The popular arts were repugnant to conservatives because they found them dangerously sensational and irrational, and therefore threatening to middle-class virtues. The popular forms also interfered with the vessels of elite culture that helped give society its grounding. Finally, they catered to the debased working classes, whose interests deserved attention only in the name of maintaining their passivity. Amid their deep pessimism and frank elitism, conservative intellectuals acknowledged that their interests and values had diverged from those of many of their fellow citizens. Despite their professed hopes for restoring an ethical consensus around their ideal expressive forms and standards, these critics were all too aware of how heterogeneous American culture had become by the early twentieth century. This difficult lesson about social differences would become a central issue as leftist and liberal intellectuals became the dominant critics of mass arts over the twentieth century. These thinkers would express far more sympathy toward groups within the popular culture audience and yet, at the same time, lose much of the conservatives' reluctant appreciation of genuine, fundamental differences with this public.

2
HEALTHY RECREATION VERSUS "EXPLOITING PLEASURE" IN THE PROGRESSIVE ERA

America's modern mass culture critique debuted in the writings of urban reformers and social workers in the first decades of the twentieth century. The mass entertainments that had been a serious but secondary concern in most of the era's journals of conservative opinion became an overriding social problem for the progressives. Reformers were affronted by a growing mass culture that violated their values and standards, but also confident that both the public and its entertainments could be elevated. The progressives' critique differed from that of their genteel contemporaries through a greater empathy for the public and a belief that people were fundamentally moral, rational, and capable of better practices. The reformers' goodwill, however, also obscured the great social gulf that separated them from the urban masses. They ignored how these differences produced different tastes and how popular standards shaped the mass entertainments. Instead, they looked to the purveyors of the new amusements for the corruption they perceived. This combination of distaste for the popular arts and determination to improve audiences introduced a theory of victimization that marks a turning point in the mass culture critique.

The most striking examples of the reformers' approach to the entertainments were the vivid stories and voluminous data they presented to illustrate their criticisms. A typical tale was told by Rheta Childe Dorr, who recounted the tragic experiences of young women of recent immigrant origins in urban dance halls. Dorr, a social worker and women's rights advocate, published a book in 1910 that included the stories of several typical working-class girls who unwittingly had become fallen women "because they thirsted for pleasure." Dorr's account featured Annie Donnelly, the fourteen-year-old daughter of an overworked cab driver, who lived in a cramped tenement with her parents, three younger siblings, and a young male boarder. Annie had no privacy in the small quarters, nor could she have friends over to visit, Dorr explained. So she had to spend her leisure time in the street. Eventually, "Annie found sitting on the doorstep and talking about nothing in particular entirely unbearable." When she got the chance to change the pattern, she slipped away with the boarder to a dance club, against her mother's wishes.

The hall was in a combination saloon and tenement house, where about thirty couples danced to popular tunes played on a piano, stirring up clouds of dust thick enough to dim the electric lights. As Dorr told the story, "In a few minutes Annie forgot her timidity, forgot the dust and the heat and the odor of stale beer, and was conscious only that the music was piercing, sweet, and that she was swinging in blissful time to it." When her companion suggested they have a refreshment, Annie declined. But he explained that in this "social club" the use of the hall came with the understanding that the patrons would buy drinks from the proprietor—it was expected. Eventually, Annie "learned to drink beer for the benefit of philanthropists who furnished dance halls rent free," and worse, "became a dance-hall habitue." There was no fundamental flaw in the young woman's character that led to this behavior, it was not because she was "viciously inclined" or "abnormal," Dorr explained, "but because she was decidedly normal in all her instincts and desires."

Annie soon learned the ways of the dance halls, first "spieling"—whirling round and round at arm's length from the partner, blowing girl's skirts "immodestly high" in Dorr's view, and effecting "a species of drunkenness which creates an instant demand for liquor, and a temporary recklessness of the possible results of strong drink." There was also the "half time" or "part time waltz," a "primitive form" of dance, "accompanied by a swaying and contorting of the hips, most indecent in its suggestion." With these influences, "Annie Donnelly's destruction was accomplished in less than a year." Dorr concluded: "The dance hall, as we have permitted it to exist, practically unregulated, has become a veritable forcing house of vice and crime in every city in the United States. It is a straight chute down which, every year, thousands of girls descend to the way of the prodigal." "Prodigal" and "unclassed" were the terms Dorr used to denote prostitutes.[1]

Reformers' other stories about mass culture were often equally damning. They included children stealing nickels from their parents in order to attend the movies; women so disgraced by their behavior at dances or amusement parks that they could not return home; and young boys witnessing crime scenes in the motion pictures and then repeating the acts after the show.

Heightening the sense of urgency about the entertainment problem were the startling attendance figures that often accompanied the dramatic narratives. Motion pictures held a greater attraction than any of the other entertainments, and the reformers' estimates of the weekly attendance for these shows in the early 1910s ranged from 20,000 in Waltham, Massachusetts, to 900,000 in Manhattan. One reformer extrapolated the urban counts and estimated that the movies served between two and three *billion* people a year.[2] Next to the motion pictures, the entertainments that received the most attention from urban reformers were the dance halls and academies.[3] A survey of New York City's recreations in 1911 estimated that there were about 200 of the dance facilities in Manhattan alone and that attendance in the halls during the winter season was between four and five million. The social worker journal *Charities and the Commons* reported in 1909 that dancing halls and academies constituted 90 percent of the "amusement program" of young girls working in the city. Statistical profiles were also common in progressives' surveys of live performance theater from vaudeville and burlesque to melodrama, and for a range of leisure outlets including bowling alleys, pool rooms, amusement parks, candy shops, penny arcades, and ice cream and soda parlors.[4]

The lesson that reformers drew from their observations was that they were facing a monumental social crisis. Urban life had fostered an entertainment business that threatened to undermine the morality of whole populations. Dorr described the dance halls, for example, as places where "the bodies and souls of thousands of girls are annually destroyed, because the young are irresistibly drawn toward joy, and because we, all of us, good people, busy people, indifferent people, unseeing people, have permitted joy to become commercialized, have turned it into a commodity to be used for money profit by the worst elements in society." Surveying the mass entertainment problem on this scale, Dorr asked, "Could a more inverted scheme of things have been devised in a madhouse?" [5]

The progressives' criticisms of popular culture started from many of the same moral objections that appeared in the genteel critique, but they went on to a new explanation of the source of these problems and a greater optimism about changing them. Their outlook combined profound worries about the potential for social upheaval and a genuine humanitarian concern for the lower classes in American cities. Their empathy helped produce a social or environmental explanation of the entertainment ills that portrayed the public more as victims of corruption rather than its accessories. They came to believe that the popular arts were remediable once the evil influences were isolated and removed. The outlines of the reformers' new critique are clearest in their treatments of motion pictures and dance halls. Older criticisms about the ethical failings of the entertainments were linked with new concerns about commercial exploiters of leisure, and reform programs were designed to try to rescue the public from both.

Reformers started from the same ground as their conservative contemporaries, believing that popular entertainments were corrupting. When they looked at the dance halls and academies, they found "low" or immoral behavior in abundance. Since many halls were affiliated with saloons and alcohol use was reported to be prevalent around all dance venues, these facilities first of all faced the full wrath of temperance passions. The head of Chicago's Juvenile Protective Association, Louise Bowen, told readers that, in the halls that sold liquor in her city, almost all boys showed intoxication by midnight. The *Outlook*, a reform-oriented journal, reported that in Cleveland's facilities, sometimes one-third of the patrons were under the influence. Other critics blamed the dance places not only for the drinking, but for its presumed effects as well. Mary Simkhovitch, director of New York's

Greenwich House Settlement, expressed a deep concern about overheated passions in the halls. In a phrase that was common in genteel criticisms, she warned that the combination of drinking and dancing was "frequently provocative of sensuality."[6]

"Tough dancing," which brought partners close physically or had them make sexually suggestive movements, heightened the reformers' fears about loosed desires in the dance places. Bowen was shocked by the "immoral dancing and open embracing" she found in most of Chicago's halls. The *Outlook* endorsed prohibiting "certain modern and indecent dances," and bemoaned the "opportunity for license and debauch" in these "grotesque" practices. John Collier of the People's Institute, a social welfare organization in New York City, wrote dramatically of "men and women depraved and turned into vampires and criminals" in commercial dance halls. Belle Israels, a former settlement worker, related that "no girl comes to the dance hall night after night and remains what she was when she began coming there." Israels added that employees of these dance facilities admitted, in confidence, "You cannot dance night after night, held in the closest of sensual embraces, with every effort made in the style of dancing to appeal to the worst that is in you, and remain unshaken by it."[7]

Motion pictures drew the ire of reformers partly for their physical features, like the dance halls. Critics worried about the effects of the films on eyesight and the dirty conditions, poor ventilation, and inadequate fire protection of many theaters. Their preoccupation with sexual encounters, of course, also made darkness a particular concern. It "afforded a cover," Louise Bowen wrote, "for familiarity and sometimes even for immorality."[8]

As with dance halls, however, the chief criticisms of motion pictures were moral objections to their subjects and the messages they carried. Reformers and social workers believed that the movies operated immediately and directly on the imaginations of viewers. The films were thought to be able to take over individuals' faculties and change their characters. Children were especially at risk, as Louise Bowen explained. She told of thirteen boys who were arrested in Chicago after they viewed a film series depicting a burglar as the hero. All "had in their possession housebreakers' tools, and all stated they had invested in these tools because they had seen these pictures and they were anxious to become gentlemanly burglars." A New Jersey court case revealed a similar awe at the purported influence of films. When a nine-year-old was arraigned for "truancy and incorrigibility," the prosecutor cited the motion picture as the central cause of the boy's behavior, and the boy's own lawyer contended that he "had been a good child at home and obedient until he developed the passion for attending moving picture shows." After placing the boy on probation, the judge announced to the court that "the moving picture shows were undoubtedly the most demoralizing force in the country to-day. The pictures had a great fascination for even adults, and the graphic portrayals of holdups, robberies, and of immoral scenes and characters, made a lasting impression on the minds of children that were demoralizing in the extreme." A New York judge went even further in another case. He asked rhetorically in his decision, "Is there any crime for which motion pictures are not responsible?"[9]

The reformers' most fundamental charges about the immoralities involved in dances and motion pictures thus overlap with the genteel criticisms. But in a sense, the progressives considered the entertainments to be even more potent because the problems were not particular to a social caste or class. In the progressives' view, evil amusements were not the separate refuges of the alien, indigent, and debauched, but sinks of immorality that could draw in any virtuous citizens who fell into weakened states. The reformers diverged yet more from the conservatives in assessing blame for the problems of the popular arts and in their view of the prospects for improving leisure. The progressives may be credited with introducing three central ideas to the mass culture critique.

The first was that the public should be absolved of responsibility for the moral affronts of the entertainments. Whereas most conservative critics held the patrons directly accountable for the quality of their entertainments, the progressives believed that bad influences in the patrons' environments largely explained these problems. The difference is most obvious in references to popular culture audiences. The sneers at "rogues," "pitiful blockheads," or "low-browed" men and women that occasionally came through the careful prose of the genteel magazines are absent in most of the reform literature. Instead, reformers such as Rheta Dorr portrayed "perfectly normal" girls wanting to enjoy the dance hall. Other approving adjectives the reformers commonly used to describe the desires of entertainment patrons—"natural," "creative," "joyful," "playful," "spirited"—suggest the audiences were honorable people with legitimate interests. The progressives did not deny the moral weaknesses of individuals but tended to see far more positive traits in people's natures. With this view of the public, reformers looked elsewhere for the source of entertainment problems. They assumed these untoward forces were alien to healthy American communities, an infection of unnatural desires.

This led to the second idea in the reformers' critique: the popularity of corrupt entertainments was a product of the manipulations of "commerce." The dance hall proprietors were particularly singled out for the evil force in their facilities. "The recreation of thousands of young people has been commercialized, and, as a result, hundreds of young girls are annually started on the road to ruin," Louise Bowen wrote of the combination of drink and dance, "for the saloonkeepers and dance hall owners have only one end in view, and that is profit." Jane Addams, the most prominent of the urban social workers, charged that American cities had "turned over the provision for public recreation to the most evil-minded and the most unscrupulous members of the community" by allowing commercial facilities to dominate leisure activities. Belle Israels argued that owners of saloon dance halls had no sense of morality beyond their cash tills. While reformers who worked with young people discouraged heterosexual relationships, afraid that "friendships" might arise, "our friend, who runs the saloon, is not afraid of any such consequence. On the contrary he realizes that in this very desire of young people to meet with one another is a splendid opportunity for him to increase his profits."[10]

"Commerce" was accused of equally sullying effects on the movies. The manager of a small-town theater, writing in the reformer journal the *Survey* in 1916, said that, for all his attempts at promoting wholesome entertainments, the movie business had found sensuality most profitable and pushed those films instead. John Collier described the effects of commerce on the motion picture as the cultivation of a debilitating addiction. "It pays commerce to develop the purely sensational side of recreation," he argued, "because in proportion as amusement becomes more sensational, the amusement seeker becomes more an habitue of it." Jane Addams saw the problem with her typical grasp of the largest implications. "We need only to look about us," she wrote, "to perceive that quite as one set of men have organized the young people into industrial enterprises in order to profit from their toil, so another set of men . . . have entered the neglected field of recreation and have organized enterprises which make profit out of their invincible love of pleasure." After recounting stories of young people ending evenings in dissipation in attempts to get the most of their recreation dollar, Addams asked whether "the disorder, the drinking, the late hours, the lack of decorum," were not "directly traceable to the commercial enterprise which administers to pleasure in order to drag it into excess because excess is more profitable." She pronounced, "We have no business thus to commercialize pleasure." [11]

Probably as indicative of the progressives' concentration on money concerns was their typical way of referring to the movie problem with mention of the admission fee. Their critical tracts carried titles such as "The Nickel Theatre" and "Five and Ten Cent Theaters," and their texts regularly used these terms to denote the facilities. The reformers' conclusion about commerce as the root of this social problem seems clear from the term that was created to refer to the movie rage: "nickel madness." [12]

The third new idea in the reformers' critique was that, because the evils in popular forms were cultivated by commerce and not indigenous to the public, the good people would naturally respond to good, reformed amusements. This notion was a call to action for the progressives because, once the profit motive was isolated as the source of corruption, programs could be created to control it. The prospect of reform likely headed off more severe measures for prohibiting these arts. The reformers' objections to the dance hall conditions, for instance, seemed ample reason to seek their elimination. Yet they rarely pursued such campaigns, and very few American cities closed dance halls altogether. Regulation efforts such as inspecting and licensing of facilities were far more common.

Some reformers promoted their own noncommercial forms of recreation rather than throwing out the offenders. Philanthropic and social organizations created centers to compete with the dance halls in several cities. In 1910, Belle Israels explained the workings of two "model" halls set up in New York by the Committee on Amusements and Vacation Resources of Working Girls. Disguise was the most notable feature, for by design it was "not known to the young people who attend them that they are anything but money-making establishments." It is unlikely, however, that patrons were deceived when they encountered the order and decorum of these cloaked halls. Practices included checking addresses of registered dancers and a rule that a young man had to be introduced formally to a woman by a staff go-between before they could dance. Special attention to girls was also written into the policy of the philanthropic hall. "The girls who come too frequently are notified, and their parents are notified that they are coming to the dance hall every night in the week," Israels wrote. "Or if the girl ceases coming we notify the parents that she is not at our dance hall now and they should see where she is." Supervision was necessary to eliminate the free behavior allowed in the commercial halls, but the hope was that it would not intrude upon the atmosphere for fun. To a striking degree, the reformers were willing to copy almost all the other features of the commercial halls or academies in creating model dance facilities. "We have gone in for confetti showers, prize waltzes and various kinds of wholesome vaudeville features," Israels explained. "We expect to go into every type of novelty that will compete with the man next door." [13]

The progressives' faith in the value of good recreation similarly moderated calls to discipline the motion pictures. The most significant attempt to control movie content, the creation of the National Board of Censorship of Motion Pictures, was in fact designed to head off more drastic measures against films. In the summer of 1907, the police commissioner of New York City had urged cancellation of all penny arcade and nickelodeon licenses in response to rising fears about their moral standards. The following year, the mayor held hearings that considered the most drastic solution—closing all the city's motion picture theaters. Reformers moved to quell these calls for prohibition, with the urging of the movie industry, by proposing a citizens committee to examine and judge films before they were shown to the public. The Board of Censorship (which later became the National Board of Review) was established in 1909.[14]

_____

While the designs of the progressives for reforming popular culture were certainly novel, they did not change entertainment habits as the progressives had hoped. By the end of the First World War and the waning of progressive reform, it was evident that public recreation efforts had had little impact. The amusement business had continued growing, and, despite a few local successes, civic recreation and regulation had done little to deter it. The efforts to subdue commercial entertainments were producing the same frustrations for the reformers as the futile attempts to reform aesthetic tastes had produced for the conservatives. Each of these crusades had in fact devolved into exalting unpopular art forms as the respective reformers grew more cynical about social improvement. To explain the progressives' failure, we must examine the sources of the critique more deeply. Just how innovative were the progressives' ideas about popular culture? The preconceptions and particular reasoning that shaped Dorr's story about Annie Donnelly are a good key to this outlook.

The reformers' moral objections to the entertainments derived from time-honored, middle-class standards. Dorr's criticism focused on the social conditions and behavior in the dance hall. Annie Donnelly was away from home with an unrelated man, unchaperoned. She was in a saloon, drinking, calling attention to herself in expressive dancing. A number of these behaviors violated the codes of many ethnic groups and classes, but all violated middle-class notions of probity, particularly for women. Women's roles were not static in the early twentieth century, but older expectations remained strong: women were to maintain moral homes, to behave with restraint and protect society against excessive passions, to be on constant guard for their reputations, and to take much of their amusement apart from men.[15]

Dorr's objections were thus very similar to those of the genteel critics because the two groups typically had the same social roots and ethical groundings. Virtually all the major figures among the reformer critics and the conservative writers were born to fathers who practiced professions. They enjoyed upper-middle-class or upper-class standards and status and were afforded the best educations. Even the obvious difference between the groups—the greater number of female writers among the reformers and social workers—appears to have affected the criticism only by encouraging a greater attention to the conditions and experiences of women and children. The female critics most often judged the entertainments along the same lines as their male contemporaries, reformer or not.

The shared backgrounds of reformers and conservatives meant that they were equally alert to the changes brought by industrialism, urban life, and especially immigration, and to the threats these posed to morality and social stability in modern America. The editors of the *Outlook*, for example, expressed their fear that first-generation Americans and other "undeveloped people" were too susceptible to the abundant evil suggestions in the modern environment. The journal referred to "the more or less rudderless human being whom we must educate into a good citizen, the child of alien parents who too often is contemptuous of the habits and maxims of his parents and ignorant of anything American but the hybrid life of a polyglot city." Most important for the criticism of popular culture, the reformers also agreed with the genteel writers that, in the face of these threats and the weaknesses of human nature, social constraints were needed for maintaining order. The public had to be directed on constructive paths in order to keep its darker impulses in check.[16]

While the two critiques had shared origins in this common social background, conservatives and reformers identified different sources for the entertainment problem because they viewed lower-class audiences differently. The way each laid blame in situations like Annie Donnelly's illustrates the contrast.

For a conservative critic such as Rollin Hartt, Donnelly's fondness for the dance hall was largely a product of her inherited character. The girl's immigrant, working-class background made her less self-controlled and more promiscuous than a woman from the responsible middle class. Her ethical and intellectual flaws clearly placed her apart from the respectable classes in the "twin streams of population" Hartt described in America. Genteel observers read the popular arts as literal expressions of the values of their producers and audiences, so the drinking, "spieling," and sexual familiarity were evidence that those like Donnelly were ruled by their passions. The sordid entertainments were a direct reflection of the moral state of the lower classes.

In Dorr's reading, however, the girl's visits and behavior in the dance hall were not due to her flawed nature but to abuses in her environment. Dorr took the girl's dancing and drinking just as literally as the conservative critic, treating them as evidence of her "fallen" character. But she looked to Donnelly's conditions more than her background for the source of the fall.

Proclaiming that the girl was not "viciously inclined," Dorr focused instead on her small living quarters and lack of private space, the presence of the boarder in her home, the amount of time she spent in the street, the severely long hours her father worked, and her parents' absence or inattention. Her implicit message was that economic exploitation had kept Donnelly's parents away from home or too distracted to supervise the children properly, forced them to take in a stranger, and left them with meager living conditions and few opportunities for constructive leisure. This deformed home life, in turn, led Annie to the dance hall, where economic exploitation merged with sexual exploitation. Her suitor and the proprietor took advantage of her natural desire for recreation by making her drink and introducing her to salacious dances. Commercial entertainment had therefore capitalized on the girl's unfortunate circumstances and compromised her in her weakened moral state. The ultimate product of these abuses, Dorr suggests, was Donnelly's thorough exploitation as a prostitute.

Certainly not all the reformers' accounts of the mass arts were this tragic, but Dorr's reflects their consensus that the chief causes of the popular culture problems were the taxing conditions of modern life. The most frequent explanations of what drove people to bad entertainments were debilitating, demoralizing work routines and the excessive stimulations of urban life.

The progressives regularly condemned the conditions of industrial labor in America out of concern for the physical and psychological health of workers.[17] In their popular culture criticism, they argued that stultifying work regimes deadened workers' sensitivities and consequently left them open to the basest emotional appeals of the entertainments. Mary McDowell of the University Settlement in Chicago wrote of the urgent need to help "the machine ridden men, women and children." "I know a bright girl eighteen years of age, who works in a room smelling of turpentine, painting and labelling thousands of cans a week," she explained to the readers of the recreation reform journal *Playground*. "By Saturday night she grows reckless. Once when her older friend begged her not to go to a certain objectionable garden, she expressed unconsciously the protest of a young nature in an unnatural environment, when she said: 'I'm so tired when Saturday night comes I don't care a damn where I go.'"[18] Howard Braucher, secretary of the reform group Playground Association of America, described the extinction of the "play spirit" in industrial workers that left them open to any artificially inspiriting recreation. "When the play spirit has been lost and the future is only one long-drawn-out work, work, work, which taxes the body, but does not engage the mind," Braucher argued, "then tragedy has reached its climax."[19] A 1912 study of the noted factory town Lowell, Massachusetts, compared contemporary work regimes with those of the early to middle nineteenth century to trace the dramatic shift to bad amusements: "Under modern industrial conditions, with automatic machinery running at high speed, the fifty-six hours a week in the cotton mills bring greater exhaustion of body and mind than the seventy hours of earlier days. Once the 'factory girls' could sit at their work and read or sew; now the operative must be alert, or else become an automaton, a part of the machinery he tends. With energy sapped, amusement is a necessity, and recreation must be a diversion."[20]

While modern labor produced an emotional stupor that drove workers to seek shocking amusements, the deluge of excitements in the twentieth-century city promoted an even greater moral callousness. "We are informed by high authority that there is nothing in the environment to which youth

Controlling the effects of the emotional stimulations of the modern city was one of the progressives' central challenges. The sort of stimulations they worried about are much in evidence in this scene of a Labor Day celebration in Buffalo, New York, 1905. (Library of Congress, LC-D401-12910)

so keenly responds as to music," wrote Jane Addams, "and yet the streets, the vaudeville shows, the five-cent theaters are full of the most blatant and vulgar songs." Addams believed that "trivial and obscene words, . . . meaningless and flippant airs" combined in music on the street "to incite that which should be controlled, to degrade that which should be exalted, to make sensuous that which might be lifted into the realm of the higher imagination." For youth in particular, she thought "it is nothing short of cruelty to over-stimulate his senses as does the modern city." An official from New York's Child Welfare Committee similarly found the "hyper-stimulus" of popular vaudeville to be too much when taken together with the "kaleidoscopic stimuli" of life in the early twentieth century. Both produced what he termed a "stimulating but disintegrating" effect.[21]

Urban enticements and industrialism sent audiences to corrupt amusements that also undermined public morality by threatening the family. The

family had been traditionally a crucial institution for instilling proper behavior. Conditions of modern life, however, were eclipsing its authority.
Louise Bowen explained that parents' concerns about the public dance halls
had initially inspired her investigations. She told how her Juvenile Protective
Association had received repeated pleas for help from mothers whose children were frequenting dance halls. Jane Addams recounted the similar frus-
tration of another parent who felt he was losing control of his family to the
entertainments. An English immigrant shopkeeper explained to her that he
felt obliged to provide his four daughters the admission to a five-cent theater
every evening. Otherwise, he feared, they might steal it from his till or even
"be driven to procure it in even more illicit ways." The shopkeeper lamented
that "this cheap show had ruined his 'ome," Addams related, and he called
the amusement "the curse of America." The director of the New York
People's Institute, Frederic Howe, portrayed family disintegration in even
starker terms in 1914, concluding that the amusement industry had "sent the
girl to the dance hall, the boy to the pool room, the father to the saloon." [22]

The reformers' new appreciation of environmental and social sources behind the popularity of entertainments had ironic consequences. It ascribed
greater influence to the popular arts, yet it focused so strongly on their manipulative potential that it discouraged consideration of how individuals
used these forms in their everyday lives. It stemmed from a greater empathy for the public, yet it simultaneously underestimated the public's ability
to choose its own most useful cultural communications and therefore made
the reformers even less engaged with the way the public perceived the world.
The key to this perverse result was that reformers considered the working
classes not simply as participants in the urban-industrial environment, but as
its victims. The focus on harsh work and living conditions defined this group
almost exclusively by its suffering. It obscured the fact that these people
remained resourceful, adaptive, thinking beings. By objectifying them as
victims, the progressives removed a dimension from their lives. They were
understood only by the ways that they reacted against their circumstances.

This new "victim" ideology became central to the Left's mass culture criticism for two generations. Its consequences were twofold. First, it blinded
reformers to the ways that different social groups understood entertainments
differently. The process of classifying entertainment patrons together as an
easily defensible group turned them into a passive, undifferentiated mass in
the reformers' minds. This group was presumed to be reduced by its envi-

ronment to the most basic human (in)sensibilities, so all members in effect became the same. The victim model thus neglected how individuals chose entertainments to fit their particular circumstances. It neglected as well the different styles or proclivities for interpreting the arts that were fostered by class, ethnicity, gender, and other interests.

The only readings of the entertainments that were credible for all, then, were the literal or scientific readings of the middle and upper classes. In this understanding, behaviors that appeared in the entertainments were direct expressions of values rather than figurative probes or fanciful challenges for these social conventions. The logic of the reformers' critique became a closed, self-sustaining system: they read salacious dances or crime-filled movies as evidence of the public's taste for immorality, which was evidence of its exploitation, which was reason to accept the victim stereotype, which discredited the public's judgment or taste and left the reformers' reading as the accepted view.[23]

The second, related effect of the victim ideology was to encourage the reformers' paternalism. With the masses so largely incapacitated, reformers felt justified in establishing their own tastes for chosen amusements as the standards for all. Entertainment audiences that were numbed and ethically weakened needed guidance to right themselves, in this logic, much as impressionable children needed guidance to work their way through difficult experiences. Reformers could therefore act as parents for these wayward citizens and prescribe their entertainments in the interest of protecting them.[24]

The effect of the victim ideology was to remove the populace from the progressives' considerations of popular culture. Consider how different the Annie Donnelly story might have been, for instance, if it were taken from the girl's own perspective.

For Donnelly, the tawdry dance hall may have seemed one of the few places where she could realize her desires and direct her own life. A working-class girl, of a recently immigrated family, living in a tenement, faced numerous physical and social constraints on her leisure: a limited amount to spend; little privacy or indoor space for socializing; her parents' particular rules for recreations; ethnic or communal proscriptions against some forms; a dearth of leisure outlets for women; and specific social rules and expectations for women from either the dominant culture or her community. The dance hall experience, though, got her away from parents and community leaders and offered the kind of glamor and excitement she could not find at home or on the street. Here, she could freely mix with men and explore her own sexuality. Dancing itself offered the physical pleasure of moving and a chance to express her desires free from many of the judging eyes she normally encountered. For an adolescent, this was a chance to challenge parental bounds and sample adult freedoms. For a recent immigrant, the hall could also represent an introduction to American ways and habits, especially the scheduled, packaged, routinized leisure patterns of industrial society.[25]

A visit to the dance hall certainly involved the risk of exploitation, as the reformers well noted. And they were certainly justified in their concern that children should not be cast into the world of adult pleasures without guidance. Dorr's concern for Donnelly, then, was certainly fitting, considering Donnelly's age.

Yet, when this insistent care was intruded upon adults as well, it became paternalism. Dorr's summary judgment that the dance hall was "a veritable forcing house of vice and crime" was much too broad to account for the satisfactions that different patrons sought there. The problem again returned to intellectuals applying scientific or literal interpretations to an entertainment that had a figurative meaning as well. By focusing so strongly on the debilitating features of working-class environments, reformers dismissed alternative readings of the popular arts. Patrons of commercial entertainments could be overworked, ill-housed, poorly educated, and generally downtrodden but still retain their own legitimate desires for freer and fuller lives.

Despite their laudable desires for protecting the victims of industrial society, then, reformers disparaged these people by neglecting their unique qualities. Because they did not appreciate the public's resourcefulness, they were unable to understand the attraction of popular culture. The most successful entertainments spoke to the strong spirits of the audiences, gave flight to people's imaginations, allowed them to sample more pleasurable lives at least temporarily or vicariously, and drew great audiences. The commercial entertainments that succeeded, then, were popular not because they took advantage of the public's weakened state and degraded desires, but because they spoke to its dreams and fantasies about how the world could work and should feel.

If we remove the ideology of victims from the reformers' mass culture critique, its consistency with the genteel views becomes apparent. The reformers' blame of "commerce" or evil entrepreneurs for bad entertainments was a recasting of the conservatives' more direct condemnations of popular tastes. When reformers attacked the biggest money-makers, in effect they attacked popular desires as they appeared in their most exaggerated forms. In the plethora of new mass arts in any one year, many failed to get the public's approval. But those that captured the popular imagination were heavily capitalized and became the biggest commercial entertainments. The bogey of "commerce" that the reformers blamed for the problem of the popular arts therefore merely represented successful attempts at communicating with the public psyche.

With the victim ideology removed, the reformers' plans for improved leisure pursuits also seem far less novel. They appear to be more an extension of the genteel hierarchy of the arts than a new order responsive to the interests of all. The progressives' rational recreation programs reflected the tastes of the Caucasian, native-born middle class that grew up amid the transformation from rural-agrarian America to an urban-industrial society. Reformers looked foremost to a particular folk culture drawn from the leisure traditions of Elizabethan England for their model of recreation. This harkening back more than three centuries was necessary because most believed folk culture was dead in early twentieth-century America. Urbanization was assumed to have destroyed a village-scale social life and also the games, caroling, and husking bees that made up earlier recreation. Reformers favored these forms precisely because they predated their own pressing urban social problems. The small-scale, neighborly folk arts were seen as healthy, exciting ways of releasing and expressing feelings as well as testimony to their community's shared moral standards. For the reformers, legitimate amusement was not all recreative activities, in other words, but the kind of sanctioned fun that they imagined had previously worked to support desirable values.[26]

When the progressives looked for a more immediate model of ideal recreation, most found some resonance of Elizabethan ways in their own childhoods. The leisure pursuits of the nineteenth century, which had supported the behavioral standards of a predominantly rural society, were equally appealing. Jane Addams's praise for "the old dances on the village green" is particularly illustrative, especially when we keep in mind her strong criticism of the "feverish search for pleasure" in contemporary dance halls. Addams believed her choice was not from nostalgic longing, but rather a rational assessment of the ways folk activities functioned. "These old forms of dancing, which have been worked out in many lands and through long experiences, safeguard unwary and dangerous expression and yet afford a vehicle through which the gaiety of youth may flow." A simple comparison of the typical rhetoric in mass entertainments criticism, stressing "excesses," "abnormality," and "distorted desires," with the seemingly naturally evolved qualities Addams upholds suggests the sea change the reformers perceived from the folk culture era.[27]

Concerted efforts to improve American recreation activities with such a local focus and a stress upon discipline and order had begun in the late nineteenth century with programs such as the provision of public sandboxes and model playgrounds for children. As the reformers' commitment grew, these programs expanded to include communal activities and social centers for adult recreation. This "play movement," as it came to be called, was operating nationwide by the second decade of the twentieth century.[28]

We can further understand the failure of the recreation reformers if we consider that their ideal forms were not only rooted in a specific historical era, but in a particular class experience within that era. Folk games, harvest festivals, and village dances were common in the sixteenth century, but other pastimes often were lewd, boisterous, and violent. In the reformers' quest for wholesome, healthy play, they focused on forms that offered to sustain the traditional values they esteemed, while ignoring the heavy drinking, whoring, cockfighting, bullbaiting and bearbaiting, and bare-knuckle boxing that equally expressed the values of many in this era. When they looked back centuries for a model to rejuvenate leisure, they did so selectively. The desires and worldviews of the poor were lost here as well.[29]

At base, the reformers, as much as the genteel critics, refused to accept different tastes in expressive arts from different social groups. This insistence on a single aesthetic standard spoke to the central concern of intellectuals of many political stripes in this era with maintaining their moral consensus. Progressives, like the conservatives, generally assumed that their standards of belief and behavior were universal and timeless. Their values were to be anchors firmly set against the tides and swells of their changing society. The notion of different but equally legitimate lifestyles existing together was alien to most of the critics and was not a desirable model for the modern society. While both reformers and conservatives recognized that the working classes did not share their views on the arts, they attributed this difference not to varying culturally rooted worldviews, but to underdeveloped tastes within one such view. For the progressives, these were remediable traits, and they set themselves to "improve" them out of existence.

————

This analysis of the logic of the reformers' critique dispels an image of the progressives as simple liberators of humanity and offers a more sober estimate of the limits of their programs. It also highlights again how the problem of growing social differences was at the center of intellectuals' efforts to define the place of "privileged intelligence" in a society with pretensions of equality. Class and ethnic prejudices colored the reformers' evaluations of the popular arts just as they had genteel criticisms, and both were separated from the lower classes by their literal readings of these forms. But where the conservatives gradually withdrew from the populace and turned social differences into firm separations, the progressives accepted the challenge of being intellectuals *within* democratic society. They worked to overcome these differences by helping the downtrodden. Their efforts at reforming entertainments ran aground on the same problem as many of their other programs: accommodating difference. The class and ethnic biases that were inherent in their worldview were inherent in their solutions to social ills as well. They met social differences with prescriptions for changes that would minimize them, and those on the receiving end often refused. Difference, then, was still not wholly accepted. As their programs for proper recreations show, they created a hierarchy of entertainments instead.

3

MODERNISM,
CULTURAL RADICALS,
AND MASS
ENTERTAINMENTS

If any group of intellectuals could have been expected to counter the prejudice against popular culture so firmly established in the United States by the early twentieth century, it was the cultural radicals of the 1910s and 1920s. These artists, writers, and critics sought, at their most ambitious, an intellectual revolution. They hoped to overturn Victorian social norms and to open the possibilities of new groundings for ethics. With regard to mass entertainments, the most important part of the radicals' challenge to sensibilities was their desire to overturn the nation's reigning aesthetic standards. The promise this movement held for the popular arts was that if the genteel order could be overcome, its proscriptions against popular forms might be discredited as well, inviting intellectuals to a new acceptance of 53 the nation's amusements. Its failing was that, while the radicals rejected the contents of the genteel hierarchy for the arts, the hierarchy itself was preserved as a useful buffer between intellectual values and often contrary popular tastes.

Cultural radicalism in America in the early 1900s was a variation of the international sweep of "modernism" that developed through the West in the late nineteenth and early twentieth centuries. This vast, heterogeneous, intellectual and imaginative force produced many of the important works of art and literature of the era. Though these efforts were inconsistent and often vaguely defined, they did share a common belief that older, established ways and understandings had become outmoded and oppressive in a world turning so dramatically modern.

One of the most important mediums of modernism in the United States in the 1910s and 1920s was the "little magazine." Artistic and literary journals such as the *Little Review*, *Broom*, and the *Dial* were "little" in that they typically attracted only a few thousand subscribers. The precarious finances of many also made for infrequent publications and short lives. Most were published in the United States, but those produced by expatriates overseas (where costs were typically much lower) also circulated in intellectual circles at home. These magazines, with their limited reach, had little direct influence on broader public opinion. Yet among groups of writers and critics such as the modernist enclaves of New York and Paris, they were read and referred to widely. They functioned as a kind of intellectual forum for developing and debating the radicals' cultural ideas, and therefore serve as important sources for understanding their perceptions of popular forms in this era.[1]

The American modernists were as disparate as was the international movement; there were significant disagreements in philosophy and matters of aesthetic taste. But while the radicals' programs for a new cultural order differed, they were linked by a shared antipathy to genteel cultural standards. They held in common a determination to reintroduce the concerns and experiences of everyday life to the arts and literature and make these forms relevant to modern America. It is most accurate, therefore, to consider not one "revolt against gentility," but rather a series of stands taken by writers against the remnants of the nineteenth-century system. Because popular entertainments had been important as a negative reference in the genteel hierarchy, examples of art that were not acceptable, their treatment by the modernists was also a prime test of how revolutionary this group might be.

————

The *Seven Arts*, although published only in 1916 and 1917, was one of the most influential modernist magazines of the early twentieth century. Edited by James Oppenheim and Waldo Frank, and influenced by writers such as Van Wyck Brooks and Randolph Bourne, the journal melded socialist politics with a loathing for genteel cultural standards and a strongly nationalist approach to the arts and letters. The *Seven Arts* did not support the most daring experiments in the arts. Its radicalism might better be described as a philosophical inclination toward change rather than a specific program built around one aesthetic style. The magazine's commitment to political support for the working classes and to bringing popular influences into the arts seemed to bode well for a new appreciation of the mass entertainments from intellectuals.[2]

"The spirit of Walt Whitman stands behind the *Seven Arts*," the magazine announced in a 1917 editorial. "What we are seeking is what he sought: that intense American nationality in which the spirit of the people is shared through its tasks and its arts, its undertakings and its songs." Whitman would serve as such a touchstone for several of the new groups of cultural radicals in the early twentieth century. For those at the *Seven Arts*, the poet's unbounded faith in the promise of American democracy and its culture became their common theme. The optimism was evident from an editorial in the first issue in November, 1916. It explained the magazine's conception that the nation had entered a "renascent period" and was on the verge, as the editors put it, of "that national self-consciousness which is the beginning of greatness." In this coming era of accomplishment, the arts would no longer be "private matters" but rather would become both "the expression of the national life," and "a means to its enhancement." The *Seven Arts* would promote this cultural awakening by encouraging "self-expression" of its writers. This freedom to plumb one's spirit, with disregard for regnant genteel standards, was central to the magazine's plan to bring new and vital arts to the public. The editors portrayed the *Seven Arts* as "not a magazine for artists, but an expression of artists for the community."[3]

While Whitman inspired the magazine's call for a populist culture, the editors initially left open the particular nature of this culture. Was the democratic spirit of America to be sought directly in popular tastes and the creations of popular artists? Or was it to be realized by more elite artists who stood at a remove from the general public, and perhaps enjoyed a greater perspective? The *Seven Arts* writers were more inclined to the latter view, and here they were most influenced by Van Wyck Brooks.

Brooks was less expansive in his sympathies than Whitman, and had an especially jaundiced view of popular culture. He presented an all-inclusive theory about the development of intellectual life in the United States that was adopted by a number of the *Seven Arts* group. Together, their interpretations of the flaws of American civilization bolstered the mass culture critique.

Brooks's themes were honed during his undergraduate studies at Harvard in the turn-of-the-century era. He was taught by professors such as Barrett Wendell and Irving Babbitt, among the university's leading Europhile aesthetes. These scholars had long insisted that American culture was artless, and that the literature of the United States was uniformly banal. Brooks absorbed their prejudices and developed an historical explanation for this supposed failure of American expression. Beginning in *The Wine of the Puritans* (1908), Brooks argued that the chief cause of the nation's aesthetic barrenness was that the society had never established deep roots in the North American soil. European peoples had lived long in their lands and absorbed the essential character of these environments before developing the arts and other trappings of civilization. But the first white settlers in North America were immigrants, so their communities could not draw upon an elemental culture in their new land. They had no native way of life that grew out of the experience of the continent. Rather, Americans had arrived as comparative sophisticates, "full-grown, modern, self-conscious men," in Brooks's telling. From the first, then, they were out of touch with their surroundings.

With no native ancestral standards to guide them in developing their culture, they had no philosophical perspective on their efforts. As a result, Brooks believed, many threw themselves into action for its own sake. There were plenty of practical problems to be solved. And in a society conquering a wilderness, immediate results were most valuable. This approach led Americans to an overexclusive concern with material matters, a mindset that Brooks identified with the ethics of commerce.

Yet others among the new Americans responded to their alien surroundings with a shift in the opposite direction. Recognizing that their European heritage did not have roots or relevance in the struggles on the raw continent, they created a philosophy that withdrew from the practical demands of their immediate environment. They resorted to what Brooks termed an "arbitrary and purely spiritual" outlook, a mystical sort of idealism.[4]

Neither of these extremes, practical or impractical, provided any firm foundation for the arts in America, as Brooks explained in *America's Coming-of-Age* (1915). The two equally unproductive principles, which he labeled "Highbrow" and "Lowbrow" after the era's shorthand for distinctions of intellect, left no middle ground for a genuine, representative expression of American life. "Human nature itself in America exists on two irreconcilable planes," Brooks wrote, "the plane of stark intellectuality and the plane of stark business." He believed poetic insight was capable of bringing thought and action together, but poetry simply could not compete with these great forces as they became further entrenched in the early twentieth century.

Brooks made a nod to Whitman and his *Seven Arts* followers by presenting the poet as the last figure capable of uniting the culture. No one since Whitman had been able to ground the idealist tradition in the realm of the practical and join the divided American. "All those things which had been separate, self-sufficient, incoordinate—action, theory, idealism, business—he cast into a crucible," Brooks wrote of Whitman's accomplishment, "and they emerged, harmonious and molten, in a fresh democratic ideal, which is based upon the whole personality."[5]

Without a contemporary Whitman, though, Brooks found nearly all American culture to be wanting; none more so than popular culture. Brooks had little personal interest in the popular arts, but his view of popular literature influenced his colleagues. According to him, the "typical best-selling novelist" was an inadvertent product of the gulf between high and low in American culture. Literature, as an academic discipline in American universities, celebrated great works and therefore was part of the venerated "highbrow" realm, Brooks explained. When contemporary writers compared their own work to such purported eminence, they were often cowed before it. The result was that they settled for the "lowbrow" realm of popular acceptance instead of striving for aesthetic effect. They wrote with such humility and meager expectations that they forfeited standards or "artistic conscience." "And the worst of it," Brooks wrote, "is that precisely these writers of irredeemable trash are often the bright, vigorous, intuitive souls who *could* make literature out of American life." While popular artists were stuck in this lowbrow orbit, though, their efforts could amount only to "richly rewarded trash." [6]

Brooks thus created a criticism of popular literature that, while based on his interpretation of American culture, overlapped the reformers' mass culture critique. Like the typical progressive critic, Brooks found the popular forms distasteful and a hindrance to better creations. Like them as well, he found that the fault for the best-sellers did not lie in the popular audience. In fact, the desires of the book-buying public did not enter at all into his considerations. Instead, he spun a theory that blamed alien forces ("highbrowism" and "lowbrowism") for corrupting the arts in much the same way the progressives blamed commercialism.

Brooks's assessment of popular literature as lowbrow or part of the business plane reduces to almost the same criticism as the reformers' blame on "commerce." They believed the ethics of the marketplace broke down moral standards and opened the public to its darker impulses. Brooks was far more concerned with the way free-market ethics cramped the souls of sensitive readers. But both sides agreed that Americans needed a different order of the arts. More precisely, Brooks and the reformers called for arts that spoke to their own life situations—educations, living standards, ethnicities, and political views—rather than the lives of the majority of Americans in the early twentieth century.

Brooks's interpretation is also significant for steering the modernists' budding interest in popular culture into a narrow preoccupation with artists' concerns. This focus on elite artistic producers disconnected the popular arts from their producers and users. Once the magazine's writers came to consider the popular arts primarily as static objects unto themselves, removed from their active role as agents in cultural communication, they were bound to misunderstand them. Intellectuals were again predisposing themselves to interpret entertainments literally, as direct statements of the values of producers and audiences, rather than texts that invited audiences to derive their own meanings. They were therefore predisposed to react to the entertainments just as literally, either supporting or rejecting the values they perceived. Thus, though the entertainments did get more notice in the *Seven Arts* than they had in conservative cultural journals, it was a particularly superficial attention.

In the magazine's first issue, it seemed that a more social reading of the popular arts was in store. Paul Rosenfeld, the resident music critic, evaluated the American scene with a scheme very much like Brooks's. Rosenfeld argued that most native symphonic composers were "ineffectual," unable to interest the public, because they had little sense of the common experience of the nation. He promoted the compositions of Horatio Parker and Stephen Foster's folk songs as better alternatives, "the one musical expression of America." Composers had to put "faith in the American destiny," he wrote. "We must go where Whitman led," and trust in the tremendous potential expressive power within America. On the surface, Rosenfeld seemed also to value the most popular new music of his day. "The music of all races and all ages, from that of Asia to the songs of our negroes and aborigines, the fierce rhythms of our rag-time, are before us," he wrote, "to teach, and to be used."[7]

An editorial by James Oppenheim the following month, however, developed the writers' damning criticism for the general run of popular culture. Also following Brooks's model, Oppenheim described two levels of "purism" in the contemporary arts. In the "high" realm were the modernist works that he thought had been stripped clean of images, stories, and feelings. These had become so rarefied, he thought, that "most of the species" was incapable of appreciating or enjoying them. For the majority of Americans, on the other hand, Oppenheim saw another kind of "purity." "Pure trash, pure vulgarity, if you will, but—pure." He repeated the indictments of previous mass culture critics: "Here are stories that are all plot, snap, ginger, and wish-fulfillment: cheap fairytales of business and adventure, turned out as by machinery. The product, though multitudinous, is uniform: and one can buy one's magazine by the color of the eyes of the girl on the cover. Here is illustration that carries rubber-stamp beauty and heroism." Oppenheim included in his condemnation "music that sets the feet dancing and turns heart-throbs into syncopation," and drama that "transplants with actuality the people of the street to the stage." He extended the conservatives' and reformers' criticisms that the popular arts exploited base passions, judging these forms to be "the art primarily of sensation, of news of common desire." Repeating again the summary judgment of the other critics, he wrote, "We say it lacks greatness: we say it is flabby and sentimental: we say that it discovers no depth and no height in the human being."[8]

Such "pure trash" was obviously not the genuine expression of the American community that the *Seven Arts* sought. For all of Rosenfeld's willingness to accommodate the ragtime beat into what he called "the song of democracy," he believed it could be only the raw material from which a recognized composer could create the desired national art. Oppenheim, in his reaction against genteel standards, argued that "raw appetite" was wiser than "fine taste," but was similarly open to only so much "lowness" in the coming great art.

Besides the denigration of audiences, what is notable in this pattern of dismissing the mass arts is how much it was predetermined by the very structure of the highbrow/lowbrow interpretation. That portrayal of extremes—idealism and opportunism, impractical and practical—as the predominant realms of life in the nation was simply too polarized to capture the complexities of the modern society. There was no room for intermediate positions in this scheme, nor for the possibility that individuals might live on several different "planes" depending on their activities over the course of a given day. The way the model prejudged entertainments was to conclude that, because they were obviously intended to operate amid the conditions of everyday life and because leisure was increasingly a part of business, they were debased by definition. Before the *Seven Arts* critics ever fully considered the question of the most suitable expression of American life, the nation's most popular constructions were already dismissed.

The high/low scheme also predisposed the *Seven Arts* critics to sustain much of the "Culture" ideology of earlier writers. They put their faith in the arts to capture certain of the society's virtues they most valued, and hoped these forms would subsequently further inspire these ideals. As this ideology emerged in the nineteenth century, it had established the popular entertainments as its benchmark for artistic failure. The new critics hardly challenged the assumption. As much as these writers may have detested genteel aesthetic standards and set themselves to dismantling that order, their plan for an American cultural renaissance effectively only changed the forms within the upper echelon of the old hierarchy rather than challenging the structure itself. The *Seven Arts* critics believed the cure for their sterile culture was not a new start with a new set of artists, but rather to have recognized artists simply draw on a broader range of native inspirations and express themselves more freely. The "bad" art of the genteel magazines, with its insistent moralism, sentimentality, and indifference to quotidian affairs had to be replaced by a new, socially engaged product. Yet still, recognized professionals were needed to provide direction and purpose for the American public.

The composer Ernest Bloch made this art bias most obvious in his analysis of American culture circa 1917. Using the highbrow/lowbrow model, he pitted the "intellectual acrobatics" of the avant-garde against the "facile taste" of the masses. The latter was, as he put it, "sinking with the love of platitude and the weight of mechanical inventions—phonograph, pianola, cinematograph." Bloch joined the *Seven Arts*'s calls for creating a "living art" from the common life of America, but also divorced that ideal from existing popular culture. After introducing the notion of an art rooted in the life of the community, he announced, "Needless to say, it cannot be the direct output of crowds; . . . however indirectly they must have contributed to its substance." Instead, such works were to be "the soul of a race speaking through the voice of the prophet in whom it has become incarnate."[9]

The most cogent criticism of this model for a democratic culture came from one of the *Seven Arts*'s own contributors, the literary critic Harold Stearns. Stearns detected the old genteel moralizing in this resort to "superior" sensibilities and feared that it would distort what was popular about the popular arts. His focus was the theater, and his immediate complaint was about "snobbish" criteria for judging performances. Most criticism derived so much from European standards that it was out of touch with the American public, he explained. The specific problem was that this criticism tended to consider the drama as "a cultural agent," a vehicle for producing an effect, rather that what Stearns insisted was its natural role as "a cultural expression," or a statement of feelings and circumstances. He explained that the function of drama was not "guiding and controlling and setting the pace for our emotional life," but rather "revealing and expressing that life." "Its business is disclosure, not discipline," Stearns proclaimed. By treating the stage as a cultural agent, critics had consistently overlooked the popular forms whose purpose was to give voice to the public rather than trying to guide it. "Even in the most conventional of the 'relief from ordinary life' or mere wish dramas there is some expression of the fermenting forces stirring in the country, thin and timid though that expression be," Stearns lectured the critics. "Because of our polite shudders at their crudeness and newness these unfinished and inchoate rebellions receive no appreciation or encouragement."

Stearns's argument for recognizing popular expression *as expression* would become perhaps the single most important new understanding of entertainments as it developed in later decades. Yet this anthropological approach to the entertainments was clearly only a limited embrace and from a lone voice in 1917. Stearns himself could not wholly shake artistic bias against the popular forms. The title of his article, "A Poor Thing, But Our Own," indicates that he hardly intended a ringing endorsement of the mass arts. Still, Stearns's critical position was worlds away from that of writers who saw the arts only as cultural agents. He realized that the literal, agential readings of the entertainments preempted the public's participation in creating meaning. As critical as Stearns was about what he called the "predominant traits" of artless American life, this did not mean that the popular arts that treated those traits were necessarily corrupting influences. Rather, they represented people engaging those traits and expressing their relationships to them in their everyday lives. Stearns saw that the mass entertainments could accurately capture the interests of the democracy, for good or bad. His defense of the popular drama was, as he wrote, "not because it satisfies the soul of man, but because it is ours." [10]

Other than Stearns's contribution, the *Seven Arts* group never lived up to its promise for stirring a fundamental reevaluation of the popular entertainments. Some of the mass arts did achieve notice as new aesthetic influences, but they never fully broke out of the old code of standards and expectations for expressive forms. Another equally promising prospect for new thinking about the entertainments, however, was presented by the magazine's other most important influence, critic Randolph Bourne.

Bourne challenged intellectuals to face the growing heterogeneity of American society. His support for cultural pluralism, the recognition of the value of many different ways of life and the need to foster such variety, seemed destined to rescue the heretofore outcast arts. Bourne was among the nation's strongest defenders of immigrants and their place in American culture, and, considering the extensive involvement of these newcomers in entertainments such as popular music, theater, and particularly motion pictures, he might well have been expected to be a champion of these mass arts. Yet, Bourne was nothing of the sort. Equally important were his worries about the entertainments in the shaping of the emerging society and his firm belief in art as a realization of spiritual values and an agent of social improvement. Instead of creating a new opening for the popular arts, Bourne charged that they threatened the vital diversity of cultures within America. He had introduced a new theme in the mass culture criticism.

Bourne was most intrigued by motion pictures. He believed them to be among the most accurate barometers of American life, marking "the norm of what happy and hearty America is attending to." He wrote in a 1915 article, "As a would-be democrat, I should like to believe passionately in the movies." That Bourne did not so believe was because of the content of the medium. Such mass entertainments, he believed, represented a new "lowbrow snobbery." Bourne wrote: "In a thousand ways it is as tyrannical and arrogant as the other culture of universities and millionaires and museums. I don't know which ought to be more offensive to a true democrat—this or the cheapness of the current life that so sadly lacks any raciness or characteristic savor. It looks as if we should have to resist the stale culture of the masses as we resist the stale culture of the aristocrat. It is very easy to be lenient and pseudo-human, and call it democracy." Compounding Bourne's disappointment was his belief that the public was prepared for better forms. Americans of the 1910s had enjoyed educational and cultural amenities, from universal schooling and free libraries to museums and inexpensive literature, far beyond those of any previous generation. "This," Bourne lamented, "is what we get out of it all." Fighting to maintain his democratic outlook, he explained that he did not mean to suggest that the public should have flocked to forms such as "Renaissance pictures or Ibsen plays or Dante." Indeed, he expressed "a certain unholy glee at this wholesale rejection of what our fathers reverenced as culture." But, Bourne added, "I don't feel any glee about what is substituted for it."[11]

Very much like the *Seven Arts* critics, then, Bourne was left looking for what he called a "third alternative" for an acceptable national cultural expression. Some other forms had to be found to avoid the extremes of the genteel hierarchy, on the one hand, and the "staleness" of mass culture on the other. The urgency of the problem was most fully expressed in his much-noted essay of 1916, "Trans-National America."

The central thrust of this article was an elegant plea for the abandonment of "melting pot" theories and programs for the complete assimilation of immigrants in the United States. Bourne urged that the notion of a single native "American" way of life be replaced by an appreciation of the nation's multiplicity of ways and traditions. "The foreign cultures have not been melted down or run together, made into some homogeneous Americanism," he explained, "but have remained distinct but cooperating to the greater glory and benefit, not only of themselves but of all the native 'Americanism' around them." The popular arts, however, threatened this acculturation.

Observing entertainments in the streets of New York City, Bourne found assimilation pressures destroying the cosmopolitan ideal. Rootless, "mass" men and women seemed to be evolving from the weakening of the immigrants' ethnic identities, and the process was being hastened by popular culture. The least common denominator among Americans' experiences was defined, in Bourne's mind, by cheap newspapers, motion pictures, popular songs, and the automobile. He saw nothing of value in this "most rudimentary" level of American culture and believed that, as immigrants lost the grounding of a distinctly ethnic way of life, they risked being integrated into their new society at these depths. "We may thrill with dread at the aggressive hyphenate" who boasts of his native culture, Bourne wrote of an imagined vainglorious immigrant, but "Just so surely as we tend to disintegrate these nuclei of nationalistic culture do we tend to create hordes of men and women without a spiritual country, cultural outlaws, without taste, without standards but those of the mob." He apparently assumed that those who indulged in the mass arts forfeited all their native character and expressiveness, describing them as "detached fragments of peoples," "the flotsam and jetsam of American life," and "the cultural wreckage of our time." Once people passed outside the integrating bonds of nationality, they were part of "the downward undertow of our civilization with its leering cheapness and falseness of taste and spiritual outlook." The ultimate result was "the absence of mind and sincere feeling which we see in our slovenly towns, our vapid moving pictures, our popular novels, and in the vacuous faces of crowds on the city street."

Bourne's conception of modern American culture therefore had no more place for the most broadly popular amusements than that of his *Seven Arts* colleagues. His castigations of the movies and popular literature for being both products and agents of the creation of mass men and women reveal a highly polarized vision of the common ways of life—the state of the public is presented as either all good or all bad. While Bourne's commitment to protecting ethnic differences was both warranted and admirable, it put him in the same predicament the progressives had faced. How could intellectuals effectively defend a disadvantaged people while still respecting their difference? His distaste for the entertainments led him to reduce the intricacies of acculturation to an overly simple moral generalization: fiercely nationalistic ethnic enclaves were intelligent and virtuous and a boon to American civilization, while those who assimilated to some degree were "half-breeds," "insipid," and en route to the ultimate degradation of mass man.

As was the Brooksians' wont with their highbrow/lowbrow scheme, Bourne fails to consider any worthwhile intermediate state for the public. Was there no practice of acculturation that allowed people to maintain their heritages while still sharing in the more general popular culture? Were the entertainments adopted wholesale and without discrimination by all? Why did many of the mass-produced arts fail to become popular and what does this reveal about the general audience?

Bourne's attitudes toward the public and its entertainments seem, then, to result in paternalism once again. Once the people became wards, a community "to be done for," they ceased being accountable fellow citizens. The characteristics of the undifferentiated "mass man" or the "mob" could thereafter be easily attributed to those who were not allowed the responsibility for their ways of life.[12]

————

As important as were Bourne and the *Seven Arts* writers for establishing a mass culture criticism for the cultural Left, theirs were not the radicals' only views about the mass arts. In the whole scope of the American avant-garde, the *Seven Arts* stood as a relatively conservative voice. Two other distinct approaches to the entertainments in the era before World War I exhibit the range of the Left's criticism.

The *Little Review* was one of the more experimental American avant-garde art journals of the early century. It took a more radical stance on both cultural problems and politics than did the *Seven Arts* and was more uniformly critical of the mass entertainments. The review was first published in 1914 in Chicago, then moved to New York in 1917. It made its mark in intellectual affairs by introducing some of the pathfinding modernist writers and artists to American audiences, most notably publishing James Joyce's *Ulysses*. Under the direction of Margaret C. Anderson, a classic Bohemian intellectual, it was one of the most fervent voices of aestheticism of the early century. As Anderson declared in a frontispiece to a 1916 issue, the *Little Review*'s belief was in "Life for Art's sake."[13]

When it came to life for the sake of new and difficult works of prose or poetic art, however, the public was not interested. The *Little Review* re-

THE LITTLE REVIEW

A MAGAZINE OF THE ARTS

MAKING NO COMPROMISE WITH THE PUBLIC TASTE

Margaret Anderson
Publisher

September, 1917

Inferior Religions   *Wyndham Lewis*
L'Homme Moyen Sensuel   *Ezra Pound*
Eeldrop and Appleplex, II: *T S. Eliot*
    The Passion for Experience

Imaginary Letters, IV: *Ezra Pound*
    The Nonsense about Art for the Many

The Children and Judas *Robert Alden Sanborn*
The Reader Critic:
    Yeats's Poems "Upon a Dying Lady"
    Gargoyles
    Phases of Crazes

To our Readers
Announcement for October

Published Monthly
MARGARET ANDERSON, Editor
EZRA POUND, Foreign Editor
24 West Sixteenth Street

15 Cents a Copy $1.50 a Year
Entered as second-class matter at Postoffiice, New York, N. Y.

The title page of the *Little Review*, 1917, bearing the magazine's haughty new motto.

mained in constant financial trouble and its circulation never rose above a few thousand. Nor did it make an effort to court a popular audience. The poet Ezra Pound, upon becoming the foreign editor in 1917, immediately announced that the review was hostile to the American people as they appeared in mass. Similar to Randolph Bourne's contempt for the homogenized citizenry, he wrote, "there is no misanthropy in a thorough contempt for the mob. There is no respect for mankind save in respect for detached individuals." The public fell further from grace when Anderson discovered the limits of its aesthetic interests in the summer of 1917. Realizing that people not only did not want "Art" but, as she put it, "hated it malignantly," Anderson responded by declaring the *Little Review* to be equally uninterested in what the populace desired. Beginning in 1917, the magazine's cover carried the slogan, "Making No Compromise with the Public Taste."[14]

Such undisguised aesthetic elitism had no use for popular forms, and, like the conservative reviews, the magazine mentioned them only infrequently. Those notices, though, were highly critical. In a 1918 piece, "The Writer and His Job," a contributor named Israel Solon lambasted the values of mass-market literature. Solon had had his articles turned down by several popular magazines, and he attributed this disinterest to the journals' over-attention to the needs of the mass public. He quoted one rejection letter: "Consider *The Saturday Evening Post*," the editor wrote. "You may say what you like about the ideas which are acceptable to the millions, or the ideas which the editors think are acceptable to the millions. It is you who know and they who are ignorant." "But," the letter continued, "where art is concerned the millions speak with authority. . . . The millions make only one demand of the artist and that is impact, force, gusto. And in doing so they make the primary, the fundamental, the essential demand. When you stop to think of it you know they are right."

When Solon stopped and thought, though, he was incensed with what he called this "religion of democracy." Condemning the public's taste for stories that were "journalism" rather than "literature," he wrote, "the meagerness of their demands is their besetting sin. It is not their virtue. Why do the millions demand so little!" Solon pointed to the financial failures of several popular magazines as evidence that the desires of the great audience had "long since passed the point of saturation." Frustrated by the apparent domination of mass culture products in American expression, Solon made a plea for the preservation of less popular, refined forms. "I do not hold forth against giving the millions what they want," he wrote, repeating the cries of the genteel critics. "All I ask is that while the millions are being so plentifully served that the thousands not be neglected."[15]

Jane Heap was perhaps the most consistent critic of the American public's tastes and expressions in the *Little Review*. In a 1918 piece, she invoked

Walt Whitman once again, but for her it was to focus objections to the popular arts and to accentuate the distance between her journal and the *Seven Arts*. Heap bristled at Whitman's oft-repeated contention that the creation of great cultural expressions required a close, supportive relationship between artists and the public. She challenged Whitman supporters to "try this 'to-have-great-poets-we-must-have-great-audiences' test on other forms of creation,—physical creation, for instance." For her, artistic creation was a most individual and intellectual practice. She wanted "peace and silence for and from the 'masses'—a happy undisturbed people." The influence of the public in the arts simply rankled an aesthete like Heap, to the point when, in 1922, she delivered one of the more tasteless gibes of all the mass culture criticism. "The movies have produced for one public only," she complained, referring to their attention to the mass audience, "until they have become their own afterbirth." [16]

The *Little Review*'s open disdain for the public's taste and its favorite arts represents one clear continuity between the conservative mass culture criticism and that of the Left in the early twentieth century. While many liberal intellectuals acted paternalistically toward the people and crusaded against offending entertainments, another, less political group was pinning its hopes on the arts to revamp the whole society. These fervent modernists differed from the genteel critics in supporting unconventional arts and in promoting intellectual insurgency, rejecting the genteel hopes for preserving older ways. Yet both the most radical and conservative programs for enlightenment through "Culture" produced the same disdain for the popular arts, considering them to be hindrances to higher achievements. This philosophical grounding for attacking the popular arts from both the Left and the Right would reinforce other criticisms of the entertainments through the century.

The narrow aestheticism of the *Little Review*'s and other avant-garde criticisms is most obvious when compared to the completely different attitude toward popular culture found in a contemporary modernist magazine, the *Soil*. Like the *Seven Arts*, the *Soil* made only a brief stand in 1916–17. Its support of arts drawn from everyday lives, however, served as an inspiration for defenders of mass amusements well into the 1920s. Editor Robert J. Coady, a New York art dealer, celebrated the national culture by praising an enormous variety of people, activities and achievements as "American Art." Coady was very familiar with the world of the elite forms and distressed at its preoccupation with shallow and fleeting styles. He denounced what he called the "ismism" in the arts. At the same time, though, he believed that it was essential for America to produce a distinctive expressive culture to link the nation. The United States, with its heterogeneity, "will be a hyphenated nation until we have an art," Coady wrote. In the first number, he outlined this desired art with two pages of examples, ranging from the Panama Canal, Edgar Allan Poe, and Coney Island to steam shovels, Ty Cobb, and the "By Heck Foxtrot." "It is not a refined granulation nor a delicate disease—it is not an ism," he said of his new definition. "It is not an illustration to a theory, it is an expression of life—a complicated life—American life." [17]

The new aesthetic canon that the *Soil* projected as a common ground for America included a great deal of popular expression. In the magazine's first number alone, which featured an inventory of expressions including ragtime, circus performers, popular dances, sports stars, the Krazy Kat comic strip, movie posters, and amusement park rides, there were articles about motion pictures and popular literature, an interview with the African American comedian Bert Williams, and a piece written by Charlie Chaplin. The Nick Carter dime novel "The Pursuit of the Lucky Clew" was featured in the first issue as well, with an introduction by Coady that supported such popular tales as worthwhile "literature" and important influences in the development of all the nation's letters. This support of the mass entertainments as valuable expressions of American life was the magazine's characteristic treatment. The articles about Williams and by Chaplin both stressed the seriousness of the business of entertainment, in contrast to the more typical critical condemnations. The pieces detailed the concentrated work and imaginative risks involved in creating popular expression, efforts that apparently equaled any of the fine arts.[18]

Coady's aesthetic, as the historian Dickran Tashjian has argued, was yet another response to Whitman's challenge of creating democratic arts for America. His lists of all the different expressions of the modern American experience appear to be directly inspired by similar inventories in Whitman's poetry. Coady's willingness to define expression so broadly and inclusively obviously separates his approach from the aesthetic elitism of the *Little Review* of the 1910s. What is less clear is how thoroughly the *Soil*'s approach broke from assumptions about the audience's passivity or victimization that had informed the reformers' mass culture critique.

If the *Soil* considered dime novels and motion pictures as good arts, what did their popularity say about the public? Was this favorable judgment a recognition of the public's role in shaping and using entertainments? Did the magazine appreciate the complex relationships among creators, the popular arts industries, and audiences? Or was Coady's effort only an enlargement of the existing aesthetic canon to include artists such as Carter, Chaplin, and Williams, an act that did not involve any rethinking of the public's role in shaping popular culture? Such questions would determine how much Coady's aesthetic differed from that of the *Seven Arts* writers and the main entertainment criticisms. The *Seven Arts*'s interpretation of Whitman's call for an art expressing the American spirit was an intellectual project—artists divining the depths of the citizenry and capturing its character. Coady's empirical approach with his lists of forms, by contrast, suggests these forms were not raw materials for artists' self-conscious creation of great art, but rather the art itself. If this definition were accepted, then the popular arts might be appreciated in a wholly different light, and the audiences that promoted these forms deserved far more credit.

Unfortunately, Coady's *Soil* did not survive long enough to offer any definitive evidence about its conception of just who should create the modernist, democratic arts. The most informed way to speculate about the *Soil*'s intent is to consider the ideas about entertainments expressed by Coady's nearest ideological successor. Dada was the aesthetic movement of the 1920s most akin to the *Soil*'s understandings of the popular arts, and it produced a similarly ambivalent judgment about their place in modern life.

Secession and *Broom* were the two chief organs of Dadaism in the United States, and Matthew Josephson, a young writer embarking on a career of radical sympathies, was its prime proponent. Dada was an international movement in the arts during the era of World War I and the early 1920s. It was based not on a set artistic style, but on a general disgust of postwar civilization. The movement sought change through philosophical challenge, questioning the root assumptions behind behavior and rejecting the tradition of logic in Western thought. Dada especially aimed to disrupt rational expression as it was presented in traditional art. The movement did not go as far as calling all art worthless, but sought to overthrow established forms in order to open a new realm of creation. The Dadaists' inspirations were the products of technology and popular culture. Recognizing that these forms were anathema to conservative leaders in the arts, they celebrated them for their shock value.[19]

American Dadaism did not show the same depths of disenchantment as

the European strains; consequently its expressions were somewhat less enraged. But the use of popular arts in the experimental magazines, following
the model of Coady's *Soil*, was no less disturbing to traditionalists. In the
first volume of *Secession*, published in Vienna in 1922, Josephson delivered
a call that would have seemed like lunacy to readers of the genteel journals.
Paraphrasing the poet Guillaume Apollinaire, an important Parisian fore-
father of Dada, he wrote, "The poet is to stop at nothing in his quest for
novelty of shape and material; he is to take advantage of the possibilities for
infinite combinations, the new equipment afforded by the cinema, phonograph, dictaphone, airplane, wireless." [20]

Writing for the *Broom* later in 1922, Josephson explained that Dada
provided young writers with a purpose, a responsibility to encompass the
"mechanical genius" of the age and to become the "fable-makers" for the
future. Social uplift was too cumbersome and limiting a purpose for such
an art, and therefore, "The work of these younger men makes no bow to the
public," he explained. "Liberated as they are from all tendencies to make
the public a little more 'highbrow' and themselves a little more 'lowbrow,'
they carry prose and poetry into new roles." He envisioned artists capturing all the facets of the urban nation in their works, especially his favorites,
the advertisements, to compose "the 'folklore' of modern times." This was
an art that involved popular expression on a grand scale. The creator was
"to plunge hardily into that effervescent revolving cacophonous milieu . . .
where the Billposters enunciate their wisdom, the Cinema transports us, the
news papers intone their gaudy jargon; where athletes play upon the fre-
netic passions of baseball crowds, and sky scrapers rise lyrically to the exotic
rhythms of jazz bands which upon waking we find to be nothing but the
drilling of pneumatic hammers on steel girders." [21]

The Dadaist conception, then, like several of the other varieties of modernism, offered aesthetic appreciation for the popular arts but made no
effort to understand the forms and their origins. The image of the artists
working the entertainments into some "better" form recalls the *Seven Arts*'s
idea of an all-knowing interpreter of American culture. And like that view,
it largely neglects the acts of interpretation that audiences performed to en-
able these arts to become popular in the first place.

It is important to recall that even this small gain for the reputation of the
entertainments was made possible largely because of the particular intellectual atmosphere that existed before World War I. The mere suggestion of

creating a great art from common lives and the popular spirit was a breakthrough of this unique and short-lived environment of ideas. It was only
then that the leftist intellectuals' faith in socialism and democracy combined with their belief in the transformative power of ideas to bring great
dreams about the potential of American civilization and the chances of cultural renaissance. Some of the faith did continue in the years after the war,
notably in some of the most avant-garde of intellectuals, but in the main
such optimism had passed.[22]

The most lasting influence of the modernists' attitudes toward the popular arts therefore came from the less hopeful decade after the war. The
disillusion and bitterness many intellectuals felt after the war's destruction
cast a general pall over cultural ideals. Most notably, by the 1920s, the links
between literary-aesthetic and political radicalism in the United States generally had been severed. The persecution of radical groups by the federal
government during the war, the first "Red Scare" after the armistice and the
nationwide raids on suspected radicals conduced by Attorney General A.
Mitchell Palmer in 1920, and the internal problems that crippled American
socialism all combined to produce a far weaker American Left in the new
decade. The influence of European artistic modernism, particularly as it
was directly imbibed by the growing number of American expatriates, also
worked to separate the agendas of the aesthetic and political avant-gardes.
For most of the cultural radicals, this fading political grounding encouraged
an even stronger development of aestheticism. The "arts," rather than "the
people and their arts," came more and more to be their chief source of value
in American life.[23]

––––––––

The *Dial* was arguably the most influential modernist journal of the
1920s in the United States. In an earlier incarnation, the *Dial* was among
the nation's strongest proponents of traditional aesthetic standards, as we
have seen. When the magazine was sold and its offices moved from Chicago
to New York City in 1918, though, it shed what the editors called its "re-
assuringly genteel tights" to become an avant-garde review. Compared to
the more extreme voices on the literary Left like *Broom* and *Secession*, the
Dial represented a more staid and serious critical approach. Its hallmark was
a new analysis of the arts on quite limited lines, an analysis that is probably
best understood in comparison to the criteria of the *Seven Arts*.[24]

The *Dial* explicitly rejected the nationalism of the *Seven Arts* and the search for indigenous art forms for America in favor of a cosmopolitan approach to expressive culture. It urged a worldwide sharing of new forms of aesthetic experience. The magazine's ideal for the arts was based on an appreciation of formal or technical beauty that was also far different from the *Seven Arts*'s stress on social purpose or utility. The "*Seven Arts* group was interested too exclusively in the soul," *Dial* editor James Sibley Watson wrote in May 1921. He attributed this approach to the writers' embrace of psychoanalysis and disparaged the system that put psychology before aesthetics. Watson characterized the critical approach of Van Wyck Brooks as moral stewardship, which only "let art come as an inconsiderable afterthought," while the *Dial*'s method was "to return from hazier emotions and sentiments to those clear, energetic, and pure sensations which lie immediately under the skin." This was a formalist approach to evaluating cultural products that was alien to the American tradition in the arts, which had long insisted on locating moral guidance in aesthetic expression. The practice and implications of the approach would not be fully developed until the New Critics of the 1930s. There was, then, a distinct air of the subversive in the *Dial*'s statements of its philosophy. Perhaps none more so than a 1922 editorial endorsing the view of the philosopher George Santayana that aesthetic perfection "may be useless or even hostile to the possible perfection of human life." [25]

Equally novel were the *Dial*'s many favorable treatments of popular amusements. A 1923 editorial comment announced that "entertainment is true nourishment, and only a small mind conceives entertainment as trivial." Watson wrote appreciatively of Charlie Chaplin's work and more broadly of the "rather blessed advantages" motion pictures enjoyed in comparison to the "legitimate" drama. Other editors and writers shared in the enthusiasm. T. S. Eliot, the *Dial*'s London correspondent, wrote glowing praise for the English music hall artist Marie Lloyd in 1922. Both the editor Scofield Thayer and critic Edmund Wilson wrote favorably of performances by Fannie Brice and W. C. Fields in the Ziegfeld Follies and of other popular musicals. Thayer was also much impressed by the Jack Dempsey-Georges Carpentier prizefight, and an editorial announced that "as our readers are well aware," "Sport . . . is a passion with us." [26]

But what exactly was the nature of this taste for the mass amusements? As with the Dadaists, the *Dial*'s disregard for the populace while it embraced the popular arts suggests it had not abandoned all of the mass culture critique. Thayer's championing of the popular stage is a case in point. He began by lamenting that so many "otherwise uninhibited" people had never stepped foot in a music hall. Thayer believed these generally wise theatergoers were missing exciting, important productions because of their insistence on a vaguely defined "good taste" and the traditional standards of the "housebroken" stage. It was the popular theaters, "mongrels" in the editor's term, that contained the greatest potential for aesthetic pleasure. "Granted our musical-comedies are chiefly twaddle, granted our vaudeville is nine-tenths sawdust," Thayer argued, "there yet does by God's bounty pretty commonly remain, in the dismallest [sic] of shows, at least one comedian, one girl, one costume, one leg, one canvas of aesthetic sheen. While the conventions of the regular theatre have driven out everybody who is alive, those of the variety-stage do permit variety, and that means, now and then, howsoever wedged, an artist."[27]

This backhanded appreciation of the popular stage was a model of the *Dial*'s approach to all the popular arts. Of themselves, the general run of these un-"housebroken" "mongrels" would likely not have captured the attention of the modernist critics. But because the magazine was determined to challenge the prevailing art orthodoxy and bring vernacular energies to expressive culture, it sought out popular forms that were outside the accepted canon. Beyond being foils against gentility, these amusements also served the *Dial* critics by presenting clean slates for applying their new system of evaluating the arts. Because most modern cultural arbiters had never considered popular forms worthwhile and therefore had not applied any system of aesthetic criteria to them, they were prime candidates for the journal's formalist criticism.

These rather narrow, purely aesthetic criteria run through the magazine's treatments of the entertainments. Watson quarreled with the *Seven Arts*, for example, about how Charlie Chaplin was properly appreciated. The *Seven Arts* had described Chaplin as "the frustrated clown that exists in the heart of every American." Watson viewed Chaplin's art, by contrast, as "a series of precise, rectangular gestures." Thayer's enjoyment of the Dempsey-Carpentier fight was similarly cerebral. Speculating about the intellectual intrigue of the prizefight spectacle, he conceded that Carpentier's legs and Dempsey's "paws" were outside the "valid form of beauty." Instead, Thayer identified the attraction as the presentation of a classic dramatic scenario. "It is the iron Indian will which inhabits the stiff straight almost archaic neck of Jack Dempsey, it is the rich verve and bright courage which live in the springing legs of Georges Carpentier," he explained, "which can hold alike the humanist and the hundred thousand."

As for the *Dial*'s self-described "passion" for American sports, this was also apparently a particular kind of love. The editorial that announced this attachment also admitted (apparently referring to baseball), "It is true that we find the actual games rather dreary, but that they should be played, and that regarding them from the grandstands should also be considered sport intrigues the intellect far more than the spectacle can interest the mind or stir the imagination." In fact, the editors explained that their liking for baseball as a "closet drama" came chiefly from reading the sportswriters' columns after the games. They believed that reporting such as Grantland Rice's was "far better critical writing than nine tenths of the criticism of art and letters published in our daily papers." These reporters practiced precisely that regard for their subject "as an end in itself, and not as a clue to something else," or in other words, as a purely formal and technical endeavor, that the magazine advocated for all the arts. "Tactics and strategy, technique and art," the *Dial* wrote of the sportswriter's practice, "compose his one passionate interest." [28]

Taken together, these opinions from the *Seven Arts, Little Review, Soil, Secession, Broom,* and *Dial* show just how weak was the cultural radicals' acceptance of the mass arts. Such forms were useful for enlivening the art world, but were invariably detached from the popular milieu in which they were shaped and tested.

There were, of course, great artists among the mass amusement creators, virtuosos who happened to apply their talents to popular media. Their genius is all the more impressive precisely because they created artistically unparalleled expressions that at the same time proved attractive to an enormous and diverse audience. These artists achieved the remarkable feat of consistently reaching a common denominator of the public's tastes and values. When the modernists singled out examples of finely honed technique or brilliant insight into contemporary life in the entertainments, then, they slighted the public's input. The forms embraced by a mass audience could not be fully understood apart from the people's experience and expression.

The artificial separation implicit in the avant-garde intellectuals' appreciation of the mass entertainments apart from the mass audience served to further the mass culture critique. It worked in much the same way as the separation between the people and the popular forms that was forged in the reformers' criticisms. The progressives believed commerce was intruding into the production of entertainments and turning the public away from its better, improvable nature. Few, therefore, appreciated how the mass arts spoke to the actual interests of the public. The modernists, by comparison, were less concerned with the state of the American masses. But in the same way they dispensed with the consideration of the people when they appropriated the popular art forms to invigorate their new aesthetic. The effect, in both cases, was to hinder intellectuals from understanding the circumstances of the public and, consequently, its real tastes and desires. The people were instead more easily stereotyped as passive, exploited, or, for the modernists, inconsequential. This separation of the popular arts from the public by liberal intellectuals would prepare the ground for later critics to make overarching claims about mass culture's damage to the society. It became easier to presume the worst effects of the ever more widely reaching mass media, because the people's actual practices of encountering and understanding the earlier entertainments were never understood.

The way this narrowed understanding of the popular arts could contribute to the mass culture critique was most evident in the writings of Gilbert Seldes, the nation's foremost authority on the popular arts in the early twentieth century. Seldes served as a managing editor and theater critic of the *Dial*, where he made his mark as a champion of the mass amusements. The critic Edmund Wilson surveyed Seldes's writings on the popular arts in 1924 and judged him to be as effective as Van Wyck Brooks or H. L. Mencken in advancing the modernists' crusade against genteel aesthetic standards. Latter-day scholars have similarly identified Seldes as a central figure in the break with the Victorian cultural order.[29]

Seldes's 1924 book, *The Seven Lively Arts*, was the most important work on the mass entertainments of the era. This book surveyed a variety of amusements from the early twentieth century: movies and burlesque shows, jazz and ragtime artists, comic strips and newspaper columnists. The opening sentences of the first chapter, a paean to director Mack Sennett's Keystone comedy films, set the tone: "For fifteen years there has existed in the United States, and in the United States alone, a form of entertainment which, seemingly without sources in the past, restored to us a kind of laughter almost unheard in modern times. It came into being by accident; it had not pretensions to art. For ten years or more it added an element of cheer-ful madness to the lives of millions and was despised and rejected by people of culture and intelligence." The problem, for Seldes, was that there was a wealth of such forms of popular cultural expression in the United States that were consistently scorned or ignored by cultural arbiters. He was de-termined to rescue the entertainments from genteel prejudice and establish them as necessary features of a complete modern life.[30]

Seldes praised the Keystone Cops films for what he called their "ani-mal frankness and health." "The Keystone offended our sense of security in dull and business-like lives," he wrote. "Few of us imagined ourselves in the frenzy of action which they set before us; none of us remained unmoved at the freedom of fancy, the wildness of imagination, the roaring, destruc-tive, careless energy which it set loose. It was an ecstasy of comic life." He lauded Fannie Brice and Al Jolson for bringing the "daemonic" element to the American stage. Jolson's "fury and exultation" and Brice's "extraordinary 'cutting loose,'" showed "their fine carelessness about our superstitions of politeness and gentility." It was not just in stage or screen performers that Seldes found intensity. He reported that, every day, 20 million people fol-lowed their heroes in several superbly executed comic strips. Funnies such as "Gasoline Alley," "Mutt and Jeff," and "For Better or Worse" provided audiences with "the freest American fantasy," Seldes wrote, and the nation's most accurate satire of manners.

The culmination of Seldes's survey of the popular arts, the two forms he praised most lavishly, were the films of Charlie Chaplin and the "Krazy Kat" comic strip of George Herriman. Chaplin was the single figure of his era who he thought was most assured of immortality. Seldes spoke of his "ado-ration" of Chaplin's work, describing how the actor "detached himself from life and began to live in another world, with a specific rhythm of his own, as if the pulse-beat in him changed and was twice or half as fast as those who surrounded him." Chaplin's vital energy, wrote Seldes, "will make him forever a school not only of acting, but of the whole creative process."

If Chaplin's abilities were timeless, "Krazy Kat" was the nation's finest contemporary expression. Seldes described the strip as "the most amusing and fantastic and satisfactory work of art produced in America to-day." Two qualities made it so wonderful: irony and fantasy. As in his impressionistic treatment of Chaplin, Seldes could not easily explain these features by ref-erences to the plot of the strip. Instead, he suggested that the preposterous material Herriman drew was a vehicle for him to apply a "touch of irony and pity" and transform the comic strip into "something profoundly true and moving."

Much of Seldes's book expressed his anger at the way these wonderful mass arts were being treated by intellectual arbiters. Most critics dismissed the popular forms out of hand, insisting on considering only work in the traditional arts, while Seldes believed the latter were typically deficient. Producers could get away with second-rate performances in classic dance, serious drama, or grand opera and still attract audiences, simply because these styles had a built-in cachet. In Seldes's words, "because they are ART." He made direct comparisons between these inferior high arts, which he called "bogus" or "counterfeit," and the lively forms. The circus was judged to be consistently more artistic than the Metropolitan Opera; Al Jolson and Fannie Brice were declared superior to John and Ethel Barrymore; Ring Lardner and Finley Peter Dunne's "Mr. Dooley" were chosen over the novelists James Cabell and Joseph Hergesheimer; Florence Ziegfeld was judged a better producer than David Belasco; and any one film by Mack Sennett or Charlie Chaplin was given the nod over all Cecil deMille's productions together.

But with the bogus thus dispatched, Seldes did not believe man could live by the lively alone. It was necessary to include both the classic and popular arts in a fully rounded life, he argued, because they served different parts of human nature. The great traditional works functioned "to associate our modern existence with that extraordinary march of mankind . . . the progress of humanity," while the need for the lively arts was apparently more biological than intellectual. In marked contrast to Seldes's effusive praise for particular popular artists, his justification for the entertainment genre as a whole was feeble. "We require, for nourishment, something fresh and transient. . . . There must be ephemera. . . . Let us see to it," he wrote, "that they are good."

Ensuring such quality in the popular arts and legitimating them in the eyes of the cultural critics was Seldes's purpose. But when his argument is reduced to its essentials, its limited embrace of the entertainments is clear. While he was challenging the range of subjects that critics normally deemed worthy of evaluation, he was hardly challenging the criteria that the critics traditionally used to evaluate the arts. His appreciation of the entertain-

Illustration in Seldes's *The Seven Lively Arts* (1924), depicting the individual popular artists he championed.

ments remained a matter of aesthetics. "Liveliness" had, for Seldes, become an artistic measure all its own. He wrote that while the "characteristic of the great arts is high seriousness, the essence of the minor arts is high levity," a kind of "exaltation, of carrying a given theme to the 'high' point." Significantly, throughout his book, he considered only the best examples of an entertainment for notice and praise. He did not champion whole categories of the popular arts because he was not interested in how they worked with their great audiences. Too many of the everyday entertainments could not meet his technical criteria for excellence.

Seldes's praises for his favorite amusements were breakthroughs in the appreciation of the popular arts, and for these he certainly deserves the recognition he has been accorded. From a longer perspective, however, the limits of his enthusiasm indirectly contributed to the criticisms of mass culture. The problem in Seldes's narrow aesthetic treatment of the popular arts was most extreme in his consideration of African American forms of jazz music. In *The Seven Lively Arts* he freely admitted that, as he put it, "our whole present music is derived from the negro," and he described how the "negro side" of jazz, "kept alive things without which our lives would be perceptibly meaner, paler; nearer to atrophy and decay."

But Seldes rejected that music in his efforts to legitimate the popular arts. He explained in a forceful paragraph:

> I am on the side of civilization. To anyone who inherits several thousand centuries of civilization, none of the things the negro offers can matter unless they are apprehended by the mind as well as the body and the spirit. . . . There will always exist wayward, instinctive, and primitive geniuses who will affect us directly, without the interposition of the intellect; but if the process of civilization continues . . . the greatest art is likely to be that in which an uncorrupted sensibility is *worked* by a creative intelligence. So far in their music the negroes have given their response to the world with an exceptional naivete, a directness of expression which has interested *our* minds as well as touched our emotions; they have shown comparatively little evidence of the functioning of *their* intelligence.

This is a contemptible racial stereotype, but also more. Because Seldes could justify the popular arts only on the basis of certain technical achievements and the perfection of a recognized method ("creative intelligence"), he was unable to appreciate fully an art form whose popularity was rooted in a less codified aesthetic. His misreading of the form reflected most unfavorably on both the artists and the audience for black jazz. Without considering the enormously complex influences behind the style—the mixing of European and African musical traditions; black, white and Creole cultures; and how all was hastened by the hothouse environment of the modern city—

Seldes could not possibly know jazz. He was especially unprepared to judge whether it was "naive" or "instinctive" because the only kind of sophistication he was prepared to recognize was that defined by the European symphonic tradition. Nor, without an understanding of the lives of African Americans, could he begin to know these peoples' tastes and interests, and therefore whether this music related to their "minds." Seldes thus ended up denigrating both jazz artists and appreciators as "primitive" because he could understand their art form only on his own narrow terms.

The music Seldes supported instead was what he termed the "complete exploitation of jazz" of the Caucasian bandleader Paul Whiteman. "All the free, the instinctive, the wild in negro jazz which could be integrated into his music he has kept," Seldes wrote of Whiteman. But "he has added to it, has worked his material, until it runs sweetly in his dynamo, without grinding or scraping. It becomes the machine which conceals the machinery." Whiteman had therefore reached precisely that expertise in an accepted form that Seldes's aesthetic required. Seldes had not considered that the jazz style he did not favor could nonetheless be a developed expression of a different culture. And without such an understanding of legitimate difference, he also could not see that Whiteman's more European-influenced jazz attracted him because it fit his own background and expectations.[31]

Seldes's treatment of jazz aptly summarizes the modernists' inadvertent contribution to the mass culture critique. As the nation's foremost proponent of the entertainments, Seldes rescued the reputations of many popular artists because they pleased his aesthetic senses. Yet he knew the popular forms only in the way he knew the elite arts—as individual and unique expressions of particular artists. Without considering the role of the public in initially shaping the entertainments and the subsequent tailoring of the arts to meet popular tastes, he could not understand how these forms were both artists' interpretations and social expressions at the same time. Appreciating only one side of the artist-audience symbiosis, Seldes and other modernists were in effect sustaining the distance from the mass public that intellectuals on the Left had opened over the early century. The acceptance of the entertainments by these professional thinkers was an unmatched opportunity for them to come to know the "common" men and women. Confronting the public's favorite expressions promised to draw the Left beyond the paternalism of the reformers and to penetrate the more complicated lives of the people. It brought the chance to reconceive these citizens as independent beings and to recognize that they were cognizant and answerable for their ways, though they might differ from the intellectuals. Because the vanguard writers limited their interest in the entertainments to artistic questions of form and technique, however, they never observed the public in all its dimensions. This contributed to the developing criticism of mass culture because it both denied the people the credit and exempted them from the blame that they deserved for their chosen pastimes.

4 SOCIAL SCIENTISTS AND "DEVIANT" ENTERTAINMENTS

The sensations of urban life that so enthused the modernists and inspired their celebrations of the popular arts at the same time caused alarm for other intellectuals. Many American social scientists in the era after World War I considered the emerging society a serious threat to the nation's existing civilization, and mass culture was prominent among their fears. The University of Chicago sociologist Ernest W. Burgess summarized the range of issues that constituted "the problem of recreation under conditions of modern city life" in 1932. For Burgess, they were patently obvious: "the insistent human *demand for stimulation*," the "growing *tendency to promiscuity* in the relations of the sexes," and "the failure of our ordinary devices of social control to function in a culturally heterogeneous and anonymous society." All the conditions, he felt, were directly linked to modern culture and centered in *"commercialized recreation."* [1]

Burgess's assessments were rooted in sociological analyses produced in the United States between the two world wars. These investigated the problems of the popular arts more explicitly and systematically than any treatments yet presented by American intellectuals. Professional social scientists introduced a new stage in the mass culture critique with the argument that mass entertainments could be both acceptable features of modern life and sources of pathology or social deviance. Popular culture analysis shifted from considering the entertainments as problems encroaching on the society to recognizing them as products of the society itself.

———

College-level sociology textbooks provide a revealing introduction to what social theorists thought about popular culture in the 1920s and 1930s. Because these books were created for classroom use, they were designed to be acceptable to the largest possible audience. They tended to concentrate on the well-studied subjects that scholars considered the focuses of their discipline. Seeking this middle ground, authors typically drew upon what was considered the most reliable literature in the field and tended toward consensus interpretations. Most of the textbooks were written from a liberal perspective. They emphasized cautious reform and regulation, social planning, and cooperation. The textbooks of the interwar period may be said to represent, then, the conceptual foundations, or what the sociologist C. Wright Mills called the "professional ideology," of his discipline. One regular topic in these textbooks, and therefore of this ideology, was the problem of mass entertainments. [2]

The popular arts expanded enormously in the United States between the world wars. Numerous magazines numbered readers in the millions. Hundreds of new radio stations were created and the number of families with radio sets went from several million in the mid-1920s to more than 25 million by World War II. Sound came to the movies, and weekly attendance was often 70 or 80 million. Professional sports attracted tens of thousands per event, and jazz became the ubiquitous sound of the city (and often the hinterlands). Equally important, the automobile provided greater access to all the entertainments, as well as a recreation in itself. Auto registrations surpassed 20 million by 1930. [3]

The general statements about the popular arts in the sociology books suggest the way the amusements unnerved investigators. Nels Anderson and Eduard Lindeman's *Urban Sociology* (1928) identified the control of mass entertainments as the preeminent concern in studies of city life. The subject was so important, they argued, because both juvenile delinquency and numerous problems of adult conduct were traceable to "the misuse of leisure." *Community Problems* (1928) by Arthur Evans Wood devoted a chapter to "The Control of Commercial Recreation" and to the premise that the amusement business had come to command the leisure of the American masses. Wood issued a somber warning: "Other civilizations have waned under the influence of vulgar amusements. It is by no means certain that ours may not do so."[4]

The most common analyses of the popular arts, however, involved a more nuanced approach that combined these criticisms of the arts with an unexpected tolerance of their existence. The treatment offered by the sociologist Maurice Davie in his *Problems of City Life: A Study in Urban Sociology* (1932) was typical. In chapters entitled "Recreation in the Machine Age" and "Commercialized Recreation," Davie wrote that popular amusements had "a large and legitimate place in the recreational life of the modern city," performing "a very definite service in increasing recreational opportunities." At the same time, though, he cited condemnations of commercial recreations for increasing the passivity of the public in its leisure, acting as a "demoralizing influence," and involving "vice, crime, and immorality."

The odd pairing of acceptance for the mass arts with diagnoses of their deviance can be traced to the two main sources of the social scientists' interpretations. One was the progressive reformers' entertainment criticisms, particularly their notion of commercial amusements as a corrupting force in healthy leisure desires. The second, more innovative influence was the body of theory that developed in the 1920s and early 1930s about the evolution of modern American society.

———

The recreation surveys of the Progressive Era continued to be influential in the years after the reforms subsided. The sociology textbooks of the interwar era were written mainly from secondary literature, and, well into the 1920s, the surveys remained the best sources on the nature and the reach of modern amusements. The particular concerns that spurred the reformers were also carried into the texts. The influence of popular entertainments on the young, for example, remained a special focus. One 1925 textbook, *Social Pathology*, proposed that these had derogatory effects on "personality," based on the findings of the social survey of Cleveland in 1920. The book contrasted the leisure pursuits of juvenile delinquents and offenders with those of "wholesome" citizens. It found that the delinquents spent most of their free time in "empty leisure and desultory activities" including "loafing on the streets, in pool halls, and bowling alleys." By contrast, the "wholesome" sounded like poster children for the reformers' "play movement." Their leisure was described as involving "a widely extended and richly diversified range of activities" such as "reading, organized games, dancing and theater-going." Most of these habits, the sociologists related, "were formed at the suggestion and under the guidance of parents, teachers, relatives and friends." Wood's *Community Problems* drew a similar conclusion from social workers' testimony about the "inevitable" connection between improper recreation and juvenile delinquency. He quoted the director of the Chicago Crime Commission: "In retracing the tortuous path of the youthful criminal, it is seldom found that the trail leads back to the playground, the diamond, the athletic field, or the Community Center. . . . A very large percentage of those apprehended have been strangers to the influences exerted by such activities. . . . The young delinquent has, in the majority of instances, grown up in the atmosphere of the saloon, the poolroom and similar hang-outs." [5]

The sociology texts also supported the argument that debasing work routines were responsible for the tawdriness of entertainments. One described the need for communal leisure "as the development of industrial society brings on minute subdivision of labor with monotonous repetition, reducing the flesh-and-blood worker to an automaton, eliminating intrinsic interest in the job, and producing fatigue." These conditions drove industrial workers not to rest, but to empty diversions and excitements, which would not happen if the work was more satisfying, sociologists explained. The attraction of the movies was similarly explained in *Problems of City Life* as a reaction to harsh labor. "In the industrial city," Davie wrote, "the theatre is the one source of mystery and romance. It is an antidote to the monotony and strain of industry." Citing the judgment of reformer John Collier that "modern conditions produce an emotional rebound that creates a demand for pleasure which is almost hysterical," *Community Problems* urged new leisure programs and facilities "so as to offset the drive of industrial and commercial life by a release of the creative energies."[6]

Sociologists in the interwar years especially singled out the conditions of urban life that had been the targets of reform when they analyzed the appeal of the mass arts. The increasing acceptance of Freudian theory in the academy brought attention to the psychological impact of city life on leisure patterns. "Disorganized" personalities and repressed urges became common interpretations. Arthur Wood psychoanalyzed the population on a grand scale, questioning the "happiness of our urban civilization" as revealed in recent literature on dance halls. In these halls, he wrote, "youth seeks adventure and romance; or it may be a degree of social recognition that is not vouchsafed through other forms of industrial or community organization. . . . Too often the quest results in a disorganization of the personal character."

In *Problems of City Life*, Davie explained that the psychological effect of urban living for most was "constant stimulation and nervous excitement." "In this jazz age," he wrote, " 'leisure' has become mainly a restless search for excitement." He quoted a list of "second- and third-hand participation": "Clicking turnstiles, Roman stadia, burning up the roads, Hollywood, jazz, gin, Coney Island, dollar-a-hole golf, comic strips, wood-pulp confession magazines and books—bad books," to endorse the reformers' view that such constant excitement without an outlet in muscular action produced "an incomplete and unhygienic life." Passive, spectator entertainments were also typically experienced among crowds in the city, Davie explained, which left individuals more susceptible to influence and to fleeting enthusiasms. These unfortunate conditions all came together in an entertainment such as the amusement park, in the sociologist's view. "Such places do not get the people away from the artificial life of the city or from the influence of mercenary motives," Davie judged. "There is scarcely anything in city life more artificial than this type of park. People even pay to get artificial bumps."[7]

These criticisms of the mass entertainments as either causes or products of modern social ills show the shared understandings between the reformers and sociologists. They differed, however, when it came to assigning responsibility for these conditions. The progressives' conception of a public waylaid by corrupt commercial influences was challenged by the sociologists' notion that the corruption came rather from the nature of the modern society itself. For the sociologists, the reformers' model of unwitting victims seemed inadequate to account for the enormous demand for mass amusements.

Lacking the faith in the public that the prewar intellectuals held, the academics settled on a less conspiratorial explanation. The culprit was the cumulative influence of the new urban environment. The sociologists created dark interpretations of city life as damaging and demoralizing and more and more treated the unwanted recreations as "natural" expressions of that life. Arthur Wood, for example, described the mass entertainment problem as "an organic phase of modern culture wherein amusements, bereft of older sanctions, have gone their ribald way under the stimulus of mechanical inventions and the profit motive." What separated Wood's view from that of the reformers was the "organic" nature he ascribed to this change, acknowledging that the impetus for the mass arts came from the nature of the masses. Wood found it futile to simply condemn the amusement business because it "could not have developed its prodigious strength had it not grown in response to popular needs." Maurice Davie readily agreed. "Entertainment caters to public taste," he wrote. "It does not create it, for it is too commercialized an undertaking."

This developing appreciation of the "demand" side of popular culture, a reemergence of the conservatives' interpretation from the early century, complicated the picture that the reformers had passed down. The progressives had developed their own sort of "demand" explanation for the attraction of these amusements, of course. They had acknowledged how industrial labor, poor living conditions, and urban overcrowding drove citizens to the nickelodeon or the dance hall. But for them these were dislocations that could be remedied to bring people back to their better natures. The sociologists, by contrast, believed the entertainment problems sprang from deeper, more entrenched habits central to modern society. As Wood phrased the sociologists' new view, "we are here dealing not with an institution but with an aspect of American civilization."[8]

To point out the sociologists' acceptance of the mass entertainments as logical expressions of modern life is not to say that these scholars favored them. Their apparent resignation in the face of this problem likely reflects two aspects of their developing outlook in the 1920s: a new sense of their professional role, and a new perspective they adopted on the way modern societies evolved. First, in the era after World War I, sociologists undertook to separate their discipline from its origins in the reform movements of the early century. In place of social inquiries geared toward remedial programs, they aimed to establish their field as an independent, value-neutral, empirical science. Attempts to stir the public to confront problems and administering solutions would be left to others.[9]

This new posture of disinterested expertise only partly explains the sociologists' fatalism in the face of the entertainment problem. A second reason was their understanding of modernization, or the way societies made the transition to contemporary ways. The hypothetical models that social scientists created to explain how rural, agrarian societies transformed into urban, industrial nations strongly influenced their expectations of the way twentieth-century America would look. The scholars thought of the United States as a society becoming thoroughly and completely modern. They also theorized that mass entertainments were the quintessential leisure forms of the modern world. The entertainments therefore became, in their eyes, the inevitable recreation of modern America. These sociological models about how modern people were expected to interact with the popular arts also had important ramifications for later mass culture criticisms.

The sociologists' modernization model compared the conditions of pre-industrial villages to those of contemporary cities. Their ideal for the way citizens should best recreate came from their conception of these villages, and squared with the reformers' visions of the face-to-face social order. Foremost, tight family and community controls guided the leisure behavior of all the citizens. By contrast, controls of any kind were fast slipping away in the thoroughly modern twentieth-century society they assumed had arrived. While progressives had been concerned about the declining role of the family in directing leisure, for example, the decline was treated as a completed change in several interwar texts. Anderson and Lindeman wrote in 1929, "When the home ceased to be a recreational center, all the traditions and habits which were identified with it vanished." The automobile was especially blamed for breaking up family outings and sending members rushing in different directions for different pursuits. In *Problems of City Life*, Davie explained, "The home in the modern city can no longer be the center of life in leisure hours. . . . All must go away when in search of pleasure and recreation." The *Social Pathology* text investigated the possible correlation between "the fact that the members of the family often seek their recreation separately" and "the occurrence of divorce, desertion, juvenile delinquency or sex irregularities."[10]

Associations of neighborhood and community, as well as family, seemed to be disappearing with the new society. The waning of traditional or "folk" ways raised questions about where people would find ethical direction. Davie saw some potential for establishing new standards for behavior, but was more immediately impressed with the society's fall from grace. He traced the shift of a large part of the population from rural to urban living to a hastening moral decline. "Our accepted traditions and rules of conduct were established under rural conditions: the new environment tends constantly to break them down," he wrote. "The growth of cities has . . . been accompanied by a certain breaking away from home ties, from church affiliations, from moral obligations." Before new rules for conduct in urban conditions were developed, "during the period of transition a certain amount of demoralization is inevitable. The impersonality and anonymity of city life tend to promote it. There is a lack of parental supervision and of the control of neighborhood opinion."[11]

Theories of other social scientists were invoked in some of the texts to compose these concerns about the modernizing society. The interaction of "primary" and "secondary" groups theorized by sociologist Charles Horton Cooley as the source of social stability was pursued in Wood's *Community Problems*. Cooley called family, neighborhood, and other local associations "primary" groups and contended that they were crucial in forming individual character. If these foundations were sound, they prepared for good "secondary" relationships with the broader community and society and thus ensured social order. Wood used Cooley's theory to argue that failing primary relationships in contemporary America were damaging social solidarity. The better amusements of an earlier day were a central part of his vision of healthier primary group relations. He cited the desirable traditions of the village green, spontaneous play, and the "simple common life," and contrasted the "romance and decent fun" of the nineteenth-century traveling circus with the degenerate lures of many modern commercial entertainments. Davie trotted out the opinions of another expert, psychologist Ordway Tead, to establish the psychic costs the public endured for this separation from folk culture and recreation. "The play of the husking bee, charades, dancing at home among friends, outdoor picnics, and other homely enjoyments is not to be sighed for simply because it is attached to a simple manner of life," Tead argued. "Its loss is to be lamented because apparently it was the more normal psychological form of play in a generation when all the claims of life on the nervous system were less wearing and exacting than is the case today." [12]

The sociology overviews, then, were presenting a model of modernizing society that suggested folk culture, and therefore communal order, was becoming extinct with the arrival of urban-industrial society. If this assumption were accepted, then misdirected play in the form of modern mass amusements was inevitable. The implications of such bad entertainment influences were clearest in considerations of motion pictures and dance halls. These entertainment offerings had received the most attention from reformers in the Progressive Era and they remained the most frequented urban amusements in the interwar years. They became a magnet for new social studies.

The sociology textbooks routinely repeated large parts of the reformers' arguments about the value and the dangers of the movies. Newer analyses based on these premises were gaining widespread attention as well. Several social science studies of motion pictures in the 1920s and early 1930s were undertaken on the assumption that the potential for the medium to change public behavior was enormous. The conclusions of these investigations differed about the effects of the medium, but the initial premise nevertheless reveals their bias. Modern audiences, it was assumed, must be susceptible to messages in the new technology. The most comprehensive examinations of the movies' social influence were the twelve-volume Payne Fund studies conducted from 1929 to 1933. The fact that such extended analyses were performed provides, as the historian Garth Jowett has described, "graphic credence to the view that the motion picture *was* a major influence in American life." The public came to know the Payne Fund series primarily through a popular condensation, *Our Movie-Made Children*. True to the premise of the studies, the book edited out the more cautious conclusions of some social scientists and presented films as a prime force in the shaping of the nation's youth. [13]

For sociologists, dance also revealed how precipitous was the decline from folk ways of recreation. Wood explained that dance had devolved from an elevating form of culture among traditional peoples in settled villages to a fruitless diversion. By his account, as people migrated into larger towns, "an-

In the interwar years, many social scientists believed the popular motion picture directly affected viewers' behavior. They assumed moviegoers, like these lined up outside a popular Chicago theater in 1927, were easily manipulated. (Chicago Historical Society, DN-68755)

cient mores fell by the wayside" and "communal amenities" were destroyed. Studies of dance halls in the 1920s found these degraded mores in volume. A much-discussed 1924 investigation of San Francisco dance halls concluded that "all of the social problems of modern life are met within the dance hall: sickness, marital difficulties, unmarried motherhood, unemployment, vocational maladjustment, desertion, feeble-mindedness, poverty, ignorance of social hygiene, of American manners and customs, lack of sex education."[14]

While the reformers had called for "substitute" halls, the new social science was intent on analyzing existing conditions. Sociological studies of the various dance venues distinguished them according to the social needs believed to be met by each type. Observers ranked the facilities according to the purported "health" of the typical relationships among patrons. Most welcome were "club" dances, which were typically held in rented halls. These were sponsored by social or ethnic organizations or neighborhood groups and therefore usually attracted a familiar clientele. Wood described that "acquaintance is intimate and not promiscuous" at these dances; Davie also thought they were "a wholesome social atmosphere."

Less acceptable were the large ballrooms, cabarets, and dance palaces. These attracted larger, more diverse crowds, and most of the dancers, predominantly young people, were reported to be previously unacquainted.

Managers of these facilities generally tried to control their patrons, Davie reported, because they recognized that the reputation of the hall was a business asset. "Trouble," though, was apparently more likely than at the club dances, because the palaces were typically located in downtown areas, "where neighborhood acquaintance, with the restraining influence which it exerts, is almost wholly lacking."

The least desirable dance places were the "closed" halls. Here, in what Wood termed a "more abject picture," the predominantly male patrons were more often poor, first-generation immigrants, or strangers to the city. Couples were usually not admitted. Instead, girls were hired to dance with the men, who paid by the tune. One study characterized the closed hall as the place where "the man without a country or a home, without much hope of an introduction to a lady, or perhaps with too great bashfulness to seek one, can buy his sociability, poor as it is, by the evening." Put even more bleakly, "He can also select, from what choice there is, of the women provided for him and find in the commercialism of the affair, a control over his partner that longer acquaintance, better understanding and perhaps more finesse, secures for the more fortunate male of more numerous social ties." [15]

The sociology interpretations thus treated the range from the club to the closed dances, from what was considered healthy to the deviant, as a direct parallel to the span from folk society to modern society. A small, tightly knit, homogeneous, face-to-face community (apparently free of market forces) was at one extreme, and a larger, more diverse, unacquainted, and less controlled population that found a common ground only in commercial relations was at the other. The importance of this method of framing the evolution of American life was its apparent implication for contemporary society. All the sociology texts recognized that the folk society, especially as it was understood in such "pure" terms, was doomed. Urban and industrial culture was spreading through most of the nation and presumed to be extinguishing the village traits. If the conditions of the closed dance hall best captured modernity, they logically also indicated the bleak fate of America.

Sociologist Elon Moore was most explicit in making this connection between the passing of the folk culture and the establishment of mass culture as the new norm. In a 1930 study, he found the same problems in the dance facilities of a midwestern university town of 35,000 as were reported in surveys of Manhattan (which by the mid-1920s estimated annual attendance at over 6 million in the dance halls). Moore described a range of patrons with varying standards of deportment in the halls of "Collegetown." Some were groups of the previously acquainted who needed no supervision "other than their own moral and social code," according to Moore. At the other extreme, groups including college men and alleged prostitutes were found drunk and doing "obscene" dances. The most significant part of Moore's study, though, was his insistence that behavior in even the most disreputable halls should be accepted as a product of the modern environment. A more regulated communal gathering was clearly his ideal, as it was for most of his fellow scholars. Moore nevertheless chided reformers for calling for sanctions against dance places. He excused what he called "the vulgarity and crassness of the dance hall," because it was not simple evil, but rather "evidence of escape or rebellion of starved or incomplete personalities."[16]

We need not accept Moore's explanation to appreciate how he was accepting depraved mass culture as an emerging normal state. This social psychological diagnosis of the most modern entertainment ills for a small, relatively privileged population suggested that the degraded mass culture order had not infected just the urban poor and recent immigrants, but might be becoming the standard for the whole nation.

The growing, albeit begrudging, acceptance by the sociologists of mass entertainments as central features of the modern society was also encouraged by their burgeoning interest in the topic of "leisure." In the interwar era, a shortening industrial work week and new labor-saving devices in the home inspired a wealth of social science investigation and theory about the time Americans spent away from the job. The consensus of these scholarly considerations was that modern civilization was producing a distinctly new way of life. As one put it, "the new leisure of our era simply must be bringing its own specific culture, its own mutation of human values."[17]

American writers on leisure in the 1920s generally agreed with the earlier theories of Simon Patten and John Collier that, because much industrial labor had become debilitating, it was no longer realistic to center the society's values in work. "The factory system, specialization, efficiency methods, have revolutionized the daily tasks of the mass of the people," wrote the sociologist Weaver Pangburn in 1922, "and contradict the idea that all work is disciplinary, that it builds character and develops a man's innate powers." If values were to be rooted in leisure instead, however, the problem was that mass culture had already cornered much of the nation's free time, and mass culture seemed to operate by its own particular standards.

Clarence Rainwater, the chronicler of the play movement, wrote regarding the motion picture camera, automobile, pictorial magazine and radio, for example, that "society seems to have failed, so far, to derive social advantages from the leisure-time uses of these recently invented technical devices beyond ephemeral crowd expressions and pecuniary gains to trafficers [*sic*]." He thought that the public "lacks suitable customs for controlling the pursuits of leisure in the interest of the common welfare."[18]

The most complete evaluation of the new culture of free time was George Barton Cutten's *The Threat of Leisure* (1926). Cutten, a psychologist and president of Colgate University, agreed that the era of work as the core of society was passing. The machine age had brought unprecedented leisure, turning Americans "from a people to whom toil was our breath to a nation of idlers, little knowing what to do with our surplus time." Like many of his scholarly contemporaries, Cutten accepted the proposition that the modern world had arrived in America, and he associated a number of debilitating leisure practices with that world. He compared the musical and artistic educations enjoyed by common people in less modern nations such as those of southern Europe to the preparations ultramodern Americans were given for enjoying leisure. The latter he found wanting. The southern Europeans were able to enjoy their leisure in forms of self-expression like folk dancing, while American workers were typically "unproductive" in their leisure. Reduced hours in the steel industry, Cutten contended, had only boosted attendance at "pool rooms, dime movies, and other places of loafing."

Self-expression and self-amusement were lost arts in the modern nation, in Cutten's argument. The public had relinquished its voice and the control of its leisure to commercial exploitation. In an argument very much like the progressives', he described how mass amusements had made expression a function of "business interests" rather than "the desires, needs, or benefits of the people." The result was bad entertainments that often damaged minds and morals. Cutten seemed both intrigued and disgusted by the scale of commercialization. "More money is spent in this country on commercialized leisure than on anything else except food, and more invested in this enterprise than anything except land," he explained. "There are more than twenty million daily admissions to the moving picture exhibitions. Last year thirty million dollars were spent in admissions to circuses in this country . . . and more than one hundred million paid admissions to sporting events." He repeated one estimate that America paid more than $100 million a year to jazz bands. The decline from self-created amusements was clear: "Think of the old folk dances, and folk music," Cutten exclaimed, "compared with the modern dances and jazz!" [19]

The understanding of the mass entertainments was directly determined by a particular model of America's modernization in Cutten's analysis, and those of many of his colleagues. These forms were believed so effective at distorting ethics and debilitating minds because the analysts thought the mass public was susceptible to ill forces as never before. Their model of modernization proposed that the people of twentieth-century, urban-industrial society were more manipulable than those of earlier cultures and that the popular arts capitalized upon that state.

A more complete environmental explanation of mass culture thus had been created by the social scientists of the 1920s and early 1930s. The earlier criticisms from reformers, linking harsh conditions of modern work and life with the commercial exploitation of leisure, were not dismissed as much as reformulated. The progressives had typically treated the bad influences of the mass arts as "outside" forces working their way into the relatively good American society. For the scholarly experts on social change, however, the untoward amusements had become products from the "inside," accepted as the expected features of contemporary civilization. With apologies to "Pogo," it seems accurate to say that, as the social scientists met the "enemy" of mass culture in the interwar period, more and more they identified it as "us."

––––––––

How would this new conception of the mass entertainments as normal parts of modern life change the mass culture critique? Were the social scientists anomalous for accepting the entertainments as genuine expressions of the public? The answers were determined by the intellectual forces that reshaped all of American social science in this period. To understand these changes, we need to digress briefly to consider the purposes social scientists ascribed to their work in the early century.

Two disciplines were central to the development of critical scientific analyses of American civilization: anthropology and sociology. Through the early twentieth century, anthropology was categorized as a biological science. This reflected the assumption, dominant in the Victorian era, that human behavior was an expression of inherent physical characteristics. A rival conception of "culture" as learned behavior had developed in the late nineteenth century, but even this was linked to a biological model of "evolving" societies. All the world's peoples were considered to be part of one huge cultural system, representing different stages of development from the "primitive" to "civilized." Natural laws were believed to control the progress of all toward the highest forms, which scholars assumed were represented by Europe and America.

The revolution against these Victorian ideas was led by the American anthropologist Franz Boas and his students. Through their empirical research, these scientists discredited universal theories of social development and denied that inherited mental traits were the chief determinants of character and culture. By the 1920s, anthropologists in the United States were developing their own approach and methods, predominantly concerned with investigating and chronicling social and cultural diversity. These investigations also brought a new penchant for criticism to the discipline.[20]

Ethnography was the key to the change, a breakthrough technique in the social sciences that became fully developed in the 1920s. The term describes the process of research in which investigators immerse themselves in a community to observe closely and record its daily life and produce detailed descriptions of the culture. For their American practitioners, ethnographic studies offered a comparative perspective from which they could critically evaluate their own society. Examinations of non-Western cultures, in particular, provided empirical evidence that was often used to stand the old model of a hierarchy of civilizations on its head. Scholars discovered valuable features of the cultures of primitive peoples and presented them in an implicit critique of many aspects of urban-industrial life.

Probably the most notable example of anthropology's melding of scholarship and criticism was Margaret Mead's *Coming of Age in Samoa* (1928). On one level, Mead's work was a straightforward study of a "primitive" culture. She was intent on documenting the features of Samoan life and debunking racial stereotypes of the culture. Yet Mead also compared Samoan practices in rearing children to American ways in order to present a clear criticism of Western patterns. Other ethnographies similarly juxtaposed less-developed but noble peoples with more advanced but flawed Western cultures. The anthropologist Ruth Benedict, for example, studied the religion of North American Indians to point up a fault of her contemporary society. Through her comparison of cultures, she criticized the social effects of religious fundamentalism in the United States and urged that morality be more divorced from religion. Benedict's masterwork, *Patterns of Culture* (1934), also used the examples of less-developed peoples to challenge Victorian moral absolutes. Another anthropologist, Robert Redfield, put contemporary American conditions in an unflattering light in a 1930 study of a Mexican village. Significantly, Redfield's work introduced "folk culture" as an "ideal type," a theoretical definition for purposes of comparison, to provide a benchmark from which social scientists could measure the development of societies. A similar ethnographic approach informed the writer Stuart Chase's *Mexico: A Study of Two Americas* (1931), which compared life in the Depression-era United States unfavorably with what he called "machineless" ways in a small, preindustrial village.[21]

The connection between these works in the 1920s and 1930s and the mass culture critique was in the assumption behind their criticisms. Such studies developed what the contemporary anthropologists George Marcus and Michael Fischer term "the ethnographic paradigm" of their discipline. This paradigm centers on "a submerged, unrelenting critique of Western civilization as capitalism." "The idea," Marcus and Fischer write in summarizing the interpretation, "was that we in the West have lost what they—the cultural other—still have, and that we can learn basic moral and practical lessons from ethnographic representations." This critical outlook puts the anthropologists and other ethnographers squarely in the mold of the new intellectuals of the twentieth century. They were a group estranged from the dominant values of their society. They were therefore critical of many of those standards and more likely to identify with groups outside the system. The anthropologists isolate three particular grounds for criticism derived from the pioneering ethnographies. Each comes from features of life seemingly lost to modern man: "primitives'" relationship with nature, their "close, intimate communal lives," and the "spiritual vision" that infused their cultures. Entertainments had, in particular, been charged with just such effects of severing connections with nature, community, and religion. But the more significant tie between this paradigm and the mass culture critique was their shared habit of treating modernity as a completely new state. Both criticisms tended to divorce artificially the new culture from earlier circumstances, as if modern life implied the negation of all that went before.[22]

The most famous ethnography of this period, one that had a pronounced influence on mass culture criticism, was Robert and Helen Lynd's *Middle-*

town (1929). Though the Lynds were not professional anthropologists, they were very familiar with ethnographic techniques, and their work was clearly designed on that model. *Middletown*, subtitled "A Study in American Culture," surveyed daily life in Muncie, Indiana, which the authors considered a typical American small city. The Lynds moved to Muncie in 1924 and stayed a year and a half performing the investigation. They compared industrial Muncie with the conditions of the city in 1890, when it was, as they described, a "placid county-seat." The nineteenth-century culture of Muncie, though by no means wholly premodern, represented for the Lynds an ideal of a "natural" communal order, much as Samoa served for Mead or the Mexican villages for Chase and Redfield. Similar to those studies also, the less advanced culture was deemed superior in many respects. For the Lynds, modern Muncie was an example of the demise of American democracy in the face of commercial values. They wrote early in the investigation, "as the study progressed it became more and more apparent that the money medium of exchange and the cluster of activities associated with its acquisition drastically condition the other activities of the people."[23]

The seeming completeness of this transition to the new century is evident from the Lynds' treatment of mass culture. There was less consideration of adjustments to the new entertainments than of the presumed major changes or dislocations they caused. The Lynds clearly believed new recreations were transforming city life. The family was becoming less important in leisure activities, and even friendships were "shallowing," they explained. For example, a typical workman was "less dependent upon his friends in his leisure" in the new century because of the opportunities presented by radios, motion pictures and automobiles. Unorganized recreations such as fishing and bicycling were giving way to thorough organization, with formal clubs replacing casual neighborhood groups. Everywhere in Muncie's leisure, the Lynds reported, "standardized pursuits are the rule; with little in their environment to stimulate originality and competitive social life to discourage it, being 'different' is rare even among the young."

Cars and movies had done the most to revolutionize leisure, according to the Lynds. The auto not only provided broader options for pastimes further afield, but the simple option of taking a drive made recreation a regular, even daily expectation for Muncie residents. Motion pictures also acted to "quicken" life, for the Lynds, in a most unwelcome manner. They cited teachers' charges about the movies bringing premature "sophistication" to

The ubiquitous American automobile, shown here in Omaha, Nebraska, in 1938, was an agent of social disintegration to some social scientist critics. (Library of Congress, LC-USF34TOI-8964-D)

the young, and a judge's suggestion that they caused delinquency, to support their theme of commercial debilitation. This powerful force had "taken Middletown unawares" and was controlled by "an ex-peanut-stand proprietor, an ex-bicycle racer and race promoter, and so on," they noted, men "whose primary concern is making money." Ultimately, in the Lynds' analysis, the people of Muncie had lost control of their amusements. While more leisure opportunities existed in 1920 than in 1890, the expansion had come at the cost of more diverse practices and the direction of the public.[24]

Middletown's comparison of the healthy nineteenth century with the misdirected modern product was also shaped by the innovative methods of sociology, the other prominent participant-observer practice of the interwar years. The Lynds were particularly engaged by the urban ethnography developed by Robert Park and his colleagues at the University of Chicago. These analyses were, in fact, the other chief social science influence on mass culture criticism in the 1920s and 1930s.

That sociology and anthropology shared the ethnographic method was a result of the intertwined development of the two fields. They were originally part of the same discipline, and separated only as a result of the turf struggles within American universities in the early twentieth century. Sociology in the early decades of the 1900s was growing away from its nineteenth-century form, similar to the way in which anthropology was redefined. In the Victorian era, sociology chiefly produced moral and philosophical treatises. Its scientific efforts were shaped by a belief in a hierarchy of cultures like that of its sister discipline. Scholars sought to identify the universal laws that were believed to direct the development of all societies. In the twentieth century, sociologists tried to transform their discipline into a more precise empirical science, a systematic and reliable body of knowledge about humanity. The sociology of modern cities, those most dramatically new and accessible human environments, was a most promising field for the retooling. The pioneering work was done by Park and others of the "Chicago school."[25]

The scholarship of the Chicago sociologists has often been labeled "anti-urban." Indeed, it is easy to go through the writings of Park, Ernest Burgess, and their colleagues and identify numerous critical references to city life. But these were not unsophisticated critics of modernity. They were liberal intellectuals concerned with the prospects for social justice in the new metropolitan civilization, and thus their work involved more than simple revulsion at twentieth-century conditions.[26]

The Chicago ethnographic investigations were designed to allow a critical comparison of cultures. Park and his colleagues were, much like the Lynds, making implicit comparisons between community life in the era before the rise of the industrial metropolis and that under the conditions of the modern city. Though the Chicagoans did not employ a particular base for measurement like 1890 Muncie, they appear to have had a model in mind. A village or small town ideal featuring primary, face-to-face relationships and strong ties of family, neighborhood, and religious groups was evident in their comparisons.

Louis Wirth's "Urbanism as a Way of Life" (1938) was the most comprehensive statement of the Chicago school's urban theories and outlines their implications for thinking about mass culture. Wirth identified the great cities as the essence of all that was "modern," both in America and the rest of the world. He contended as well that the influence of these metropolises, where mankind had been "farther removed from organic nature" than ever before, extended beyond their physical boundaries to almost all aspects of contemporary culture.[27]

Wirth identified three characteristics of the urban population—size, density, and heterogeneity—that he believed were directly responsible for changing both social structures and personalities in city environments. His findings were based on ethnographic research, and an imagined rural-folk society served as the ideal type against which he made his comparisons. In Wirth's theory, urban living had a centrifugal force on the community, loosening bonds and casting individuals away from the core of their old social order. The traditional ties of family and neighborhood were slackened, impersonal and superficial relationships increased, normative standards for conduct weakened, and, consequently, a common moral order disappeared. In the mobility and instability of the city, the "pecuniary nexus," or commerce, became the most serviceable medium for personal relations or association. With so little of substance to hold the people together and give grounding to their lives, they tended to act collectively as "fluid masses" rather than stable groups.

Taken together, these urban conditions, as presented by Wirth and his colleagues, fostered increased "disorganization," or "deviancy"—an inability to match behaviors with conditions—for both individuals and groups. Many of their studies concentrated on this pathology. The titles in the University of Chicago Sociological Series, and other books written in the Sociology department, are illustrative: *Suicide, The Hobo, Family Disorganization, The Gang, Domestic Discord, The Gold Coast and the Slum, The Jackroller, The Ghetto, Vice in Chicago*, and *Mental Disorders in Urban Areas*. These works bore out Robert Park's 1915 keynote interpretation that drove the Chicago research agenda: "Everyone is more or less on his own in a city. The consequence is that man, translated to the city, has become a problem to himself and to society in a way and to an extent that he never was before."[28]

For the Chicago sociologists and the textbook writers who used their scholarship, mass entertainments had become a part of urban disorganization. Wirth, for example, equated popular amusements with all the other human needs exploited by commerce in the new cities. He described urban recreation as typically either "passive spectatorism" or "sensational record-smashing feats, . . . catering to thrills and furnishing means of escape from drudgery, monotony, and routine." Park termed modern leisure "mainly a restless search for excitement," a "romantic quest which finds its most out-rageous expression in the dance halls and jazz parlors." This restlessness was, for him, an indication of "mental instability" and a surrender in the face of modern challenges. "It is in the improvident use of our leisure, I suspect," wrote Park, "that the greatest wastes in American life occur."[29]

Paul Cressey's *The Taxi-Dance Hall* was the closest examination of com-mercial recreation produced by the Chicago scholars, and Ernest Burgess's introduction offered a précis of this critical approach. The problem of over-excitement in mass entertainments the sociologist attributed to the eclipse of American community over the previous half century. "In the city," he ex-plained, "the expression of the fundamental human craving for stimulation appears often to be dissociated from the normal routine of family and neigh-borhood life." The village of an earlier age provided for this need of rousing activity through "wholesome expression" in the community's normal activi-ties or in the lure of pioneering ventures to the West. In the modern era, though, the older community's recreations, based in the family and neigh-borhood, had retreated before the huge and glittering urban attractions.

Burgess presented a long list of modern amusement enterprises as evi-dence of this enormous social change. From professional baseball and national prizefights to autos, radios, motion pictures, Miss America con-tests, nightclubs, the decline of the neighborhood saloon and the rise of the speakeasy, recreation had shifted away from local control to the "out-side world." The city practice of commercializing amusement and physically separating leisure pursuits from home and community life had the effect of further dividing people's lives. The "pursuit of thrills and excitement," Burgess believed, became "a segmented interest detached from the other interests of the person."

All these outlets that drew entertainment from the home and neighbor-hood presented fundamental problems of control for those in authority. Burgess characterized nearly all the mass amusements as requiring a par-ticipation "little beyond the stimulation of individual emotion" and found "little or no function for social integration" in the new forms. Separated from the direction of kith and kin, and requiring such little commitment of any kind from its audiences, the new recreation threatened to foster aimless moral free agents caroming like pinballs from thrill to spurious thrill.[30]

Cressey's text itself amply supported the theme of mass entertainment as part of urban disorganization. The "taxi-dance" was a form of the "closed" dance hall. Women there were available as partners for male patrons for the cost of a ticket. (The "taxi-dance" term referred to this timed rate service.) Reformers were aghast at these halls, calling them thinly veiled prostitution rings. In striking contrast, though, Cressey professed acceptance for the taxi-dance hall as a legitimate urban recreation. In a clear reproach to reformers, he insisted the rise of these facilities was "not the result of the perverse machinations of a little group of wilful men." Instead, the taxi-dance hall was "the natural result of certain social forces, of certain basic human desires and interests, and of human nature itself when confronted with a particular physical setting and with certain social situations." Cressey found the commercial recreation to be a product of the same social forces that produced vice, crime, and family disruptions. "In the last analysis," he wrote, "the problem of the taxi-dance hall can be regarded as the problem of the modern city."[31]

––––––––

Cressey's conclusions, like the other social scientists' association of entertainments with urban pathology, were consistent with the model of modernization that underlay much of the ethnography of the 1920s and early 1930s. Mass entertainments were considered as the typical modern forms of expression in a theory that explained social change as a thoroughgoing transition from a rural or folk culture to an urban mass culture. Scholars were usually careful to stress that they were discussing this transformation in schematic terms. In hopes of understanding the broadest outlines of modernization for particular cultures, they explained, they were using ideal types to create profiles of two kinds of "pure" societies that never actually existed. A "pure," static folk society was as much an invention as was an urban society of wholly unprecedented conditions and behaviors.

At this theoretical remove, though, the more complicated experiences of change in real societies were easily ignored or glossed over. By so often expressing modernization in terms of ideal types and accentuating the extremes of the development process, the tendency was to distort the complexities of such change and overestimate its completeness. Even an account such as Wirth's "Urbanism as a Way of Life," which cautioned against expecting an abrupt discontinuity between the rural and urban personality types, left readers with a lasting impression of the extremes. By presenting only the two poles for consideration, the article gave the sense of a stark break in social development.[32]

This exaggeration by ideal types was often built upon rather unscientific comparative methods. For example, Wirth and the urban sociologists focused their research on pathological modern conditions. To establish these conditions as unique products of the city environment, they had to compare them to earlier, more agrarian cultures of the preindustrial era. Their footnotes suggest, however, that they did not closely investigate these earlier cultures themselves. And they certainly did not pursue them with the same rigor they applied to the studies of contemporary communities. Rather, they employed an ideal type in the sociology literature, a model society frozen in time, as their base line. The likely result of their comparison of the modern city to an artificial standard of "folk culture," then, was an overestimation of change. The anthropology works were inclined to distorted comparisons that were mirror images of those found in the sociology practice. They concentrated their empirical investigations on undeveloped societies. Their implicit comparisons to modern life were typically not based on direct or systematic study of contemporary conditions. Mismeasurement of social shifts was therefore equally likely. This is not to suggest that the rural-folk/urban-mass comparisons by the ethnographers were all wrong or intentionally misleading. Ideal types were eminently useful for establishing a scientific approach for these disciplines, and analyses like Wirth's, for example, are still unsurpassed for their clarity and scope. The use of ideal types does, however, paint social change in such broad strokes that it skews the precise nature of the particular shifts that are involved.

Without deeply studying the mass entertainments, for example, the social theorists cast them in their ideal type as primary symbols of the modern order. For Stuart Chase, the amusement park, motion picture, and comic strip were the antitheses of the recreation life of the "machineless men" of the happy Mexican villages. For the Lynds, they were prime cogs in Muncie's new industrial order. For Burgess and the Chicago analysts, they represented the prototypical problems of modern city life. What was missing in these assumptions about what the entertainments meant was an appreciation of the unevenness and the fits and starts of the change to the mass arts. Such overly broad conceptions cannot account for the particular ways people chose to enjoy, or perhaps ignore, entertainments. What were the patrons seeking in their leisure? Did they patronize the popular arts in groups, or alone? Who exercised authority if they were in such groups and how did this affect the amusement experience? How did people's thinking before the entertainment compare to that afterward? These are just a few of the questions that would be necessary to ask and to answer in order to discern how mass culture operated amid the other influences in people's lives. A comparison may be made between Americans' "migration" to the new mass culture order and immigrants' experiences in the United States. Both are complex stories of accommodation and resistance to new conditions, and, in each case, the process of change was partial, halting, and incomplete. An overly neat juxtaposition of folk and mass culture ideal types is therefore as misleading as a simple theory of assimilation.

The enormous powers the social theorists credited to mass culture, therefore, could have been as much a product of the theorists' models of social change as of any observed force. Modernizing influences were portrayed as acting on the existing society in a zero-sum equation. For every instance of new behaviors there was expected to be an equal diminution of old ways. By documenting new, "disorganized" facets of the city, the decline of "community" or folkways was implied. The effect of the zero-sum model for social change was to dismiss the possibility that "folk" characteristics could survive alongside the new ways. The existence of an intermediate stage between folk and mass culture was also effectively ruled out. Framed in these abstract terms, if the "folk" did not simply reject or ignore commercial recreations, their patronage of these offerings was taken as an indication that they were "de-folked" and were therefore becoming manipulable urban masses. The people's ability to at once enjoy and act selectively among the influences of these expressive forms, determining meaning, ignoring irrelevant content, and making messages fit into their own worldviews, is never considered. There was no room in such a scheme for independent-minded or responsible popular culture patrons.[33]

Like other Left intellectual groups of the early twentieth century, the social scientists had conflicting messages about the popular arts. They presented new ideas that helped to dismantle the earlier conservative criticisms of popular entertainments and at the same time added support to the new mass culture critique. On the optimistic side, where the progressive reformers established amusement and good leisure as legitimate needs, and the modernists found aesthetic beauty in several entertainment forms, the sociologists of the interwar period showed that the scorned mass amusements were natural products of the modern environment. They accepted the forms as reflections of life in urbanizing America. By linking the problem of mass culture to the fundamental forces of economics and demography that were remaking America, they discredited older criticisms of entertainments that were based on the public's purported moral failings. But the social scientists' treatment also encouraged despair at the popular arts. Because they also found modern society rife with pathology, their defense of the entertainments had the effect of painting these forms as agents and evidences of "disease." In the process of relieving the people of direct responsibility for their bad amusements, they paid only limited attention to the way people used the amusements and how they actually coped with the forces of the new society. Most often, they assumed that the worst effects of modernity had intruded. The social theorists presented, then, what the historian Thomas Bender describes as "a logic of history rather than a historically-grounded account of social change." By failing to examine adequately the public's actual experience of mass entertainments, the "logic" that treated mass culture as an indomitable threat to American life gained yet more credence.[34]

5 AMERICAN COMMUNISM AND POPULAR ENTERTAINMENTS

"What are the bulk of the working masses in this country reading?" asked correspondent Myra Page in the American Communist Party's *Daily Worker* in 1931. Her question, often extended to include what workers were seeing, hearing, and doing away from their jobs, was asked repeatedly by radical writers from the latter 1920s through the 1930s, and always with despair.

"Get into any street car or subway train in the industrial centers, or go into working class homes in the Middle West, in New England or Southern textile areas, or where sailors hang out," Page wrote, "and besides the local capitalist sheet, you'll find—one or more copies of *Liberty*, *Collier's*, *Saturday Evening Post*, *True Story*, *Argosy*, or others of these flourishing weeds of 5 and 10 cent magazines." Often, she added, "one of the sentimental, reactionary women's magazines is also at hand." These journals, which she labeled "dope-peddlers," had combined circulations of more than 15 million, with the *Post* and *Liberty* alone each claiming more than 2 million paid subscribers. The most dispiriting fact was that, while these magazines reached an audience beyond industrial and agricultural laborers, Page realized that "the bulk of them are workers." A similarly unhappy estimate about the reach of popular culture was reported by the novelist Louis Adamic three years later. Adamic was convinced, after a year's travel around the United States observing the habits of workers, that "ninety-nine and one-half percent" of the proletariat was "beyond the reach of radical printed propaganda or serious, honest writing of any sort." Virtually paraphrasing Page's findings, Adamic's answer to "What does the working class read?" was, "hardly anything" besides local newspapers "and an occasional copy of *Liberty, True Stories, Wild West Tales*, or *Screen Romances*." [1]

Such laments were typical of the mass culture criticisms offered by the most rebellious writers on the Left in the Great Depression era. Their objections to entertainments forms were pointed and angry. Page condemned popular literature, for example, as capitalist propaganda "fed the masses under the guise of 'love,' or 'adventure,' or 'true' stories." She scoffed at the magazines' presentation of America as a society of unlimited opportunity for those who were diligent, thrifty, and fair in their dealings with employers. The entertaining stories that inevitably celebrated law, order, and private property she found equally affronting. "America is the land of democracy where peace and harmony of interests reigns between the classes," Page wrote in describing the dominant message of the mass literature, "and strikes are a thing of the past except when a few wild-eyed reds get loose and stir up trouble before they can be locked up and put safely out of the way." Not only conditions in America, but international concerns were distorted as well, she charged. The editorials and fiction of the adventure magazines romanticized imperialism and colonialism and were increasingly being used by capitalists to "whip up sentiment for military preparedness and war."

The American Communists' condemnations went beyond popular literature to include the stage, screen, and other mass arts. Motion pictures were thoroughly excoriated in the Party press in the early 1930s. A *New Masses* film critic in 1934 described the movie industry as "a gigantic propaganda factory for every feeble and vicious and half-false way of life." American Communism's most developed analysis of the film, Harry Alan Potamkin's

The Eyes of the Movie (1934), similarly described most American pictures as engineered "escape" into worlds of fancy that served the interests of the ruling classes. "Repeated succession of such films makes the audience, 'the self-respecting petty bourgeoisie and the working class,' forgetful of their plight—that at least is the hope of the class serving this dish," Potamkin argued. Even the mere inklings of revolt were squelched by the medium. "As more and more doubt creeps into the audience through the pressure of circumstance and positive radical education, the illusions served will be augmented to overwhelm dissent."[2]

The popular stage was strafed as well. The Communist *Student Review* in 1933 depicted theater as obsessed with "sex neuroticism and trivialities," bent on "the avoidance of major social themes." The following year, the publication issued a blanket censure to all of Broadway for its social irresponsibility. Jazz fared little better. The music critic for the *New Masses* denounced it as "pseudo-music," of "trivial character and unrelated to reality or higher aspirations," while one letter writer to the magazine simply insisted that such music could never serve workers' needs. "Mozart composed for a romantic bourgeoisie," she wrote. "The jazz artist composes for a bastard capitalistic generation."[3]

Communist cultural views in the early 1930s enjoyed a fair prominence as a significant number of American writers and artists joined the political Left. The Communist perspective on entertainments reached readers across the nation through Party journals, newspapers, and the fellow-traveler press. On their face, these views seemed to be founded on dramatically new grounds: the notion of unavoidable class conflict and the belief that working-class audiences were being systematically exploited. Yet the mass culture critique produced by these most radical of America's twentieth-century critics also continued to employ many of the same themes of earlier, more moderate intellectuals. What most distinguished the Communists from earlier critics is that they were allied to a mass movement and therefore were more aware of the practical impact of their ideas for "common" people than were many of the other critics. The differences that remained between the critics' prescriptions and the practices of the rank and file, however, again highlight how intellectuals consistently misread entertainments.

Communist Party headquarters, New York City, ca. 1934, including the offices of the *Daily Worker*, the newspaper that best exhibited the Party's changing line on popular entertainments. (Robert F. Wagner Labor Archives, New York University)

The mass culture criticism of American Communists consisted of three fairly distinct periods. Though the criticisms did not necessarily shift at any precise dates, they may be roughly outlined as the "Proletarian Culture" era ("Proletcult" in the intellectuals' shorthand) from 1928 to 1932; a period of more lenient attitudes toward the popular arts that overlapped with the Popular Front and lasted from 1932 to 1936; and a renewed hard-line era from 1936 through the Second World War.

The Proletarian Culture movement that developed in the United States in the late 1920s and early 1930s aimed to change the much-lamented facts of the working classes' popular culture tastes by weaning them from the bourgeois arts and letters. Intellectuals hoped to establish a unique order of expressive forms by and for the working class. Though the movement's theoreticians quarreled over who might create this art and over its content, their broad goal was to create forms relevant to the experience of the American proletariat and to encourage its revolutionary consciousness.

The American proletarian culture program closely reflected the evolving Soviet policy in the arts. The precise degree of control that the Soviet Union exerted over the American Communist Party in the interwar era remains a subject of intense scholarly debate. But as far as these cultural policies are concerned, American radicals appear to have taken their cues consistently from the Soviet example, beginning with the Party's inception in the United States after World War I.

These cues were not always clear or consistent. Efforts to cultivate worker-artists and establish a distinct working-class culture had developed haphazardly in the Soviet Union after the Bolshevik Revolution. The arts (in any form) had to be a lesser priority for a society attempting such a dramatic restructuring. Also, proletarian culture lacked the most powerful doctrinal imprimatur because it had never been mentioned in the writings of Karl Marx or Friedrich Engels. The program was in fact opposed by both prominent leaders of the revolution, Vladimir Lenin and Leon Trotsky, because they feared it would force too much structure on imaginative expression. Without such important sanction, those officials who favored the program were forced to pursue it outside Communist Party channels. Proletarian culture was most shaped by disputes among competing literary movements. Only by the last years of the 1920s, after the expulsion of the Trotskyists and a shake-up among the literary groups, did the proletarian culture movement become the central force in Soviet letters.[4]

In the United States, the chief early advocate of the proletarian arts, and the critic who would become the most recognized Communist commentator of the 1920s and 1930s, was Michael Gold. Gold was the pen name adopted by Irwin Granich. He was the child of Jewish immigrants and had grown up in the slums of New York's East Side. Leaving school at age twelve, he held a number of odd jobs in his youth while he trained himself as a journalist and a writer of radical poetry, plays, and novels. He was attracted to anarchist politics and a Bohemian lifestyle, joined the radical labor organization Industrial Workers of the World, and spent nearly two years in Mexico during World War I to avoid the draft. After the war, Granich returned to the United States and resumed his journalistic career, writing as

"Michael Gold" to protect himself against Attorney General A. Mitchell Palmer's persecutions of radicals.

In 1921, while the new Soviet culture program was gestating, Gold published the first call for proletarian literature in the United States. "Towards a Proletarian Art" was typical of most avant-garde cultural pronouncements of the 1920s: Gold's purpose was to flay the genteel tradition in American letters as much as it was to promote revolutionary new practices in the arts. Gold thought that he had achieved a complete knowledge of life from his experiences in the tenements. He proudly called himself "Mike" to celebrate his simple roots. Like some of the modernists who sought to introduce everyday experiences into the arts, he sought to establish the value of his own experiences as cultural expression. More broadly, he urged that arts should be created that would express the realities of the lives of the workers, without shame or apology. The proletarian culture program under way in the Soviet Union was encouraging the masses to express their "divinity," and Gold called for America to follow suit. He counseled aspiring writers to ignore the leading stylists and fashionable intellectual techniques of the day: "The boy in the tenement must not learn of their art." Instead, they should follow his lead and cultivate the resources of their own environment. "Art," he wrote, "is the tenement pouring out its soul through us, its most sensitive and articulate sons and daughters." [5]

This proletarian approach spelled yet more trouble for mass culture. Gold's analysis of the reigning philosophies in the American arts reduces to a scheme very much like Van Wyck Brooks's highbrow/lowbrow explanation. At one pole of the arts world, Gold suggested, there was a "decadent" order of aesthetes such as the writers for the *Little Review*, who championed "pure art" as man's highest achievement. These, he believed, were destined to produce only empty expressions divorced from real life. At the other pole was a more pervasive force, popular culture. He regarded the popular arts as equally degraded and sterile as the aesthetes' forms, and cited as his chief example the *Saturday Evening Post*. "Plutocratic, feudal America, made up of cockney, white-collar slaves, sordid, golf-playing, spruce overseers, and the Masters, speaks through this school," Gold wrote. "The writers are amazingly expert technicians who perform a definite function in the industrial dynasty. They feed the masses the opium of cheap romanticism, and turn their thoughts from the concrete to the impossible. They gild the filth in which we live; they make heroes out of slave-drivers, and saints out of vultures. But they cannot create a great art."[6]

The concerns that Gold expressed were an interesting combination of disgust toward comfortable lifestyles, fears of the cultural exploitation of the people, and art criticism. They suggest how his criticism could serve the radical intellectuals' divergent interests simultaneously. Gold was at once displaying his sophistication amid vanguard aesthetic ideas while preserving his credentials as a champion of the common people.

Gold's criticisms also indicate that a Marxian perspective on mass culture, rare as it may have been in the America of 1921, was nonetheless familiar for its similarities to the established mass culture critique. Gold had adopted the dominant assumptions of Left intellectuals of the early twentieth century about the public's capabilities for selecting their appropriate expressive culture. The parallel between his *Little Review/Saturday Evening Post* dichotomy in American culture and Brooks's highbrow/lowbrow version is significant. Brooks's scheme was premised on Americans' lack of an indigenous cultural tradition; he believed that, consequently, their way of life tended toward misguided extremes, ill suited to contemporary society. Gold's view similarly assumed that there had yet to be a core for the nation's culture that faithfully represented workers' experiences. Therefore, he wrote off the possibility that the working class could have produced any true expression of its particular interests. In both Brooks's and Gold's interpretations, the implication was that intellectuals were the only hope to bring the creation of such an authentic aesthetic order from scratch—Brooks with the nationally minded artists and Gold with the tenements' most astute sons and daughters.

Gold shared with the progressives a view of the public as victims of the socioeconomic system that assumed the mass entertainments to be victimizing agents rather than reflections of the people. The working class could not indulge in the dominant culture as represented by the *Saturday Evening Post*, for example, and still preserve its dignity. Like Randolph Bourne's argument that the mass arts ruined the inherent cultural nobility of the new immigrant, the amusements developed a "false consciousness" among workers, turning the potential revolutionaries into bland ciphers. Like both Bourne and the reformers, too, Gold failed to consider whether workers had any input in the creation of the mass expressions. Gold's simple model of exploitation ignored the interactions between classes and across ethnic divisions that produced mass culture. Like previous intellectuals who assumed the entertainments thoroughly overwhelmed the public, Gold did not consider that the people might adopt or discard entertainments to suit their needs and thereby influence creators of the popular arts through their demands. There was no room in his theory, in other words, for any form of what Raymond Williams termed an "alternative" culture: one distinct from the dominant order but not arrayed against it. Direct opposition to the entertainments was the only option for workers.[7]

This Manichean conception of Americans' relations with the arts was typical in the radicals' entertainment criticism. It reflects the strongly moralistic, often puritanical judgments the Communists made about cultural forms. Gold, for example, launched another diatribe against the *Saturday Evening Post* in 1922 that portrayed the magazine in distinctly "sinful" terms. Responding to its 2.5 million weekly circulation, Gold wrote, "Oh! the filthy lackey rag, so fat, shiny, gorged with advertisements, putrid with prosperity like the bulky, diamonded duenna of a bawdy-house!" He again referred to the stories of success as "spiritual opium," and to the editors' claim that they were "giving the people what they want," he jeered, "Pimps, dope peddlers and gold brick merchants have the same apology for their professions." This popular literature represented, for Gold, all the illicit pleasures that his community had to defend against and those that had proven to be timeless lures of secular civilization. Similar images of debased sexual habits and narcotic dazes were typical in official Soviet charges against entertainments such as jazz music, for example. "False" stimulations were presumed to be administered to the proletariat by capitalists to dissuade or distract them from pursuing their freedom in revolt.[8]

Besides Gold's diatribes, this puritanical tone toward the entertainments appeared in the sporadic treatments of workers' culture in the American Communist press in the 1920s. Robert Minor, a radical cartoonist, wrote in the *Daily Worker* in 1925 castigating the hapless *Saturday Evening Post* as the epitome of degraded art in capitalist societies. To make a living under capitalism, a creator had to "subject himself to a process of elimination of artistic qualities, comparable to the process thru which a street-walker is subjected by long practice of her profession of mock-love," Minor explained. "The prostituted artist becomes sleek and witty, but nevertheless remains a flatulent mock-artist." Under the title "Mammonart and Communist Art," a writer named Robin Dunbar denounced Mark Twain and Jack London in the *Daily Worker* as artists who debauched themselves in their attempts to achieve popularity. Dunbar described works such as *Tom Sawyer* and *Huckleberry Finn* as "childish" books, "composed by childish minded men, who never grew up, or if they did grow up, became corrupted by sycofancy [*sic*], parasitism, and class c[o]llaboration." Warming to the task, Dunbar also employed the new and supposedly spotlessly moral proletarian theaters of the Soviet Union to flay the bourgeois stage for its "nude women" and "adulterous wives." "The dirty, the pornografic [*sic*], the lewd, the drunken, the low, the bummy, the bourgeois in short is shown the gutter and the healthy worker . . . is given the center of the stage." The proletarian theater was strictly for workers, Dunbar explained, "not for lounge lizards, and jazz hounds and sex degenerates, who moan and whime [*sic*] in Oscar Wildean monotones about not sufficiently satisfying their degenerate appetites, their sadistic cravings, their abnormal thirsts." [9]

The American Communists' prudish streak and practice of casting culture in strict good-versus-evil terms fit their conception of themselves as the last righteous souls in a depraved society. Yet, as with any policies offered in the name of a mass movement, the important determination is how much of the Party was represented by these pronouncements. The nature of the American Party's membership in the 1920s suggests that the cultural verdicts spoke for intellectual leaders rather than the rank and file. Robert Wolf, a *New Masses* editor, explained to the Communist Academy in Moscow in late 1927 that there were between ten and twenty thousand people in the revolutionary movement in the United States, and less than three thousand spoke English. Studies have indicated that by the mid-1920s, when the Party's foreign-language federations were disbanded, Finnish speakers and Eastern Europeans together accounted for approximately three-quarters of the membership, and only 10 percent spoke English. When Party leaders created the American entertainment criticism (in English), they therefore likely had little input from the kinds of workers who typically patronized these forms most. Nor could they easily discuss these other members' experiences with the entertainments to test their victimization model. Explaining how some of these fellow Communists could patronize the popular arts and yet remain politically mobilized would certainly have complicated the mass culture critique. While American Party leaders were directed only by the broad constraints that came from the U.S.S.R., their perceptions were largely formed in a vacuum. They attacked what their own prejudices told them must be ill effects from the amusements.[10]

The proletarian cultural movement in the United States gained its greatest influence after the international Party initiated what it termed the "Third Period" in 1928. Acting on the belief that the world was now on the brink of class revolution and the proletariat ready to assume its leading role in the change, Josef Stalin engineered this sharply militant turn in the movement. The Communist Party called for an "intensification of the class war on the cultural front," and adopted a much stronger stand against bourgeois culture. The proletarian arts program was elevated to a central role in the worldwide revolutionary crusade.

In the United States, the change was marked by Mike Gold's appointment to direct the *New Masses* and the journal's conversion to championing the working-class arts. The *New Masses* had been founded in 1926 as a nominally independent organ. It was considered a voice of Left politics but was not linked to any particular program. By 1928, its politics were realigned and it adopted workers' literature. More concretely, the magazine formed the John Reed Club of New York in 1929 to foster young proletarian artists. The club, which soon spread nationwide and produced a network of literary magazines, adopted the motto "Art is a Class Weapon." It welcomed both Party members and sympathizers and therefore attracted a variety of politically involved writers and artists. The Reed Club was enrolled in the International Union of Revolutionary Writers and, as part of Moscow's attempts to coordinate universally the arts, it sent delegates to a 1930 conference in the Ukraine for instructions in developing the American proletarian movement.[11]

The effects of the new cultural hard line on Left intellectuals' attitudes toward mass entertainments are evident from changes in the Communist and fellow-traveler press. In the latter 1920s, Gold's criticisms were more radical than that of the party organ, the *Daily Worker*. The paper devoted most of a page each day to cultural news and found the popular arts worthy of much coverage. The *Daily Worker* reviewed motion pictures and the theater, for instance, reported on the circus and featured pictures of stage and screen stars. In addition, most of its reporting on commercial amusements showed no signs of political slant. By 1931, in the Third Period crackdown, the coverage of entertainments had disappeared from daily editions of the paper. Virtually all the popular culture mentions that remained were book reviews in a special Saturday section. In early 1933, even this weekend section was gone, and there was virtually no coverage of popular culture in the publication.[12]

Excitement about the potential of the proletarian culture movement seemed to peak in the early 1930s as the Depression deepened and many American writers and artists were increasingly radicalized. The intellectuals' interest in "workers' culture" did not necessarily mean, though, that it was the workers' own expressions that they supported. The question of how much the proletariat should be involved in creating the Communists' desired culture emerged among Party intellectuals soon after the Bolshevik Revolution and remained a subject of debate for decades. For a number of leftist cultural experts in the United States, the proper workers' culture was to be along the lines of the *Seven Arts*'s ideal for a national art: recognized artists were to divine the popular interest and then express it through their particular techniques. Some intellectuals, then, could regard the shift to proletarian culture as an opportunity for aesthetic rejuvenation in the United States as much as a commitment to the working class. This may explain how several important writers who supported modernism in the 1920s made the shift to the proletarian culture movement while maintaining the same hostility to mass culture. To put it bluntly, the avant-garde critics did not necessarily have to change their characteristic disregard for the desires of the masses to become Communist cultural arbiters.

Radical criticism of the motion picture offers a vivid example. *Experimental Cinema*, a nonpolitical journal devoted to film as a modern art form, was founded in Philadelphia in 1930. Its first number was dominated by concerns of cinematic theory and technique. An article by the editor Lewis Jacobs, for example, used the modernists' vocabulary to castigate filmmakers for ignoring their medium's unique capabilities. Instead of "allowing the plasticities of its instruments to limit and govern their visions," Jacobs wrote of American movie producers, they "project their celluloid results in concocted plastics (funded from their previous aesthetic pilferings) and moral recipes suited to the evanescent demand of the many." Within a year, though, the magazine ceased publication, reorganized under the same editors, and reappeared in February 1931 announcing its new "proletarian basis" and "close relationship with the labor movement in America." The editors vowed to help produce films "which will serve to give cohesion to the movement among the masses of movie-goers and which will serve to counteract amongst these masses the stupefying opiate of the Hollywood product." The radical bent was evident in charges that the movies were acting as a tool for the nation's imperialist policies in Central America, and the possibility was raised as well that the medium could be turned toward manipulating the public of the United States.[13]

For editor Jacobs, this shift to the proletarian culture movement brought remarkably little change to his critical attitudes. In his new radical persona, he still showed far less concern with workers' expression or their heightened revolutionary consciousness than with the potential of the new political order for solving the artistic problems of American films. "In America, the film, the one absolute and vital cultural force of our time, is completely imbedded in the ideas and doctrines of a reactionary class," he began a 1931 article. "The bourgeois currents behind the puerilities of the film are dead to any promise of unfoldment within the lens. Only the ethos of class-struggle contains any hope for a new transformation of the film in America." Jacobs compared the American movie situation to that of the Soviet Union. There, the revolutionary ethos had inspired stunning new techniques in the medium. The Soviets' new political order promised to free moviemakers to develop their aesthetic ideas to the utmost and at the same time elevate them to positions of social leadership. "Directors there," he wrote of the Soviet situation, "define the revolutionary working class reality and ideology." The best example was Sergei Eisenstein, whose films *Potemkin* and *Ten Days That Shook the World* had "evolved autonomous laws of cinematic form sharply related to the needs of the Russian masses." Jacobs wrote that Eisenstein transformed film "from a bourgeois opiate into an intense experience in which the spectator becomes a participant in a new and orphic conception."[14]

Harry Alan Potamkin, the recognized dean of Communist film critics in the early 1930s, made a more substantive change than Jacobs, shifting from a criticism based on aesthetics to one of social and political concerns. Yet he also similarly maintained his disdain for popular productions. In the 1920s, Potamkin, a poet and editor of a literary magazine, was taken with the early developments of the "New Criticism" and its focus on the formal properties of expressive culture. His film criticism of the late 1920s stressed matters of structure, composition, and technique, analyzing the "internal" qualities of the motion picture. "The film which does not dwell upon itself," he wrote in a characteristic phrase, "does not realize itself." Potamkin developed strong political attitudes in the early years of the Depression, and in 1930, now a firm Marxist, he became the film critic of the *New Masses*. His concentration shifted from the formal properties of the medium to its ideological underpinnings. *The Eyes of the Movie*, a compilation of his writings, opened: "The movie was born in the laboratory and reared in the counting-house. It is the benevolent monster of the four I's: Inventor, Investor, Impresario, Imperialist. The second and fourth eyes are the guiding ones. They pilot the course of the motion picture. The course is so piloted that it is favorable to the equilibrium of the ruling class, and unfavorable to the working class."

Potamkin had suggested in 1931 that Hollywood served as America's mythical "holy city," the center for modern pilgrimage and the epitome of the nation's values. He wrote that the movies constituted a new religion, and, following the Marxist treatment of religion as a false ideology to delude the masses, he excoriated the medium. To those who defended the movies on the grounds that they were cathartic experiences that purged audiences of cares, he countered that "what it leaves in the body systemic is more vicious than what it sets free." The movie's malign function was "to free from all the pores the currents of criticism that might ultimately assail consent. They go off as steam. Its function is to obscure all the major issues by calling them profane or by stressing the trivial." He concluded, "Holy Hollywood is Holy America, is the Holy Alliance and Entente of capitalist society."[15]

Both Potamkin and Jacobs claimed they had made the political shift, from relative disinterest in the mass audience to making the working classes their chief concern. But for both this made little change in their presumption of the public's cultural limitations. They were not moved to investigate the proletarians' actual experience and use of the film because, like the earlier critics, they believed the masses were powerless before the images. Part of the attraction of the Soviet cultural model for such thinkers, it may be suggested, was that it preserved intellectuals' detachment. For all the model's apparent liberation of the masses, the public's preferences did not become the gauge for setting Communist cultural standards. The state, through its experts, decreed the proper content of the arts.

Though American radical critics had no such powers to suppress the people's desires, their model of the way entertainments operated effected a similar kind of cultural disfranchisement. The Communist-inspired mass culture critique of the Third Period presented a black-and-white picture of thorough domination. It depicted an overpowering socioeconomic and ideological system subjugating an enfeebled public. In the face of compulsion and manipulation, popular needs and desires were presumed to be misconceived or distorted. Potamkin, for instance, accepted that the masses were virtually defenseless before the messages in bourgeois films. He took the movies' popularity as evidence that they were the most effective possible manipulators. "Most people are eye-minded," he argued. "The things their eyes see become the things that affect them." Images portrayed repeatedly in films therefore "become the beliefs of the impressionable audience, whose mind receives the suggestions like wax and retains them like marble." [16]

Other radical critics showed this same conception of the American public as a helpless, atomistic "mass" in the face of the entertainments. Late in 1931, Philip Sterling wrote a scathing article for the *New Masses* on the purported effects of popular music in manipulating Americans during World War I. He began by recounting a 1918 scene on a troop transport that had been torpedoed. The soldiers, about to go down with the ship, were singing the popular tune "Where do we go from here, boys." Sterling called the incident a "triumph" for "Tin Pan Alley" and described this and four hundred other published war songs as "the magic sounds which turned America into an army of whirling dervishes bent for destruction, death and chaos." George M. Cohan, the creator of "Over There" and other wartime tunes, was cited as the chief of the "piano prostitutes" and was charged with fostering the martial spirit only to hide the realities of the awful conflict in sweet lyric stories. "Mr. Cohan could claim the distinction," Sterling wrote, "of having sent more young men to their deaths than any other living 'artist' in America."

The importance of this interpretation is that Sterling believed the exploitation was so complete, and also that the public of 1931 would be equally lemminglike for the latest popular music pipers. This expectation of people's immediate, positive response to suggestion informed his fears that in the next war, Tin Pan Alley, now advanced beyond sheet music and pianos, "will din a new message of mass suicide to unprecedented numbers of workers over the radio and through the talkies." The only escape he could conceive from another world tragedy (and "the deluge of nauseating songs") was in the promise of international peace contained in another, presumably non-propagandistic, musical form: the socialist "Internationale." [17]

The idea of mass entertainments victimizing the helpless remained evident as well in the Third Period in the drug addiction metaphor pressed by Mike Gold. Depicting mass entertainment patrons as junkies, prostrated by their affliction, justified the critics' view of the public as necessarily irresponsible with the popular arts. The people needed to be detoxified before they could determine their best interests.

Gold argued in 1931 that capitalist propaganda surrounded Americans in every advertisement, short story, child's primer, and popular jazz song. He described newspaper reporting as especially blameworthy for its obsession with "sport, sex and crime." "The masses are hypnotized," and people are "robots," he argued, because the main purpose of capitalist culture was to delude their sensibilities, "fill their minds with any nonsense that will divert them from thinking." The Soviet model was heralded as the proper course. Gold described how millions of newspapers were sold daily in the U.S.S.R. that contained not a word of crime news. He contended this was because the Soviet people did not want such stories, and had never developed a habit for them as Americans had. In the final analysis, popular culture forms were a cynical exploitation of human weaknesses. "They say the people want it. But the people do not want it," Gold wrote, restating the *Saturday Evening Post* indictment of a decade earlier. "Cocaine peddlers have the same alibi. . . . The coke fiend does not 'want it'—he has had the misfortune to form a terrible habit, and instead of helping cure him, certain shrewd businessmen keep him in bondage."[18]

Gold's image of citizens drawn to the popular arts out of impairment, and against their better natures, could well have been taken from a reformer's tract in the Progressive Era. This similarity merits attention. The criticisms of mass entertainments that grew from the "play movement" of the 1910s and the Communists' Proletcult program of the late 1920s and 1930s differed sharply in their ultimate solutions: the progressives trusting in reform of the socioeconomic system and the Communists seeking revolution. Consequently, the Communists' condemnations of popular forms were more virulent. The movements did share, though, an assumption about the nature of Americans' interactions with the mass arts and the damage they believed it inflicted. As the reformers saw dance halls and motion picture theaters as dangerous retreats for the industrially debilitated, where their weakness would be further exploited by agents of commerce, so the Communists believed popular music, literature, and film encouraged the degraded to be content with their situation, and narcotized them to potentially greater social evils. Both the play movement, with its encouragement of rural folk practices, playgrounds, and "substitute" dance halls, and Proletcult, with its production of workers' books, arts, and films, sought to shift the existing public entertainment habits. Each claimed that the wholly new entertainment order it sought to create would be a more authentic representation of the masses' needs. The ultimate failure of both the progressives and Communists to wean the public from the popular arts left critics yet more awed by what they presumed was the thorough control mass culture had achieved. Both movements had, of course, denied that the popular entertainments were rooted in the interests and values of the public, and that the public could resist their influence.

———

By 1935, when the major overview, *Proletarian Literature in the United States*, was published, the working-class culture movement in America had already begun a precipitous decline. The direction again came from the Soviet Union. By the early 1930s, Stalin's ruthless programs for industrialization and the collectivization of agriculture had proved only partly successful. Vast strides had been made in transforming the U.S.S.R. into a dominant modern power, at the cost of millions of lives. But it was yet no match for more advanced economies. This inadequacy was glaring, and especially frightening to Soviet leaders aware of the rising threat of fascism, particularly Nazism. It sent the U.S.S.R. searching for strong allies. The result was an almost complete about-face in the Soviets' approach to the liberal democracies. The declaration of the Popular Front against War and Fascism at the Seventh Comintern Congress in 1935 encouraged worldwide political cooperation with progressive non-Communists, and, notably, it brought new policies for the arts. As Stalin pursued better relations with the Western powers, Moscow found a whole new tolerance for bourgeois culture.

The Popular Front shift brought the dismantling of the proletarian culture program in favor of independent, national guidelines for the arts. The John Reed Clubs were disbanded in 1935, and discussion of the proletarian arts in the Left press rapidly declined in the succeeding years. As indigenous influences in the United States were allowed increasing precedence over a specific Soviet line, there was some leeway for considering the mass arts as legitimate parts of the nation's culture.[19]

For example, the *New Masses*, a proletarian culture journal under Mike Gold's direction in the late 1920s and early 1930s, opened its standards to some degree. The criticisms of motion pictures, which had toed the Party line in Harry Potamkin's years as the journal's chief critic, became less for-mulaic as reviews paid more attention to the entertainment provided by the medium. By the later 1930s, many notices, though often critical of the level of intelligence displayed in movies, showed little of the predictable radical rhetoric. The *Daily Worker*, as well, liberalized its policies in cultural mat-ters. The coverage of entertainments that had disappeared from its pages in the early 1930s returned with daily reviews of mass amusements in the latter half of the decade and a new full-page sports section.

The shifting fortunes of popular entertainments among Left intellectuals are especially evident in the concerns of the League of American Writers. This was a group of prominent professional writers, both Communists and fellow-travelers, that was created to replace the John Reed Clubs as the leading radical voice in the arts. The new, less sectarian approach is evi-dent from the League's initial membership, which included writers such as Ernest Hemingway and Archibald MacLeish who had displayed only nomi-nal leftist politics. That several of the authors had achieved public acclaim and some commercial success also suggests the League offered some open-ing toward more popular forms.

The successive congresses of the League over the latter 1930s show, as well, this steady liberalization of the Left line toward the mass arts. The first meeting, which formally established the League in the spring of 1935, had come before the official declaration of the Popular Front. It reflected both the writers' obeisance to proletarian culture standards and the chaf-ing of many at the requirements of that order. The American Communist Party's secretary, Earl Browder, addressed the Congress to clarify the official policies in the arts. He explained that there was no set line in aesthetic pro-duction, no fixed standard for automatically separating works "into sheep and goats." To best support the Party, he urged that writers simply produce their best work. "We do not want to take good writers," Browder said, "and make bad strike leaders out of them." [20]

The 1937 Writers' Congress, well into the Popular Front era, showed less concern for proletarian forms and greater attention to the encroachments of fascism at home and abroad. Its openness to popular culture was high-lighted by a remarkable address from the Hollywood humor writer Donald Ogden Stewart. Stewart explained to the gathering that he suspected his appearance was intended to serve as the "Horrible Example," the Congress's equivalent to the old temperance lecturer's ploy of trotting out a dissipated, destitute figure to expose the dangers of drink. In his case, the vice to be laid bare was ten years of writing popular movie plots. The intended effect, he announced, was that "when you go shuddering to bed tonight you can get down on your knees and pray, 'Dear God, please don't let me become like Donald Ogden Stewart. Amen.'"

Stewart's speech before the Congress does not appear, though, to have been simply a chance for comic relief or for gloating from high-minded noncommercial writers. Rather, he delivered an address quite critical of the state of American culture, and he encouraged radical action to change the society. The implicit message in his appearance was that producing mass amusements was not incompatible with a critical social conscience. Entertainments, one might suspect from Stewart's presentation, were not necessarily reactionary. In the Popular Front atmosphere, then, with critics on guard foremost against blatant fascism, what previously looked like dangerous bourgeois propaganda seemed comparatively innocuous. At the end of the 1937 Congress, Stewart was even elected as the new president of the League.[21]

The Third Writers' Congress in 1939 paid the most attention to issues of mass entertainments, including sessions on writing popular literature, the potentials of radio for radical writers, and a report on motion pictures. The classic question of Left artists, "Why are we having so little success reaching the mass audience?," arose once again. But this time they found a less comforting response. "I accuse writers of being snobs," Hope Hale said in one meeting. Hale, a short-story writer for a variety of journals from *Modern Romances* to the *New Yorker*, pointed out that all the radicals' pronounced dedication to the working class had produced only inbred intellectual discussions with no relevance to the proletariat. "While we were eating our cake of devotion to the masses and having our cake of arty self-indulgence too," she lectured the writers, "the workers have not waited. They have been reading. Millions of them have made their own selections of literature that answered in some way their needs." Citing the monthly circulation of two million of the realistic fiction tabloid *True Story*, Hale contended that the magazine was an indispensable medium for social messages. Potentially, if radical writers could overcome their pretensions, such mass fare could also carry radical ideas. "We have been too snooty, or too lazy," Hale said, "to learn the difficult technique of making truths live in terms of people's lives."[22]

The Third Congress's session on radio was also clearly designed to challenge simplistic mass culture criticisms among radical writers. Stewart reported that CBS script director Max Wylie offered a challenge to the writers to consider radio work, and that he found the idea well received. Wylie also warned the group about being "snooty" toward the medium, and encouraged them to think of the mass radio audience as a boon to their cause, their best means of conveying arguments for freedom.[23]

This apparent growing acceptance of popular culture by Left intellectuals during the Popular Front era can be easily explained, and in fact dismissed, as simple manipulations of the American Communist Party from Moscow. The cultivation of bourgeois intellectuals to defend the Soviet Union, according to this interpretation, led logically to a decline in criticism. And the liberalism so prominent at the 1939 Writers' Congress does seem a clear example of the surrender of radicalism. But this explanation of Moscow's control as the sole force in reforming intellectuals' popular culture attitudes may be too easy. It ignores the possibility that changes in thinking about these arts may have occurred within the Party to effect this shift. It also overlooks new ideas about the entertainments that were being developed by a varied group of American intellectuals by the 1930s.[24]

The effects of the rise of international fascism in causing a reevaluation of American life should not be discounted. The threat encouraged many writers to extol American virtues to counter enemies who were promoting rabid varieties of nationalism. In retrospect, however, we can see that there were also longer-term developments in the nation that likely played a role in the changing image of popular culture by the late 1930s.

This decade witnessed a more widespread acceptance of the urban, cosmopolitan culture than ever before, as numerous scholars have suggested. Several of the most effective media for carrying the ethos of this new way of life, motion pictures and nightclubs for instance, had been limited primarily to cities in the earlier decades of the century. The 1930s witnessed their spread to encompass most of the United States. For radio, the carrier of popular music and humor that were prime vehicles of the new culture, the Depression era was again the crucial period of growth. The commercial wireless had appeared only in 1922, but by 1934 60 percent of American homes owned the magic box. The penetration of the new culture was not just through the new media, however, but also came within existing popular literature. Leo Lowenthal has shown how the profiles of personalities that

The nationwide reach of the mass media, as evidenced by the range of magazine offerings at this Omaha, Nebraska, newsstand in 1938, effected a growing acceptance of mass entertainments by intellectuals toward the middle of the century. (Library of Congress, LC-USF34TOI-8939-D)

had appeared in mass magazines of the early century had shifted to mass culture concerns as midcentury approached. The leaders from business and politics who had been sketched in earlier decades often had been replaced, by 1940, with heroes from the world of entertainment. By the latter 1920s as well, the new culture had brought changes in the images businesses used to attract the public's attention. The enormous success of new confession and tabloid magazines such as *True Story* and the *Daily Graphic*, together with the influence of the movies, had changed the style of national magazine advertising toward entertainment formulas. The spread of the new media and their messages by the 1930s, then, probably best qualify this era as the advent of a national mass-media culture for the United States.[25]

The steady growth and pervasion of the mass arts over the early century likely also influenced intellectuals' perceptions over time. The "Lost Generation" of American writers, those born in the 1890s or the first few years of the 1900s was, significantly, also the first group to grow up in the age of modern urban entertainments. These creative minds, whom the critic Malcolm Cowley has shown to be so influential in twentieth-century culture, had by the 1930s lived most of their lives with the entertainments. Their writings suggest an easy acquaintance with the forms and values of popular culture. Familiarity with the amusements was, of course, no guarantee that the intellectuals would spare them their contempt. But decades of exposure to the new culture made it less likely that the criticisms would come from a complete ignorance of mass culture. As the "Lost Generation" became "found" by the eve of the Depression, and most members returned from their physical or spiritual expatriations, it evolved into an American intellectual cohort more aware of popular expression than probably any since the Civil War era. Perhaps this explains the change in the most famous of the intelligentsia's treatments of American life. The critics' encyclopedic castigation of the national culture after World War I, edited by Harold Stearns as *Civilization in the United States* (1922), contained no discussion of entertainment media. But when the topic was reevaluated far more sympathetically in 1938 in *America Now*, again under Stearns direction, a paper on movies and radio was prominently featured.[26]

———————

While the Depression era may very well mark a turning point in American intellectuals' attitudes toward the entertainments, it was certainly no sea change. While criticisms of the mass arts declined in the Popular Front years, and some critics found virtues in these forms, most culture experts still shunned them. The Communists in particular, now at the peak of their influence in the latter 1930s, launched a folk culture program to try once again to replace commercial expressions. They cultivated rural traditions, those expressly detached from the mass media, in hopes of better serving the American proletariat. The center of the Communists' effort was the adoption of American folk songs in the late 1930s and early 1940s. Before this period, radical organizations in the United States such as the Industrial Workers of the World or the Socialist Party had not placed any particular value on what was considered native folk music. The political tunes of these movements reflect catholic tastes, their songbooks including European labor songs, American patriotic songs, takeoffs on hymns, and popular music of the day. Even in the Third Period of the late 1920s and early 1930s, the Communists' search for a uniquely proletarian music had dismissed folk songs. A "Composers Collective" of professional writers was formed instead to pursue the class-specific idiom. Though few of these formally trained composers were members of the Party, they closely followed its instructions to root out bourgeois influences in creating proletarian works. While condemning, for instance, "sentimental anesthetics from Broadway," they rejected presumably pure American folk songs because most were considered insufficiently militant. "Not all folk-tunes are suitable for the revolutionary movement," wrote Charles Seeger, a frequent spokesman for the composers. "Many of them are complacent, melancholy, defeatist—originally intended to make slaves endure their lot—pretty, but not the stuff for a militant proletariat to feed upon." [27]

The Popular Front brought a substantial change. The composers' creations were designed primarily for formal choruses, hardly suited for spontaneous use in strikes or protests. New mass songs with vernacular roots had developed in the Depression years, though, and had proven effective with workers. Most of the Collective's members never became complete converts to folk and popular songs as the proper musical expression of the proletariat, but they did make concessions. The evolution can be seen in the *Workers Song Book*, a compilation of the Collective's compositions published in 1934, which included no tunes derived from folk or popular sources. A 1937 version, however, under the significantly different title *Songs of the People*, devoted nearly half of its pages to widely known tunes.[28]

The omnipresent Mike Gold took up the defense of folk expression early in 1936. His stance highlights the nature of the American Communists' opening toward popular culture. Ray and Lida Auville, Communist folksingers from the Great Smoky Mountains of Tennessee, had produced a book of radical songs in 1934 that drew much interest in Party circles. Members of the Composers Collective who reviewed the book, however, found fault. One notice in the *New Masses* categorized the Auvilles' songs as failed revolutionary art, falling on the aesthetic scale somewhere between the production of folk poets and the more sophisticated works of proletarian artists. Their melodies, "typical Tin Pan Alley stuff," according to the reviewer, were the Auvilles' great downfall. These tunes meant well, they were "symptomatic of the growing desire of America's workers—so long fed on musical scraps and rubbish—to have a music and a musical outlook of their own," but were apparently still far from that ideal.[29]

This critique and another, describing the Auvilles' music as "a hybrid mixture of jazz and balladry," raised Gold's populist ire. In his *Daily Worker* column, he intimated that Ray Auville was as valuable to the revolutionary cause for his exciting "fiddling" as were those refined musicians who "play the violin." Gold described the Auvilles' music as "the real thing, folk song in the making, workers' music coming right out of the soil." He took the composers' spokesman to task for missing the advance that was represented in this turning of traditional expression to new and radical use. "It is sectarian and utopian," he scolded the critic, "to use Arnold Schoenberg or [Igor] Stravinsky as a yardstick by which to measure working class music."

Gold's defense sounded like a breakthrough, a sectarian's embrace of pluralism in musical tastes. Yet once again, the specter of mass culture lurked behind his position. Intertwined with his support of the Auvilles was a suggestion that the issue was not the worth of folk song itself, but the potential of this music to replace popular commercial forms. In answer to his own question, "What songs do the masses of America now sing?" Gold listed traditional ballads, folk tunes, and "the semi-jazz things concocted by Tin Pan Alley." "This is the reality," he wrote, "and to leap from that into Schoenberg seems to me a desertion of the masses." But put in these terms, the folk songs sound suspiciously like a concession. This new proletarian voice seemed the lesser evil between demeaned popular forms and impracticable elite arts, rather than a music valuable in itself.[30]

Gold's conflicted sympathies are indicative of the general compromise over mass culture that was reached in the Communist ranks in the Popular Front years. Party critics were more willing than in earlier years to look to the expressions of the American people for the sources of a workers' culture but still drew the line at the arts produced for commerce. They were hard pressed, consequently, to find untainted, innocent emanations of the modern public among a largely urban population. The Party's preferred songs most often had a rural flavor, and its favorite performers were equally rustic: Woody Guthrie, Burl Ives, Will Geer, Aunt Molly Jackson, and the Almanac Singers.[31]

This search by American Communists for a usable national tradition outside the growing mass culture was firmly in the American mold. It is best understood in relation to the larger discovery of folk life and value by American thinkers in the 1930s. The analyses of the social scientists in the 1920s and early 1930s, which developed an implicit criticism of contemporary American culture and praised premodern ways of living, found support from a number of groups in the twentieth-century United States. The "folk" were venerated in ways as different as Henry Ford's celebration of rural life at his museum in Dearborn, Michigan, and the Agrarian intellectuals' literary praises for antebellum Southern folklife. Similar allegiances were involved in New Deal relief efforts, such as the arts programs that recorded American folklore and music. These varied efforts all shared the Communists' aversion to modern, urban, commercial popular culture. Each sought in some way to preserve folklife and expression from contemporary degradation.[32]

Alongside and sometimes overlapping these efforts at preserving traditional popular expression, however, was an emerging analysis that understood folk culture as a more dynamic force. Established folk culture scholars such as Constance Rourke were important in this movement. In her *American Humor* (1931) and the posthumously published *Roots of American Culture* (1942), Rourke recollected past popular entertainment forms and hailed them as the stuff from which the highest American arts had grown. She attacked doctrinaire Marxist critics, in particular, for dismissing older vernacular literature while they attempted to create proletarian forms. Rourke broke from the artificial distinctions between "commercial" artists and those less well remunerated, considering those who performed for pay as well as amateurs in what she called "streams of popular expression." Another professional scholar, Robert W. Gordon, the first director of the Archive of American Folk Song at the Library of Congress (1928), explained the complex relationship between folk and commercial popular expression. Purportedly "pure" folk music had been drawn from the style and content of vaudeville songs, Gordon found, as well as contributed material to those "commercial" culture forms in the nineteenth century. Rural audiences heard the songs of white minstrel troupes, and eventually used the material to create new forms of "folk" music, in a rich dynamic.[33]

A number of other writers who were not "folk" culturists were also increasingly willing by the 1930s to consider the modern mass entertainments as real popular expressions and valuable parts of a thriving culture. Their ideas began to show how arbitrary were the strict distinctions critics established between "folk," and "popular" or mass forms. Examples include a 1937 article by the intellectual historian Merle Curti that gave serious consideration to the place of the dime novel in American thought. He examined how the books reflected the public's values and contended that these were a "true 'proletarian' literature" that radical critics had overlooked in the quest for workers' expression. By 1938, Charles Seeger of the Composers Collective was praising the integration of folk and "high art" music with jazz and swing, urging that "each has something the other needs for its well-being and the well-being of the country." The critic Sigmund Spaeth, writing in 1936, also intimated that the black idiom, which was once despised as the antithesis of civilization, had so infused different forms of American music that it was part of the vital core of the nation's culture. The editors of *Scribner's* magazine in 1938 even presented an extended series on "magazines that sell," including articles on "love pulps" and "confession magazines," and seriously analyzed them as legitimate expressions of the public's desires.

None of these examinations was wholly uncritical of the entertainments. But more important, their existence is evidence that some American intellectuals were not satisfied with the notion of an extinct "folk" in the modern United States and did not believe the critics' portrayal of a passive, endlessly manipulable mass public. Some thinkers were considering instead how Americans actually used popular culture forms. They presented a picture of an American people much more attuned to, and assertive of, their needs than were the duped protorevolutionaries of the leftists' model. By rejecting the assumption that entertainments were simply packaged evils, propaganda or false consciousness, these newer sympathetic treatments were also the forerunners of the popular culture studies that would become prominent in the next generation.[34]

The appreciation of the "folk," then, came in two very different varieties in the 1930s. One celebrated rural cultures as they were frozen at an arbitrary time, and the other considered the folk to be a modernizing people who were adjusting to new conditions. The mass culture criticism of Left and liberal intellectuals in the early twentieth century had been based on an understanding of the American public much closer to the "frozen folk" notion. The people were assumed to lead unchanging, unadapting lives, and they were therefore overwhelmed by new forces that were presumed to originate outside their communities and their interests. The Communists' adoption of this same line on the entertainments shows that, despite their direction from abroad, they were squarely in the emerging pattern of the mass culture critique.

The example that best summarizes the mass entertainments criticisms of Communist and fellow-traveler critics over the late 1920s and 1930s and highlights the inherent problems in maintaining the idea of the passive, victimized public is the treatment of popular jazz music during the Third Period. In considering jazz, the radicals' simplistic analyses of exploiters and exploited failed most completely. Jazz simply could not be dismissed by Communist critics as perfunctorily as they did the other mass arts, because it was largely the creation of African Americans, a classic "victimized" group.

The grounding of jazz in the black community became particularly important with the beginning of the Third Period. Before then, Communist policies, though quick to defend blacks, had been intent on treating black and white problems together as parts of the larger class struggle. With the radical turn in 1928, however, the Comintern declared African Americans in the South to be an independent "nation," a community of common language, history, customs, and territory whose right to self-determination had to be championed. Black radicals were redefined as nationalist revolutionaries who also happened to be soldiers in the fight to overthrow capitalism. This new approach took specific form in edicts like those at the 1930 Kharkov International Conference on proletarian culture, which pledged American groups to defend this potential black militancy by fighting against "white chauvinism" in the United States.[35]

The Party's new commitment to African Americans was not easily squared with its antipathy toward their music. Jazz was treated as a debased genre by most Communist critics in this era. The novelist Maxim Gorky issued the most influential of the Soviet critiques in 1928. Calling jazz "the music of the gross" and of unchecked libido, Gorky saw it as both a cause and effect of the moral collapse of bourgeois civilization. Leaders of the proletarian culture movement also denounced jazz as a dangerous inroad of the degenerate West and went so far as campaigning to ban the saxophone from the U.S.S.R. Soviet officials further pressed the attack, prohibiting jazz from schools and radio stations and threatening those who imported or played American jazz records with stiff fines and six-month prison terms.[36]

Dutiful American Communist critics followed the Soviet lead, denouncing the music as vulgar and dismissing the fans as "jazz hounds." The critics' problem was how to deal with this unwelcome black cultural initiative without criticizing black people. Most often, they resorted to the established criticism canard of underestimating the public. They caricatured African Americans as "pure victims," people presumed to have been thoroughly incapacitated by their oppression. The critics then used blacks' plight as justification for relieving them of responsibility for their music. The program of the Workers Cultural Federation, the proletarian arts group, for instance, described northern blacks as paralyzed by cultural patronization. Black artists were described as being "kept at the level of a blues-singer and tap-dancer for the amusement of tired businessmen and white thrillhounds." Mike Gold similarly found exploitation in whites' interference with black art. He accused Carl Van Vechten, the noted white promoter and literary doyen of the Harlem Renaissance cultural scene, of foisting a "cabaret obsession" on young artists. "Gin, jazz and sex—that is all that stirs him in our world," Gold wrote of Van Vechten, "and he has imparted his tastes to the young Negro literateurs." When blacks found their "true" voice in the revolutionary movement, however, Gold predicted, "It will be a voice of storm, beauty and pain, no saxophone clowning, but Beethoven's majesty and Wagner's might, sombre as the night with the vast Negro suffering, but with red stars burning bright for revolt." [37]

Another argument the Communist critics pursued to spare blacks from their criticisms was to posit a "good" jazz against the bad. This good form, writers contended, sprang from the folk experiences of blacks and reflected their oppression. It was therefore a true proletarian art and had nothing to do with the exploitative "bourgeois" jazz that grew out of Tin Pan Alley and vulgar commercial motives. The music critic of the *Daily Worker* in 1933, Charles Edward Smith, pursued the contrast by posing "true," "hot jazz" as the antithesis of commercial popular forms. Smith argued that the effect of the bourgeois music was "to hoodwink the masses and divert them from revolutionary class struggles," while the proletarian form emphasized oppression and helped to foster class solidarity.[38]

This attempt to erect boundaries within jazz was imaginative, but unfounded. Jazz was a commercial form from its inception, played in brothels, clubs, and New Orleans advertising wagons. The transit of the jazz musician from sporting house to stage to recording set did not fundamentally change his art or its relation to his audience. The effort to create two jazzes does again, however, reveal just how consistent were the Left's arguments of the

1930s with the earlier mass culture criticisms. Earlier writers had similarly attempted to separate genuine "folk" entertainments from what they viewed as artificial and exploitative commercial forms. They had also assumed an amusement's monetary success was evidence of a perversion of popular values. And like the other critics who had insisted on firm differences between "folk" and "mass" arts, the whole criticism was wrapped up in the Communists' beliefs about the effects of mass forms. Finding unwelcome characteristics in entertainment audiences, they presumed to understand the people well enough to know these were not naturally occurring traits and attacked them as evil encroachments. They did not acknowledge the possibility that the people might have acquired the traits of their own choice.[39]

As much as the far Left critics shared with previous censors of the entertainments, there was an important distinction. The Communists had thousands of rank and file followers whose experiences with the entertainments could have tempered and refined the intellectuals' judgments. Their attitudes certainly seemed different. Popular jazz enjoyed favor with the Party's members despite the intellectuals' disdain. In the spring of 1930, following New York City's first major demonstration in the wake of the Depression, Harlem's Communists organized an interracial dance featuring the jazz star Duke Ellington to show Party solidarity. In the latter 1920s and early 1930s as well, the seasonal balls and carnivals sponsored by the *New Masses* enjoyed the music of the "Vernon Andrade Renaissance Orchestra," billed as "Harlem's Best Jazz Band!" This apparently easier fit between Marxist doctrine and good entertainment at the grass roots was captured by *Fortune* magazine in a visit to a Communist summer camp in 1934. The highlight of the camp weekend, according to the report, was the Saturday night meeting, "when you can listen to songs like 'Poor Mister Morgan Cannot Pay His Income Tax' and sing the 'Internationale' yourself with clenched fist upraised." "But," the story informed, "after the mass meeting the floor is cleared and everyone dances gayly to petty bourgeois jazz."[40]

That these comrades could consider themselves good Marxists and enjoy popular jazz at the same time should perhaps have given the critics pause. Even more, though, it should have alerted them to how people could be intelligent, responsible, and even ideologically correct, yet still find enjoyment in a mass entertainment. The embrace of jazz at the grass roots, without ill effect, was vivid evidence of the misunderstanding that continued to inform the the mass culture critique. The motive force behind the critique was Left intellectuals' desire to defend an idealized public that likely never existed. The Communist intellectuals' misperception of working-class Americans in just this way, as a static, passive, premodern folk, was what made their critique plausible. Their romanticizing of the people made the victimization model a self-fulfilling prophecy.

6

THE COSMOPOLITAN
INTELLECTUAL CRITIQUE:
PARTISAN REVIEW

The era of the Great Depression was a watershed in intellectuals' conceptions about the popular arts. Cultural critics showed a growing appreciation of the common people and their tastes and desires. And beyond the populist atmosphere, the entertainments provided many with a chance to forget at least temporarily their economic woes. By this period as well, entertainment media and techniques had achieved national penetration, and, having existed for more than a generation, they had become second nature in most Americans' lives.

This favorable environment might well have diminished or even brought an end to the mass culture critique, if not for the efforts of the "New York Intellectuals." This emerging intelligentsia, which scholars today recognize as one of the more influential intellectual cadres of the twentieth century,   137 almost single-handedly revitalized the critique of the popular arts. It combined the two dominant strands of criticism that had been defined over the early century—one concerned with elevating the public through the arts, and the other with protecting the people from being exploited by entertainments—in a new argument that made mass culture a pressing concern once again. The New Yorkers' brash judgments brought out more than ever before the assumption that had underpinned the earlier critique: the guidance of intellectuals was indispensable for rescuing the masses from their enjoyments.

————

The New York group's attacks on popular entertainments grew out of a sophisticated philosophical rationale they created to support their tastes in the arts. This philosophy, and in turn their entertainments criticism, strongly reflects the social backgrounds of the writers and their aspirations to intellectual standing.

The roots of the New York intellectual group were in the far Left political efforts of the Depression. A most important segment had come together around *Partisan Review*, a literary magazine founded in New York in 1934 as the organ of the Communist Party's John Reed Club. The club was an instrument of the Communist proletarian culture movement, and its members were responsible for cultivating militant voices both of and for the American working class. Almost from the journal's beginning, however, it was apparent that the *Partisan Review* writers had serious differences with the Party's design. They valued the arts, particularly literature, too highly to support just any artist with a leftist message. They would not be content with an aesthetic that was so limiting, nor with such a limited role in the radical program.[1]

An editorial in the first volume of *Partisan Review* in the summer of 1934, written by the magazine's chief voices, William Phillips and Philip Rahv, established the group's insistence on exacting aesthetic standards. The piece welcomed the recent growth of agitational, revolutionary writing but found serious failings in most of this literature. The main problem was the simple intrusiveness of the "leftist" style. So much of radical fiction consisted of thinly veiled harangues, what the editors described as attempts "to force the reader's responses through a barrage of sloganized and inorganic writing," that it ceased to be art. Such literature "distorts and vulgarizes the complexity of human nature," Phillips and Rahv contended. They bemoaned that this same facile agitation appeared in at least three-quarters of the poems and short story manuscripts they received at the magazine.

To discourage this vulgar approach to the revolutionary arts, *Partisan Review* challenged the Party's reigning cultural theories and sought to instill right thinking among its leaders. The upstart New York writers first issued gentle rebukes to several of American Communism's important critics (most notably Michael Gold and *New Masses*'s literary editor Granville Hicks) for their lax aesthetic standards. Next they launched themselves into the momentous battles over Party doctrine. They charged that "leftism," the flawed literary approach, resulted from a misunderstanding of Marx. The creators and defenders of the sloganizing stories were misinterpreting Marx's explanation of the relationship between the economic and cultural features of capitalist societies. The New York critics maintained that the society's cultural "superstructure," including its arts and letters, was not shaped exclusively by the relationships at its economic "base." The arts were not, in other words, a simple and direct effusion of the class situation. They were, rather, the product of multiple influences (economics admittedly foremost among them). Ideally, cultural expression captured these complex motivations. This obviously made the task of radical litterateurs far more difficult. In the scheme of the *Partisan Review* editors, no longer would proletarian writers be sanctioned for composing simple political primers. They were expected to attempt a politically inspired "art." The prime importance of this first major statement from *Partisan Review* is its definition of "good" literature and art as the obverse of media carrying more direct or immediately affective messages. The contrast was in fact a clear parallel to the dichotomy between "Culture" and popular entertainments set up by genteel critics in the late nineteenth and early twentieth centuries. How, though, could these radical writers—professed egalitarians—find such agreement with that hierarchical order? The answers lie in how these critics originally came to their positions, and their conception of the responsibilities of cultural arbiters.[2]

The New York intellectual group was composed primarily of young writers from Jewish families recently arrived in the United States. The parents of Phillips and Rahv, for example, had come in the early twentieth century. Phillips, whose family name had been changed from Litvinsky, was born in New York in 1907 and grew up in the Bronx. An accomplished student, he completed college and earned a master's degree in English. By the early 1930s, he was working as an instructor at New York University. Rahv was born Ivan Greenbaum in 1908 in a village in the Ukraine. Following his father, he emigrated to America in 1922. After high school in Rhode Island, he worked in advertising on the West Coast before coming to New York in 1932. Unemployed, and at times homeless, he took advantage of the shelter of the city's public library and began to study literature.[3]

These personal histories, similar to the general backgrounds of a number of the other New York writers, help to explain their intellectual bent. As with the children of tens of thousands of other recently arrived families, Phillips, Rahv, and their colleagues undoubtedly felt some desire to step away from their family backgrounds and assimilate American ways. Because they were Jewish immigrants, though, this transition was all the more difficult. They faced hostility from a society that was both xenophobic, consistently blaming immigrants for social ills and periodically moving to exclude them, and insistently Christian. Not wholly content with their parents' way of life, nor able to adopt the dominant culture of their new land (while still maintaining their dignity), these immigrants faced a potentially deep alienation. Their best hope for a satisfactory integration in America was to create their own third way. They found just such an alternative in the life of the mind.

The New Yorkers' culture was not created wholly from new cloth. "Brainwork" was important to both their old and new societies. Intellectual attainment was revered in the Jewish community, providing a necessary support for the literary bases of Judaism. It remained a most important part of the immigrants' culture, despite the growing secularism of this era. By the early twentieth century as well, the American system of higher education was firmly established as a social and economic influence. The rewards of a career as a professional thinker were growing, and an ideal of a meritocratic society based upon intellectual attainment found strong support.

Yet if the life of the mind offered an intriguing assimilative strategy for the New York Intellectuals, would their ideas and values, their stock in trade, be drawn from the Old World or the New? For critics such as Phillips and Rahv, a third route again proved most attractive. They chose a cosmopolitan approach. European modernism offered a highly intellectualized world of the arts in the early twentieth century. At the same time, it maintained a critical distance from the mainstream of American culture. Mastery of the high moderns therefore offered a respectable means to escape the ghetto, through the imagination, and potentially through a literary career.[4]

Most young Jewish men did not, of course, follow this ideal of avant-garde intellectualism as an alternative to assimilation. The key influence for writers such as Phillips and Rahv seems to have been an early introduction to literature, and particularly to modernist approaches. Rahv recalled that when he was eight or nine years old, he received books by Fyodor Dostoyevsky and Leo Tolstoy from a Russian soldier, and Phillips has written that it was his teenage years and very early twenties that were formative: "My literary and intellectual development was rooted in the '20s, in the experience of modernism: my world was bounded on all sides by Eliot, Pound, Joyce, the Cubists, Mondrian, etc."[5]

Marxism served an intellectual function similar to modernism for the New York group. It offered a needed middle ground between the influences of the immigrant neighborhood and the national mainstream. First, it provided the writers with a defense of their community and an understanding of their struggles. Capitalist exploitation explained the plight of their families and friends. It also went beyond that to provide an explanation of how American society, and indeed most of the world, worked. Radicalism was a standard social conception that a number of Jews had brought from Europe. The literary critic Irving Howe described how in his East Bronx neighborhood in the early 1930s, "almost everyone seemed to be a socialist of one sort or another." For many immigrant Jews, he explained, the radical stance was not just a political choice, but "an encompassing culture, a style of perceiving and judging through which to structure their lives."[6]

Marxism also maintained a distance or buffer from American life for these critics, the political counterpart of modernism. The explanation of why the *Partisan Review* group gravitated to Communism, among all the varieties of socialism, can be seen as part of this ethic of cultivating the most advanced, consciously discomfiting sensibilities. The example of the Soviet Union made Communism more attractive because there the Party had a proven record of social achievement, beyond any other leftist movement. Foremost among the radical groups as well, the Communists trumpeted their concerns for cultural achievement. The Party offered therefore not only change, but the promise that a better, higher order of intellect and social organization was near at hand. The apparently easy accommodation to Communism by some modernist aesthetes in the early 1930s suggests how close these movements seemed to be in the early years of the Depression. A revolutionized socioeconomic order was poised to clear the way for a new cultural flowering.[7]

The New York Intellectuals, then, in cultivating these allegiances to Communism and avant-garde aesthetics, chose to maintain a constant tension in their relationship with American culture. This role of a "professional opposition" especially fit their certainty in their own intellectual abilities. They believed their's were the most advanced literary and political views and that these beliefs stood as the primary progressive force in the United States. This supreme self-confidence is even more striking considering that many of these men were still in their mid-twenties at the time of the founding of *Partisan Review* in 1934. "We were," as William Phillips recalled, "cocky kids."[8]

Ambition and confidence were evident in the *Partisan Review* project from the start. The history of the magazine shows how it brought the Marxist-Modernist outlook to the forefront in American criticism. Not content to follow the intention of Communist literary leaders and produce an organ of new and unknown proletarian writers, Phillips and Rahv began publishing established bourgeois writers. The *Review*'s attractive mix of good literature and radical theory soon rivaled that of the *New Masses*, the Party's designated flagship magazine. The senior journal responded swiftly. At the end of 1934, Granville Hicks suggested "reorganizing" the revolutionary press, reminding readers that the *New Masses* was the designated principal showcase of revolutionary thought and literature. Hicks scolded the upstart editors for publishing too many writers who were not members of the John Reed Club and who could easily publish elsewhere. He also challenged the new magazine's practice of reviewing the same books that were being treated in the pages of his own journal. The best indication of his pique was his suggestion that, if *Partisan Review* was not going to stay in its place as the organ of the Reed Club, "it ought to be primarily devoted to long, theoretical critical essays." An exile to the Siberia of the cerebral.[9]

The New York writers would not be so easily dismissed, however. The more they were pressed to stay on the Party reservation, the more they pursued their own intellectual course. With the Communists celebrating the proletarian arts, the *Partisan Review* critics increasingly shunned these arts designed for the masses. In 1934, for example, Phillips (in another journal) berated proletarian poets for ignoring the aesthetic breakthroughs achieved by James Joyce, Ezra Pound, and T. S. Eliot. Finding only "banality and tawdriness" in the proletarians' own work, he argued that they had to understand these best examples if they were to hope to create a worthwhile art. To ignore the modernist tradition was "to posit an immaculate conception for the proletariat and its literature; to deny the greatness or relevance of great bourgeois art works."[10]

Rahv similarly defended modernist forms and unveiled *Partisan Review*'s view of the popular arts and proletarian arts as merely two sides of the same coin. Degraded art was degraded art, in the editor's view, whatever interest it was serving. Rahv made the point in two steps. First, he leveled the familiar Communist charge that popular bourgeois writings victimized the working classes. He assumed, as had all the mass culture critics since the progressives, that the entertainments were creations that came not from the public's tastes and values, but from manipulators pursuing their own interests. He described the process as a "chloroforming technique," anesthetizing the people so they could be reconciled to capitalism: "It is the commercial writers who command the largest market and who affect the masses directly; they are the open instrument of propertied class interest in letters. On the subjective side this is reflected in the moronic level of this body of writing and its utter lack of integrity — in dealing with mass propaganda the bourgeoisie takes no chances."

But rather than offering "strike stories" or other proletarian propaganda as a corrective, Rahv's second step was to ignore Party policy and champion modernist forms. He chided "doctrinaire" leftists who would not recognize the more subtle opposition to capitalism built into modernist works. The writing of the "advanced intellectuals" showed none of this "shallow optimism" and "open cash-valuation of life," he explained, but was instead "an art that articulates despair, that slashes certain forms of philistinism, and that even indulges in virulent social criticism (usually not stated in class terms, but deflected through various crooked mirrors)."

Rahv recognized that this "advanced" work had produced no political action to date, but he saw the Depression as a force to trigger those effects. The fault of the avant-garde had been that its despair with bourgeois life had "idealized negation," he believed. Such literature, in other words, became satisfied with a simple naysaying stance, an aesthetic divorced from social concerns. These "fetters of aesthetic and metaphysical consolation" in modernist letters would be broken, however, in the coming class struggle. The artists would be turned toward direct political commitments. Art and politics would prove inseparable as despair led to social revolt. In Rahv's wordplay on the title of Eliot's famous poem, "the waste land" could thus become "a flower garden." [11]

For the mass culture critique, the effect of this melding of modernism and Marxism was to remove the critics yet further from the realities of most Americans' lives. Considering the people to be passive victims of commercial entertainments, and believing that the only effective cultural countermeasure was to cultivate the most difficult arts, the critics once again depicted the public as helpless. The people's only hope was to be saved by their intellectual leaders. The problem for the mass public, according to the *Partisan Review* logic, was that, short of an immediate revolution in its tastes and intellectual capabilities, any arts it would understand and enjoy were manipulative trash. Developing the full potential of the avant-garde arts was the New Yorkers' only solution, then, trusting that, after the revolution, the masses would eventually embrace the forms as well.

Few of the *Partisan Review* set were poets or novelists, but they believed themselves nonetheless crucial in encouraging modernism because professional criticism was every bit as important as the literature itself. Once again, though, there was no place for the popular audience in these lofty intellectual realms. Phillips and Rahv championed their theoretical criticism at the first League of American Writers' Congress in 1935, responding specifically to the charge that their immersion in criticism abandoned the more immediate needs of the proletariat. "Those who attack theory invent private 'Marxian' rationalizations by making the intelligence of the mythical reader-ignoramus the norm of the critical level," they wrote. "This reader-ignoramus cannot understand involved analyses, it seems, and must be protected from mental overstrain." But rather than arguing that the public was being underestimated, and showing how theory was accessible to the rank and file, Phillips and Rahv chose to impugn their critics. "Perhaps it is really themselves that the rationalizers are protecting," they wrote. Having thus dismissed the interests of the mass public, they went on to promote themselves even further, contending that criticism was actually a higher intellectual calling than mere production of literary or artistic works. It was the literary theorists and critics, according to the editors, who brought cultural advance and were therefore exempt from direct responsibility for the proletariat. A form such as drama was easily understood by mass audiences and could therefore be considered successful in an "agitational" role. But breakthroughs in thinking came only from criticism, which was intended only for those already intimately familiar with aesthetic issues. It could not be judged by how many "can easily digest it." Criticism, then, need only answer to the demands of the cognoscenti.[12]

This elevation of modernism and its criticism to the status of superior consciousness, together with the New Yorkers' understanding of class conflict, left the intellectuals at loggerheads with virtually all the popular arts and entertainments. What the people understood and enjoyed was, almost by definition, an accommodation with the class and aesthetic enemy and therefore a retreat from the revolutionary cosmopolitan order.

The *Partisan Review* appraisal of mass entertainments was, then, steadily reproducing the same false duality presented by most of the earlier mass culture critics. Popular entertainments could not represent the genuine interests of the people. By assuming from the first that the mass audience was composed of passive victims open to any messages, the critics were never forced to consider how popular input affected the creation of entertainments. Because the critics also often misunderstood the nature of the working classes, presuming that these, their political allies, held values similar to their own, they could only propose a conspiracy to account for the proletarian tastes they observed. The entertainments the intellectuals detested must have been manipulating or duping their working-class friends. In such a self-centered understanding, the New York critics could cast all the arts in Manichean terms. They were either redemptive, or purely destructive. What was not clearly opposed to mainstream culture was therefore dangerous.

———

As the editors' allegiance to modernism became more pronounced, and their distaste for popular culture all the more clear, *Partisan Review* was obviously rushing headlong out of the proletarian orbit. The process was hastened by the New Yorkers' split with the Communists. The Party's announcement of the Popular Front policy in 1935, and the resulting disbanding of the Reed Clubs, pulled out the financial props from under *Partisan Review*. It folded the following year. With their institutional tie severed, the New Yorkers turned sharply against the Party.

The fallen *Partisan Review* did not rest for long. It was revived in 1937, this time as a journal of independent, anti-Stalinist radicalism. This reorganization, with the split from the Party and the addition of several new writers to the editorial board, seemed a dramatic break. It brought remarkably few changes, however, to the magazine's cultural line.[13]

The new *Partisan Review* group found renewed confidence, as well as prominent sanction for their ideals, in the writings of former revolutionary leader Leon Trotsky. After he was targeted as an opponent of the Soviet leadership at the Moscow trials, Trotsky had become something of a living political martyr. His star had risen steadily with the anti-Stalinist Left. The Moscow trials were shows of institutionalized terror that Josef Stalin conducted in the mid-1930s, forcing his political opponents to confess responsibility for incredible traitorous crimes and pay with their lives. With the *Partisan Review* editors now denouncing Communist policies, identifying with Trotsky provided them a model for an independent radicalism and the sense that they were carrying the torch of true, "pure" Marxism. Here was a leader who shared their understanding of how the revolutionary impetus had been twisted and sullied. Trotsky also served as something of a role model for the New Yorkers. An intellectual, an accomplished writer and literary critic, and a man who had wielded great influence in the world of practical politics, he was the *beau ideal* for these young men who hoped to revolutionize American society.[14]

Of all his writings, Trotsky's cultural theories were most inspiring for the *Partisan Review* critics. The "Old Man," as his disciples called him, had been rejecting any prescribed proletarian culture for more than a decade. In his *Literature and Revolution* (1924), he described the arts of the Soviet Union as being in a state of transition as the nation worked toward a classless order. Until that perfect order was achieved, he said, a "universal" revolutionary culture could not be established. Trotsky, like the New Yorkers, also conceived of the arts as a realm of superior understanding or insight removed from everyday concerns. He therefore believed that advocates of workers' forms were foolish to think that the masses, with no background in artistic matters, could create their own cultural expression from scratch.

Those at *Partisan Review* were also attracted to Trotsky's support of great literature. "It is childish to think that bourgeois *belles lettres* can make a breach in class solidarity," he wrote. "What the worker will take from Shakespeare, Goethe, Pushkin, or Dostoyevsky will be a more complex idea of human personality, of its passions and feelings, a deeper and profounder understanding of its psychic forces and of the role of the subconscious, etc."[15]

True to their initial "cockiness," the *Partisan Review* critics treated their new, independent radical position of 1937 as evidence of a dawning cultural epoch. Phillips and Rahv interpreted their break with the Party as an indication of a major shift in the history of political literature. Together with the decline of revolutionary works in the new Popular Front period, the editors judged there was sufficient evidence to declare that an era was over. They therefore began to weigh its achievement. The Communists' contributions to art had been minimal because of their misguided conception of Marxism, according to Phillips and Rahv. Their theatrical works depicting class struggle, for instance, were dismissed as blind to "character creation" and "tragic consciousness." "If the gilded dramaturgy of Broadway merely enacted the platitudes of its class," the editors wrote, "the Left theater contented itself with rehearsing tedious sermons of proletarian virtue." Working-class poetry, which trumpeted the imminence of revolution, was similarly rebuked for its banality. The proletarian critics Granville Hicks and Mike Gold were reproached as "vulgarizers of Marxism," responsible for the whole mess.

In what seemed to be an odd association, Phillips and Rahv identified a fault similar to that of the Communists in American efforts at writing modernist literature. Both, they argued, had failed to achieve a modern consciousness. In their hammering on the strike theme in agitational works, the Communists had never delved into "the enormously complex meanings" involved in revolution. And while American writers of the Lost Generation had returned from Europe with interests in the modern and its "complex meanings," the editors believed that "in reality their modernism was no more than a cultural veneer glossing the old village furniture." Most of the self-proclaimed avant-garde, they charged, had acquired advanced styles but never the developed worldview to direct these talents. So "instead of advanced poets we got advanced technicians." [16]

On their face, these charges seem to be just more evidence of the New Yorkers' hypercritical approach. But the connection between these two condemnations reveals the criteria that the group was developing to measure all the arts and letters: conflict and complexity. What the editors identified as the connection between the proletarian arts and Lost Generation modernism was a shared anti-intellectual bias. This theme is most revealing for the *Partisan Review* criticism, and one that writers in the magazine's circle would repeat for decades. As the sociological insight underlying the New

Yorkers' criticism, it also involved a new scheme compared to the mass culture fears of the earlier century.

Simply put, the *Partisan Review* writers' new critique branded ideas or aesthetic expressions that did not willingly embrace the complexity and uncertainty of modern life as anti-intellectual and reactionary. Both the "arty" pseudo-avant-garde American modernists and the proletarian propagandists failed to show a sufficient sophistication with the cosmopolitan, urban society, and had established no theoretical grounding to guide their works. Their naivete, wrote Phillips and Rahv, drew literature "below urban levels" into "the sheer 'idiocy of the village.'" The editors shuddered to think that literary criticism, "almost a pure product of the city," was being composed "by people who regard their own spontaneous responses as valid judgments."

Dwight Macdonald, one of the new editors for the revived *Partisan Review*, best developed the implications of the conflict and complexity standards for evaluating popular culture. His vehicle was a review of the humor style of the *New Yorker* magazine. "More persistently than any other magazine the *New Yorker* has exploited a distinctive attitude towards modern life. The typical *New Yorker* writer has given up the struggle to make sense out of a world which daily grows more complicated," Macdonald argued. "His stock of data is strictly limited to the inconsequential. His *Weltanschauung*—a term which would greatly irritate him—is the crudest sort of philistine 'common sense.'" These failings were not necessarily because the writers were inadequate, in Macdonald's view, but rather the result of a "pruning" of talents and "intellectual amputations" by which the magazine deliberately spared its readers from uncomfortable realities.

Looking back, such criticism appears to be part of the efforts of artists and critics over the early twentieth century to subdue gentility and to bring all of life's harsher truths into public discussion. But more specific to the 1930s, Macdonald's was a statement of the cultural critics' sense of purpose. He was calling for intellectuals to take their proper place as agents for redeeming American society. Anything less than a direct grappling with the most difficult problems of the day, set against this responsibility, was considered a moral failing. Popular culture, of course, failed just so. "In times like these," Macdonald wrote of the *New Yorker*'s subjects and treatments, "there is something monstrously inhuman in the deliberate cultivation of the trivial." [17]

By 1937 then, the New York Intellectuals had erected their taste and proficiency with the existential dilemmas of modernist literature as the measure for all American culture. The contrast they proposed, between "criticism" and the "city" on one hand and "spontaneous response" with its implication of naivete and error on the other, made the critic the essential figure for cultural progress. This *Partisan Review* ideal of intellectuality and complexity did produce some good in certain pursuits. It was particularly effective, for instance, in bringing a greater sophistication to literary and social analyses. Its great failing, though, was as a prescriptive model for how the arts should serve people.

The kind of modernist art forms that the New Yorkers promoted amounted to a harsh cultural regimen for the public. They embraced rootlessness and all manner of destabilizing sensations. Taken to its extreme, the logic of the New Yorkers' ideal encouraged forfeiting the whole gamut of primary, integrating social forces for the sake of living in the unknowable, contradictory, often irrational culture developed in the avant-garde outlook. A way of life based on the comfort and order of family, community, and religious faith was deemed inferior to a system that required an embrace of almost constant change.

This requirement that the public adjust its sensibilities and welcome new arts also marks a transition in the leftist mass culture critique by the latter 1930s. Though the people were not yet given full responsibility for the content of the popular entertainments (a notion that most on the Left had discarded since the turn of the century), they were beginning to be held more accountable for their state. Starting with the new *Partisan Review* critics, the public was more likely to be criticized by Left critics for not rejecting or at least moving away from degraded amusements. The audience itself, in other words, was becoming more identified as a source as well as a victim of the mass culture problem.

This concern about the public is evident from the changing image of the American "masses" that the New York critics were developing. The masses identified as victims of the entertainments in the criticisms of reformers and social scientists in earlier decades had typically been portrayed as atomistic individuals and normless souls. They had been yanked out of the bonds of traditional primary groups by the modernization process, in the view of those critics, and were adrift amid the influences of urban life. The image of the masses presented by the *Partisan Review* writers, though, was nearly reversed. It depicted a people too firmly ensconced in older group ties and ways, too secure and comfortable in its pragmatic approach to social problems. Such a criticism had, of course, informed a few of the earlier modernist attacks on the entertainments. But beginning with the New Yorkers, Left intellectuals' suspicions that the shortcomings of the masses led to the problems of mass culture began overlapping with explanations from the Right.

The culmination of this subtle shifting of the mass culture critique, from a simple model of victimization to an understanding that accorded the public some responsibility for its entertainments, came in a series of *Partisan Review* articles in the late 1930s. Dwight Macdonald wrote three pieces charting the development of the Soviet cinema, explaining how political interference had ruined the once world-renowned Soviet art and manipulated the public. He made comparisons between the Soviet situation and Hollywood at every step to establish the destructiveness of each. Macdonald's explanation of this exploitation then drew a response from a new critic, Clement Greenberg, with an even bleaker interpretation. The radicals' defense of the masses appeared to be growing ever more strained.

Macdonald's argument began with his fond recollections of seeing Soviet films such as Sergei Eisenstein's *The Cruiser Potemkin* and *Ten Days That Shook the World* in the mid-1920s. He recalled sensing that he was witnessing "*the* great modern art." Film provided him, and his fellow "avant-garde illuminati," with the quintessential modernist experience, "a deep and dynamic contact with twentieth-century life." Between 1925 and 1929, several Soviet cinema producers had rejected the theatrical and realistic styles of early filmmakers and experimented with techniques from expressionism to montage to newsreel documentaries. Given its fullest expression in the work of directors such as Eisenstein and V. I. Pudovkin (*The End of St. Petersburg*, *Storm over Asia*), the Soviet cinema had most closely fulfilled the modernist ideal of a thoroughly contemporary aesthetic expression, an art unique to its medium.[18]

But as quickly as the Soviet film had flowered, Macdonald explained, it had withered under the political meddling of the "Third Period." The prominence of the Soviet directors initially earned their films an exemption from the proletarian culture requirements of 1928. Movies were, however, eventually reorganized under the Five Year Plan. Artistic experiments were squelched and directors were reassigned to simplistic propaganda projects, convincing the Soviet public about the value of collectivization and industrial transformation for the country. In 1938, Macdonald wrote, "Every single one of the radical innovations which Eisenstein and his peers introduced . . . has been discarded—officially proscribed, indeed." With the banishing of these "formalist" or "bourgeois" abstract artistic techniques, by the late 1930s the Soviets were producing mainly run-of-the-mill entertainments. "Their films differ from those of Hollywood," Macdonald wrote, "only in being technically less competent."

The attacks by the Stalinist regime on modernist artists extended beyond the motion pictures. Macdonald roundly condemned all the efforts to force the arts to communicate directly to the Soviet people: "Socialist realism is nothing more complicated than Stalinist politics applied to art. In architecture, it means classical colonnades; in literature, the banal historical novels of an Alexis Tolstoy; in music, the 'tuneful' marching songs of Dzerzhinsky; in painting, the realistic French school of the last century, whose influence, outside the U.S.S.R., is today traceable chiefly in bar-room art."

Most galling were the direct attacks on the modernist heroes of the New York Intellectuals. Macdonald was enraged by a *Pravda* description of James Joyce's "Ulysses" as reminiscent "of the delirious babblings of a mad philosopher who has mixed all the known languages into one monstrous mess." He repeatedly condemned Stalin for his order to Dimitri Shostakovitch "to abandon his discordant modern technique in favor of melodies the toiling masses could whistle on their way to work." [19]

Having thoroughly censured Soviet policy and ennobled modernism, Macdonald turned to the question of where the broader public might fit in his avant-garde society. Could the tastes and capabilities of the modern masses, whether Soviet or American, possibly be squared with modernism? And if not, would the radical intellectuals be forced to forfeit their working-class allies to either the Soviet or American form of popular culture?

Focusing on the Soviet situation, Macdonald began with the proposition that Stalinist arts programs had been able to succeed only because they had found favor with the public. He addressed this "Problem of Mass Taste" with a comparison of two art exhibitions in Moscow. The Museum of Western Art featured a collection of works by famous modernist painters such as Paul Cezanne and Pablo Picasso. The Tretyakov Gallery contained the works of what Macdonald described as the "Russian academicians" of the nineteenth century, featuring realistic "battle scenes and winter sunsets." The public's choice between the avant-garde and traditional popular styles was obvious from attendance at the galleries: "The Museum of Western Art is always empty, the Tretyakov always crowded." To explain the lack of interest in the modern, Macdonald quoted the opinion of one lay viewer about the "formalist" paintings. "They are stupidities," said one woman, echoing the State's denunciations of Joyce and Shostakovitch, "which it would be better not to show." [20]

Macdonald, however, refused to believe this rejection was a natural, innocent reaction. He resisted the idea that the popular audience would, of its own choice, reject the moderns. Because Macdonald was schooled in the Left's concept of the public as passive victims, with desires foisted upon them, he looked for a manipulator in the process. Stalin had to be behind the twisting of popular tastes. Choosing one of the popular "academic" artists to make his point, Macdonald asked, "Why, after all, should ignorant peasants prefer [Ilya] Repin to Picasso, whose abstract technique is at least as relevant to their own primitive folk art as is the former's realistic style?" "No," he concluded, "if the masses crowd into the Tretyakov, it is largely because they have been conditioned to shun 'formalism' and to admire 'socialist realism.' The regime has conducted this conditioning with its usual thoroughness, and for its own political ends." [21]

This argument about the conditioning of the masses hearkened back to Phillips and Rahv's contention that the acceptance of advanced art in the United States was being held back by the public's bourgeois training. They claimed such problems would be remedied by the new thinking introduced by the revolution. Once again with Macdonald, the people are portrayed as little more than simple automatons, available and amenable to direct indoctrination with the ideology of a particular reigning group.

Like so many on the Left since the early century, these intellectuals misunderstood the popular arts because they failed to go beyond their empathy for the underprivileged masses to respect them for their own unique tastes and traits. Again, as with the critics before them, this misconception of a passive, malleable public reinforced the intellectuals' paternalist sensibilities. Who else could rescue the masses from their manipulation and exploitation?

The New York Intellectuals read this assumption of mass malleability into the past as well, creating an historical explanation of the need for the critical talents of modernist intellectuals. The chief instance was Clement

Greenberg's 1939 response to Macdonald, "Avant-Garde and Kitsch," which became one of the century's seminal articles about mass culture.

Greenberg, an aspiring art critic making do as a customs clerk in New York in the late 1930s, took exception to Macdonald's version of cultural history. He wrote a letter to *Partisan Review*, in particular to correct the notion that the masses had ever enjoyed an era free from the influence of their betters. The misconception was that the public had lived for centuries with no contact with the dominant bourgeois arts.

> It must be pointed out that in the West, if not everywhere else as well, the ruling class has always to some extent imposed a crude version of its own cultural bias upon those it ruled, if only in the matter of choosing diversions. Chromeotypes, popular music and magazine fiction reflect and take their sustenance from the academicized simulacra of the genuine art of the past. There is a constant seepage from top to bottom, and kitsch (a wonderful German word that covers all this crap) is the common sewer.[22]

In the article that Greenberg developed from these thoughts, he wrote that the central quandary of modern culture was that "one and the same civilization produces simultaneously two such different things as a poem by T. S. Eliot and a Tin Pan Alley song, or a painting by Braque and a *Saturday Evening Post* cover." "All four are on the order of culture," he wrote, "and ostensibly, parts of the same culture and products of the same society." Greenberg, of course, knew how this heterogeneous order had come about.

The source was the simultaneous emergence of arts that were critical of social conventions, and of commercial entertainments. Greenberg lavished praise on avant-garde art, crediting it with a "superior consciousness of society." Bohemian artists had become so valuable, according to his argument, because they had absorbed the emerging radical political consciousness of the middle to late nineteenth century ("even if unconsciously for the most part") and actively resisted the manipulations of the dominant society. They eventually rejected all politics but settled into what Greenberg described as their indispensable role in modern life: "not to 'experiment,' but to find a path along which it would be possible to keep culture *moving* in the midst of ideological confusion and violence."

In this same era, there also emerged the entertainment industry. "Where there is an avant-garde," Greenberg instructed, "generally we also find a rear guard." While revolutionary forces in art and literature were developing, a "gigantic apparition" of popular culture or kitsch was arising alongside: "popular, commercial art and literature with their chromeotypes, magazine covers, illustrations, ads, slick and pulp fiction, comics, Tin Pan Alley music, tap dancing, Hollywood movies, etc., etc." Greenberg traced the rise of kitsch to the industrial revolution, urbanization and universal literacy, arguing that "peasants who settled in the cities as proletariat and petty bourgeois learned to read and write for the sake of efficiency, but they did not win the leisure and comfort necessary for the enjoyment of the city's traditional culture." Because these new city groups were also distanced from the folk arts they had enjoyed in the countryside, "ersatz culture" was created to offer "the diversion that only culture of some sort can provide."

Greenberg's views about the value of this kitsch were unequivocal. "Kitsch is mechanical and operates by formulas. Kitsch is vicarious experiences and faked sensations. . . . Kitsch is the epitome of all that is spurious in the life of our times. Kitsch pretends to demand nothing of its customers except their money—not even their time."

Of crucial importance for the developing mass culture critique, though, was Greenberg's explanation of why kitsch had proven so irresistible. His argument rebuts Macdonald on every point. Macdonald had portrayed the common people as powerless in the face of political dictates regarding culture. But he did maintain the possibility that a public conditioned to one form of culture could potentially be conditioned to another under different guidance. Greenberg denied even this faint hope.

To make this point, "Avant-garde and Kitsch" returned to the example of the "ignorant Russian peasant" standing in front of the paintings by Repin and Picasso. Greenberg wrote that it was very natural that the peasant would choose the former as his favorite. It was not that he had been conditioned to like social realism, as Macdonald held, but the choice rather was a reflection of human nature. In a Repin battle scene, "the peasant recognizes and sees things in the way in which he recognizes and sees things outside of pictures—there is no discontinuity between art and life," Greenberg wrote. "The peasant is also pleased by the wealth of self-evident meanings which he finds in the picture: 'it tells a story.'" To appreciate Picasso's message, on the other hand, the "cultivated spectator" would depend on "the result of reflection upon the immediate impression left by the plastic values." It was this additional stage of effort involved in interpreting "genuine" art, Green-

Norman Rockwell's "New Television Antenna" (1949) is both a depiction of the new television entertainment that concerned many postwar critics and itself an example of the kind of comfortable, "middlebrow" art that disgusted the New York Intellectuals. (printed by permission of the Norman Rockwell Family Trust, copyright © 1949 the Norman Rockwell Family Trust)

berg thought, that introduced the public to a particular realm of transcendent values. He believed these values were attainable in no other way. Those products that could be passively understood were, in comparison, "predigested," or synthetic art.

Lest his readers forget that this dichotomy was even more advanced in the West, Greenberg made a specific reference to his native popular culture.

"It is lucky, however, for Repin that the peasant is protected from the products of American capitalism," he wrote, "for he would not stand a chance next to a *Saturday Evening Post* cover by Norman Rockwell."

Greenberg's interpretation is another sign of the turning point in the mass culture critique that the *Partisan Review* writers had forged. His forthright acknowledgement of the difference in tastes between the mass public and intellectuals was an idea the Left would be forced to consider in later decades. But his implication was that there was an even larger wedge between the radical intellectuals and their working-class confreres. If the public was naturally inclined to kitsch, while modernism was the only source of transcendent values and cultural "movement," where could the twain meet? In the scenario that Greenberg presented, the prospects for revolutionary change in fact looked better without the masses' involvement.

Greenberg chose not to press the matter, focusing instead on those revolutionary comrades he most trusted. The freedom of advanced artists, especially their freedom from the popular audience, needed defending all the more. The ability of popular expression to distract and deter the artist and intellectual was a prime danger. Introducing what would become a favorite theme of post–World War II mass culture critics, Greenberg worried that popular forms and their profits were attracting members of the avant-garde away from art (he mentions John Steinbeck as a "puzzling borderline case"). Indeed, the myriad forms and levels of popular art were threatening to swamp the (already tiny) audience for high culture:

> Traps are laid even in those areas, so to speak, that are the preserves of genuine culture. It is not enough today, in a country like ours, to have an inclination toward the latter; one must have a true passion for it that will give him the power to resist the faked article that surrounds and presses in on him from the moment he is old enough to look at the funny papers. Kitsch is deceptive. It has many different levels, and some of them are high enough to be dangerous to the naive seeker of true light.[23]

As the New York Intellectuals set themselves firmly behind the modernist "true light," they brought an important change to the mass culture critique over the 1930s. From their start in the Communist orbit with its simplistic model of entertainments as tools of economic exploitation, they had come to suspect that the public contributed significantly to its own degradation. As the *Partisan Review* critics began to consider that the tastes and interests of intellectuals and the working classes were divergent, they pursued the modernist arts (and criticism) all the more as the key to cultural salvation. The result of the New Yorkers' merging of the two dominant criticisms of the early century was, then, the creation of an even wider chasm between mass culture audiences and the critics. The charge that popular entertainments interfered with the elevation of the public through superior art, and the charge that the entertainments manipulated a presumably passive, helpless public, were both based on the assumption that the people were wholly without their own purpose and direction. Joining these two bases of the criticism therefore served to reinforce the intellectuals' condescension. As the *Partisan Review* critics struggled to maintain even the paternalist concern for the public shared by earlier Left writers, their affinity with the elitism of many conservative mass culture critics became all the more apparent.

7

DWIGHT MACDONALD AND THE CULMINATION OF THE MASS CULTURE CRITIQUE

Dwight Macdonald's auspicious debut in *Partisan Review* in the late 1930s would alone merit his inclusion in the history of popular culture criticism in the twentieth century. It was not until the 1940s and 1950s, however, when the intellectuals' condemnations of popular entertainments reached their greatest intensity, that Macdonald became the most read and recognized mass culture critic in the United States.[1]

Macdonald prized his role as the central American voice on the mass arts. In his later years, he told an interviewer, "Almost my only big idea I've had in my life, that I exploited far too much perhaps, is this mass culture business." He even claimed to have originated the phrase "mass culture." It was just this ardor with regard to the popular arts that made his views so central to the critique in the twentieth century. Macdonald's was an extremely lively intellect. His own changing ideas, together with his openness to the influences of his fellow critics, brought a series of revisions in his attacks on the entertainments. Better than any other source, these capture the evolution of the mass culture criticism. Macdonald both brought the problem to its peak of public concern and pushed the Left entertainment criticism to its logical extreme, where Left and Right attitudes overlapped. His writings were the culmination of the entertainment condemnations of the first half of the century and the spur that in recent years has moved intellectuals to examine the condemnations critically themselves.[2]

Macdonald was born in New York City in 1906. His mother was a homemaker from a wealthy family and his father a struggling law student who would continue to struggle through his professional career. He was educated at private schools, Phillips Exeter Academy, and then Yale. Macdonald recalled he was "always a rebel." If so, this was a distinctly haughty kind of revolt. At Exeter, he created an exclusive group, the "Hedonists" (fellow students considered it the "Genius Club," he claimed), whose three members distinguished themselves by wearing fancy ties and monocles and carrying canes. They styled themselves after Oscar Wilde and H. L. Mencken, took as their theme, "*Pour Epater les Bourgeois*," and put out two issues of their own magazine, fittingly titled, *Masquerade*.[3]

Such superciliousness nearly got Macdonald thrown out of college in an episode that might be considered his first formal tangle with the problem of popular culture. Macdonald considered himself a superior intellect, and he objected to professors who simplified or popularized difficult material for the less gifted. He took his stand against the practice in 1927 by attacking William Lyon Phelps, an English professor who had taught at Yale for more than three decades. Phelps was an accomplished lecturer but was known more for keeping athletes eligible than for his academic demands. Phelps also had made a successful career of lectures, articles in mass magazines, a newspaper column, and eventually radio reviews popularizing the literary classics and making them palatable and accessible to the American public. Macdonald bridled at what he felt was Phelps's cheapening of the intellectual tradition, and in a bold editorial for the *Yale Lit.*, he called for the professor to stop teaching Shakespeare. Because of his charge that Phelps was incompetent, Macdonald was threatened with expulsion. The incident

Dwight Macdonald, the nation's foremost mass culture critic, in the 1940s. (Dwight Macdonald Papers, Manuscripts and Archives, Yale University Library)

was so important to him that, decades later, he still wrote about "the crowd-pleasing pop-romantic antics certain eminent English profs went in for to hold the interest of a lecture hall full of future stockbrokers."[4]

Macdonald's cultural outlook from his youth, then, might best be described as effete prejudices writ large. The appeal he found in Mencken's attacks on democracy and popular taste and Wilde's sophisticated cynicism were at base little different from the disdain for the American public that conservative critics had shown in the genteel magazines of the early century. A highbrow intellectual culture was held before the public as the single path to social virtue. As with the other aesthetic idealists who sought to reform the public through the arts, Macdonald attacked any development, such as Phelps's teaching and popularizing efforts, that might threaten the value of higher forms. Macdonald said, in retrospect, that his feeling of separation from his fellows began at Exeter and Yale, when he began to think of himself as an intellectual. His initial criticism of the popular arts, then, was rooted in an acknowledgement of the differences in American tastes and values much like that conception of "twin streams of population" that had informed conservative critics.[5]

Developments in Macdonald's criticism also were shaped in part by his career path. After a brief, failed attempt in a management training program at Macy's, he went to work in 1929 as a staff writer for *Fortune* magazine, the new business journal of Henry Luce's growing media empire. Ironically, this job with a decidedly conservative magazine developed Macdonald as a radical journalist. His experience with mainstream, commercial American journalism, which lasted until 1936, convinced the young man that he understood the production of American mass culture. The *Fortune* experience also schooled his revolutionary attitudes. The firsthand knowledge of the workings of American capitalism made him increasingly skeptical about the system. Particularly important was the impression that he formed about the nation's leading businessmen. These captains of industry were "idiots," "coarse and stupid," "narrow, uncultivated and commonplace," Macdonald thought, reinforcing his sense that there was a fundamental emptiness in mainstream American culture.[6]

Macdonald maintained his faith in the ability of the arts to reorient society and continued his aesthetic criticism in the early Depression years by writing for the *Miscellany* (1929–33), a small literary magazine he published with a group of college friends. His writings continued to show his iconoclasm, but also his developing sense of the artists' and intellectuals' responsibility to lead modern society. Macdonald dismissed the poetry of T. S. Eliot and Robinson Jeffers, for example, as artistic dodges, retreats from the problem of defining direction amid the chaotic values of the twentieth century. Eliot's seeming refusal to fulfill this role, his confounding of communication with his deliberately obscure technique in *The Waste Land*, appeared to Macdonald not as a revolutionary approach to sensibilities but a withdrawal from the intellectual's necessary commitment.[7]

While Macdonald agreed with his contemporary highbrow critics that the taste of the public was degraded, he felt this was no excuse for artists to retreat from responsibility. If the masses were demeaned, that was all the more reason to offer good work. His position was evident in his rough handling of Jeffers. Macdonald cited the poet's difficult, despairing verse as further evidence of social decay, and labeled him, together with James Joyce, as "portents of dissolution" rather than the vanguard of a new literary movement. He bemoaned the contemporary scene, "when the mob has burst into letters, when no publishing house but panders to the vulgarity of mass taste," but insisted that the arts continue to try to communicate some direction to the people.[8]

The ray of cultural hope that remained for Macdonald was the moving picture. In the initial issue of the *Miscellany*, he praised a group of films, both native and foreign, as the greatest art of the twentieth century and compared the films favorably with some of the classic creations of any era. The sheer newness of the movies struck Macdonald as an invaluable opportunity to experiment with techniques and approaches to develop the art. Another advantage for the new medium (he mentions that "talkies" were only a year old at this time) was that the movies were not yet established as an "art" in critical circles. Because they were not set off in this way and subject to particular aesthetic criteria, they remained closer to the public. By the late 1920s, critics had erected a rigid division in the arts between what they considered "good" and what was "popular," Macdonald explained. He believed the greatest forms could overcome this artificial barrier, both pleasing the experts and communicating to a broad, inclusive public. Movie directors, still experimenting with the potentials of their art, were able to satisfy such heterogeneous audiences. "The soil is deep enough to nourish the highest trunks," Macdonald wrote, and "the most abundantly spreading branches." He believed that the entertainment could therefore serve as a central cultural touchstone for all citizens. Just as religion had for centuries brought together disparate peoples, the motion picture could be the "meeting place of the great and the small, the powerful and the weak."[9]

Here, in the new film medium, Macdonald recognized a means for the exercise of cultural direction and leadership that could bridge the gap between mass taste and artistic expression. Entertainment could provide, in his words, "the common ground for the artist and the layman." In the same spirit as the reformers and social workers of the early century, then, Macdonald rejected the public's tastes in the arts as debased but held out the hope that new entertainments could attract the people to better standards that would provide a needed element of consensus in the heterogeneous society.

Macdonald's approach was similar to the progressives', too, because for both the goal of reformed tastes took precedence over the public's right to determine its own standards. This thinking is evident from his initial embrace of the Soviet movies. Macdonald's first attraction to the Soviet Union in the early 1930s, before he discovered Communism's political appeal, was for what he perceived as the nation's aesthetic openness. In the Soviets' Third Period celebration of the proletariat, the government decreed the messages in the arts and that they be geared to the public's level, thereby ensuring that Soviet moviemakers had a common ground with the audience from the start. These constraints the artists faced in the content of their work, though, allowed them more freedom in developing their styles. "The Russian director has his orders plainly enough about the political tone of his pictures, but he is free to express this just as he pleases," Macdonald argued. "He can be as bold and subtle and experimental as he wants as far as his technique is concerned; and this is the kind of freedom the artist must have." The Communists' proletarian culture dictates in effect created the same shared understandings across society that Christianity had once provided. The solid foundation of a ready-made audience had permitted Dante, Milton, Bach and untold numbers of artists to experiment with their styles as they communicated their religious experiences.

The Soviet arts system was especially attractive to Macdonald because it was sharply different from the seemingly centerless, vastly plural world of the modern United States. There, without such common understandings, the bottom line of commercial success was the primary force determining both form and content. Because the movies in America had to communicate full and complete messages, rather than merely alluding to shared understandings, directors were hamstrung. He "must not bewilder his audience by telling his story in a subtle or original way," Macdonald wrote of the filmmaker's limits. "Every picture must be capable of being grasped by the 120,000,000 Lords and Masters of America, which means that every picture must come as close to mediocrity as humanly possible."

This was Macdonald's fullest statement of his mass culture criticism to date, and it puts his values in the clearest light. The intellectual direction provided by the arts was for him of paramount importance in society. He was unconcerned with other forces that aspired to direct the society, to the point that he accepted the imposition of a universal system like Communism if it offered a firm social foundation for the arts. Also, because he was so at odds with the public's tastes and standards, he could only condemn America's free market for the arts. Recognizing the people's choices and meeting their demands interfered with the uplift he sought to bring them. Macdonald thus sounded like most other elitist critics of the early century when he complained that the failure of the American movie directors was "because his master, the mob, prefers the easily shallow, the safely dead." [10]

Steeled with this determination to bring aesthetic reform to American society and overcome vulgar public tastes, Macdonald proceeded to recreate himself as a professional friend of the masses. He subdued his air of superiority toward the people from his earlier entertainments criticisms, only to adopt a paternalist posture that equally misunderstood their nature.

The quirky way Macdonald made his move to the radical Left was unique to his personality. He recalled becoming a "mild fellow-traveler" with the Communist Party as early as 1932, but a 1934 article he wrote for *Fortune* about the American wing of the Party showed little interest in the group. This piece must of course be considered in light of the magazine's capitalist philosophy and the constraints he must have understood. Yet it was clear that Macdonald's bemusement at the weakness and dullness of the organization outweighed his admitted attraction to the Communists' stance as "professional friends of the underdog." [11]

Subsequently, though, Macdonald's experience at *Fortune* convinced him that American businessmen were "inferior people," and his radical leanings must have increased. When the Communists brought him to a meeting and sought his membership, his superior attitude still kept him apart. "When I left I said to myself, my God, these people, they're just simply wobbits," he explained. "They don't have any brains and they're scared to death of each other and they have no sense of humor, no *life*!" He began to read Communist theory, however, in the summer of 1935 (Marx he found "quite boring. Not my style at all.") and finally became actively engaged in politics in 1937. The transcripts of the Moscow Trials had a most important political influence for Macdonald, as for many American intellectuals growing wary of the Soviet leadership. He admitted he was not immune to Stalin's case against purported conspirator enemies, but he was outraged by the obvious frame-up of Leon Trotsky that was presented. He soon became involved in John Dewey's Trotsky Defense Committee, a mixed group of American liberals and radicals that investigated the charges against the revolutionary leader and helped him resettle in Mexico. He joined the Trotskyist, or Socialist Workers Party, in late 1939.[12]

Macdonald's transition from liberal to radical and vague Communist to anti-Stalinist was not, then, in its outlines very different from many others on the Left. What is striking is how quickly it occurred. The other obvious anomaly was that he had moved left while continuing his well-paid work for *Fortune*. But that association came to a quick end as well. After writing a highly critical series on U.S. Steel Corporation in 1936 (which, in draft form, bore an introductory quotation from Lenin's *Imperialism*) and forcing a showdown with his editors, he resigned from the magazine.[13]

Macdonald's path crossed that of the other New York Intellectuals in the spring of 1937. Frederick Dupee, his friend and fellow editor at the *Miscellany*, was organizing the new *Partisan Review* and introduced him to William Phillips. After what Phillips described as an all-day argument he and Philip Rahv had with Macdonald to straighten out his lingering Communist leanings, Macdonald joined the new editorial staff. While he was never a thoroughgoing literary man like Rahv or Phillips, Macdonald's ideal for cultural transformation meshed neatly with their Marxist modernism. His objections to popular taste were also easily incorporated in the group's hostility to the Popular Front cultural policies.

Macdonald's *Partisan Review* articles in 1938 and 1939 on the Soviet cinema (discussed in Chapter 6), portraying a public conditioned to reject its own natural tastes, placed him clearly in the mold of earlier Left critics who believed the entertainments exploited the masses. Their interpretation of the blame for this situation appealed to Macdonald in his new position as champion of the working public. He could no longer condemn the desires of those he had called the "mob" without explaining himself. But the charges against entertainments put forth by reformers and radicals permitted hostility to mass taste in the name of redeeming the masses. By insisting that the entertainments were exploitations of the public's weaknesses rather than representations of its genuine tastes and values, the critics recast the "mob" in a more sympathetic light. The people were now passive victims, helpless souls needing care. As a newly minted radical critic, Macdonald could therefore continue many of his earlier elitist habits, rejecting the people's entertainment choices while insisting that he was doing so out of concern for their interests.

By the early 1940s, as Macdonald's radicalism was just cresting, his ideas increasingly diverged from those of the other editors of *Partisan Review*. As they slowly distanced themselves from revolutionary politics, they were suspicious of Macdonald's allegiances and thought he wanted to "politicize" the magazine too much. After the Pearl Harbor attack, Macdonald took an outspoken stand against American entrance into World War II, and the clashes with other editors proved insurmountable. He resigned from the journal in the summer of 1943.[14]

The break from *Partisan Review* proved to be fruitful for Macdonald, allowing him to concentrate more on his favorite issues, such as popular culture. In February 1944, he introduced a magazine called *Politics*, for which he served as owner, publisher, editor, and chief contributor. The title, which was suggested by sociologist C. Wright Mills, reflected Macdonald's conviction that questions of power and leadership were central to all modern problems. This remarkable journal published a number of leading American and European thinkers over its five-year life and was known for presenting the liveliest opinions of the early postwar era. Most important for the entertainment critique, *Politics* provided Macdonald a regular forum for presenting his evolving ideas in the form he most favored: short, pointed, critical articles and commentaries. In the first issue, he inaugurated a regular column on the popular arts with a complete overview of the problem of mass entertainments.[15]

"A Theory of Popular Culture" was organized, like Clement Greenberg's "Avant-Garde and Kitsch," around the modern division between the mass and elite arts. "For about a century," Macdonald wrote, "Western culture has really been two cultures: the traditional kind—let us call it 'High Culture'—that is chronicled in the textbooks, and a 'Popular Culture' manufactured wholesale for the mass market." He believed the history of this culture pattern was generally understood. As democracy spread through most of the West, accompanied by increasing literacy, the "upper-class monopoly of culture" was broken. The masses demanded arts, and their desires were met by eager capitalists. Technological advances allowed for cheaper and larger production of books and periodicals, music, and even architectural features.

In the latest stages, entertainment entrepreneurs produced media such as movies and radio that were geared specifically to the mass audience.

This "Popular Culture," according to Macdonald, was a completely new product created to serve the equally new social order. Before the twentieth century, there had been a unique culture of the common people, which he called "Folk Art." The distinguishing characteristic of this order was that it "grew from below" in society: it was a direct expression by the people reflecting their own experiences. The new popular arts, by contrast, were imposed from above. Macdonald described them as "manufactured by technicians hired by the ruling class and working within the framework of High Culture." The result was that these new entertainments exploited the people, turning them away from their natural, genuine interests. Popular Culture "manipulates the cultural needs of the masses," he argued, "in order to make a profit for their rulers."

Macdonald's theory, then, grew out of the entertainment criticisms developed by the reformers and political radicals and adopted the flawed modernization theory of the interwar era social scientists. Like the reformers and radicals, Macdonald assumed commercial entertainments were produced without any influence or control from the public. He therefore considered the subjects and standards of these media as alien, artificial tastes intended to draw the people away from their true, better natures. This interpretation of a helpless, passive public was supported, in turn, by the social scientists' theory that America was changing from a rural-folk society based on strong family and communal ties to an urban-industrial society based on superficial, impersonal relationships. Macdonald accepted that this change had occurred and believed that it was total: all "folk" characteristics were destroyed in the transition, and the people adopted all the modern ways in a zero-sum exchange. He consequently believed "folk art" of any type—expression shaped by its audience—had to be extinct.

What Macdonald added to the existing condemnation of entertainments were the charges about their purported effects on "high" culture. Fears that the popular arts threatened to undermine better forms had been voiced for decades by conservative aesthetes and more recently by modernist critics. The attraction of that bygone era of strictly divided folk art and high culture was therefore twofold. The common people were free from manipulation, according to Macdonald, but at the same time the aristocratic arts were free to ignore what he called "the crude tastes of the masses." Like the aesthetic idealists both traditional and modernist, he lashed out at the popular arts for drawing audiences away from the elite arts, threatening the only "living" part of modern expression and the locus of higher ideals and inspirations. Referring to an "infection" that "cannot be localized," Macdonald warned, "Folk Art perished speedily at the hands of Popular Culture; the death struggles of High Culture are more protracted, but they are taking place."

The kind of "High Culture" that Macdonald feared for was the avant-garde order promoted by his fellow New York Intellectuals. Arthur Rimbaud, James Joyce, Igor Stravinsky, and Pablo Picasso were his ideal aesthetic creators. Each had "made a desperate attempt to fence off some area where the serious artist could still function" in the early twentieth century. They had "created a new compartmentation of culture, on the basis of aristocracy of talent rather than social power." Vanguard artists thus joined the radical political movements of the era in challenging the status quo. That many of the aesthetic revolutionaries were disdainful of the working classes Macdonald freely admitted. He never considered, however, how his own revolutionary elitism had shaped his understanding of the American masses.

With the prospects for political revolution remote by 1944, the fate of aesthetic change had become all the more important. Macdonald was convinced that the mass arts were simply gutting modernism. Avant-garde art was losing its competition with popular art on all fronts: sponsorship, the allegiance of creators, and audiences. He suggested that a "Gresham's Law" existed in respect to culture: "Bad stuff drives out the good, and the worst drives out the bad" because "the bad is more easily enjoyed than the good." [16]

The demise of the avant-garde order was leaving many writers and artists no other option but to go into commercial work. The increasing sophistication of some kinds of popular culture gave many "serious" writers attractive outlets for their work that threatened to remove them permanently from "outsider" status. Macdonald cited the move of literary critic Edmund Wilson to the *New Yorker*, the writing of Kay Boyle being serialized in the *Saturday Evening Post*, and the appearance of a number of avant-garde writers in the *New York Times Book Review* as evidence that commercial imperatives threatened to overwhelm the whole of American high culture. More immediately, he added in a footnote, "The problem this tendency—which applies to political writing too—raises for the future of a magazine like *Politics* is obvious."

Finally, Macdonald sought to establish why this power of popular entertainments should engage all intellectuals. "The whole problem of popular culture," he wrote, "involves one's conception of the role of the common people in modern history. It is, basically, a political question." The Spanish philosopher José Ortega y Gasset authored one such concept, proposing that the surge of democracy in modern societies — the "revolt of the masses" — had to be countered by reestablishing firm class distinctions. Macdonald rejected this notion as a prescription for further exploitation. His own solution was a vaguely defined "new order" that presumably would promote social democracy and his cherished aristocratic arts at the same time. Macdonald wrote that the "revolt of the masses" had not proceeded far enough and that popular culture "has not been popular enough." Drawing on the vision of a postrevolutionary, classless culture suggested by Trotsky and the *Partisan Review* writers, he believed that the masses, once unencumbered, would adopt more refined tastes and the avant-garde would be preserved.[17]

The change in the role of the popular arts in society from Macdonald's earlier *Miscellany* discussion to this "theory" is startling. In 1929, he had envisioned entertainment as the common ground between classes, a bridge across social differences. In 1944, the mass arts were portrayed as dangerous precisely because they filled this intermediate position. They were now accused of drawing the working classes away from their true nature and dragging the elite arts beneath their potential. The changed perspective again indicates how adopting the reductionist model of class exploitation led Macdonald to caricature the public. While in his 1929 piece he acknowledged distinct differences between "powerful" and "weak," and "artist" and "layman," the lessers were assumed capable of determining their own needs for arts and their judgments were honored. In the cruder portrayal of conflict in the latter article, though, he envisioned the power differences in terms of two "watertight compartments" of high and folk culture. Entertainment purveyors lured the masses from their protected realm into the no-man's-land between the genuine cultures. The legitimate needs and desires of the people could never be realized in this hybrid mass culture region, in Macdonald's explanation. So if they ventured into it they were without any influence or control, and were defenseless against domination.

Macdonald's theory was true to its roots in earlier Left entertainment criticisms in its inconsistencies as well. Like the early modernists who embraced a few mass artists whom they admired while often condemning the genres they worked in, Macdonald enjoyed a number of contemporary popular arts and wanted to preserve them from the exploitation indictment. He therefore discarded his charges when it came to the films of Charlie Chaplin or D. W. Griffith, Walt Disney's early cartoons, jazz music, or the comic strips Krazy Kat or Thimble Theatre. Searching for a justification, he argued that these examples were not in the debased middle ground of mass art, but rather were instances where "the old compartmentation is restored." They were popular, but their essence was either "Folk Art" or "Avant-gardist High Culture." The public was safe from harm in these particular instances.[18]

———

Macdonald's "Popular Culture" essay appeared again twice in revised editions over the next sixteen years, first as "A Theory of Mass Culture" in 1953 and then as "Masscult and Midcult" in 1960. These were the writings that made Macdonald's reputation as the nation's authority on the social impact of entertainments, and they were very consistent; in each revision, most of the previous text was unchanged. The new ideas that were added at each update, the result of Macdonald's openness to other critics, do, however, provide indispensable clues to the ideas that sparked the last evolution of the entertainment critique. The changes Macdonald made in each rewriting can be used to isolate the intellectual changes of the postwar era that brought mass culture fears to their peak.[19]

Most apparent in the changes from 1944 to 1953 is Macdonald's own increasing sense that his criticism was making no headway and that he had to be on the defensive. He seemed to be concerned much less with radical social change, for example, than with preserving artistic achievements. Avant-garde high culture, which he treated previously as a lever for erecting the classless cosmopolitan order, was coming to supersede that order altogether.

In "A Theory of Mass Culture," the sheer number of new entertainment media was a prime concern. Macdonald had mentioned radio and the movies as new technologies in the earlier article. In 1953, he added comic books, detective stories, science fiction, and television to the list. He identified these as media specifically created by mass culture, where "the serious artist rarely ventures." Indeed, the change in the title of the article from "Popular Culture" to "Mass Culture" was the result of these new circumstances. The "mass" arts that Macdonald was considering were distinguished by being "solely and directly an article for mass consumption, like chewing gum." These differed from some popular arts in the past, such as Charles Dickens's stories, which were examples of high culture attracting a vast audience. To be critical of all that was "popular" would therefore be to cast his net too widely.

More and more, Macdonald recognized that the entertainments he most despised were those created solely with popularity in mind. As an example, he cited the novels of G. A. Henty, a contemporary of Dickens who also achieved a fair following. The difference between the two authors was that Dickens was "an artist, communicating his individual vision to other individuals, while Henty was an impersonal manufacturer of an impersonal commodity for the masses." Macdonald was thus narrowing the object of his criticism, with a criterion that was nothing more than his own taste. Dickens, like Chaplin, Griffith, jazz, and Disney, was evidence that valuable entertainments were produced and appreciated by vast audiences in Macdonald's purported age of cultural degradation. To maintain his interpretation, Macdonald had to limit his field of evidence.[20]

The Hentys were in ascendance in American culture seemingly everywhere Macdonald looked in the early 1950s, and the refuges of individual communication were being swamped. One new section in the 1953 piece described mass culture as "a dynamic, revolutionary force, breaking down the old barriers of class, tradition, taste, and dissolving all cultural distinctions." The "compartment" of Folk Art Macdonald proposed in the earlier piece had been broken down by the homogenizing force of mass culture. He seemed resigned to leave the public to its fate. "If there were a clearly defined cultural *elite*" in the United States, then the masses could have their *kitsch* and the *elite* could have its High Culture, with everybody happy," he argued. But "the boundary line is blurred," wrote Macdonald, who therefore thought his criticism was necessary to preserve aesthetic values.[21]

This siege of boundaries and barriers that Macdonald chronicled reflected his growing fears of "mass society" as the postwar era advanced. By 1953, his concerns about entertainment audiences susceptible to manipulation had grown into a section of "Mass Culture" entitled "The Problem of the Masses." His theme was that most of the public was lost to any political or cultural reclamation. Macdonald explicitly criticized earlier leftist views of the entertainment problem, with no hint that he was repudiating his own stance. "Marxian radicals and liberals . . . see the masses as intrinsically healthy but as dupes and victims of cultural exploitation by the Lords of *kitsch*—in the style of Rousseau's 'noble savage' idea," he wrote. "If only the masses were offered good stuff instead of *kitsch*, how they would eat it up! How the level of Mass Culture would rise!" This earlier view was inherently wrong, in Macdonald's new explanation, because people organized into "masses" were incapable of anything having to do with culture. His definition of mass society was: "A large quantity of people unable to express themselves as human beings because they are related to one another neither as individuals nor as members of communities—indeed, they are not related *to each other* at all, but only to something distant, abstract, non-human," such as a system of industrial production or a party or State. He described the organization of the public as masses as a forfeiture of their "human" qualities and contended that the true arts could only be produced for such human beings.[22]

The connection between mass society and its cultural expression Macdonald explained from much the same sociological scheme. A "folk" or a "people" were, in his definition, "a group of individuals linked to each other by common interests, work, traditions, values, and sentiments." The scale of these relationships was such that the influence of individuals was always felt. By contrast, he described the mass society man as "solitary," "uniform," and "undifferentiated" from those around him, and thus unable to have his "creativity nourished by a rich combination of individualism and communalism." The result was that "a mass society, like a crowd, is so undifferentiated and loosely structured that its atoms, in so far as human values go, tend to cohere only along the line of the least common denominator; its morality sinks to that of its most brutal and primitive members, its taste to that of the least sensitive and most ignorant." Macdonald argued that mass culture purveyors were taking "this collective monstrosity" as their target audience for the arts and were, therefore, hastening massification.[23]

These worries about mass society and entertainments are again an extension of the social scientists' modernization model. The interpretation was particularly persuasive to Macdonald because it fit his own observations and experiences in the 1940s and early 1950s and because it was reinforced by some of his most eminent intellectual contemporaries.

The world situation of the early 1940s particularly spurred Macdonald's fears about massification. Most everywhere, it seemed, individual human agency or control was being eliminated. This theme was obvious in his last article as an editor of *Partisan Review* in 1943, an attempt to account for the failure of Marx's revolutionary prophecy. Macdonald wrote that, while private capitalism was declining in the world, as Marx had predicted, it was not the working class that was set to take control. Rather, "a new political bureaucracy" had seized power in developed societies. He believed that this "bureaucratic collectivism" was an infection that progressed from simple state intervention in social affairs to the eventual establishment of fascism. While he did not think it precluded revolutionary action, Macdonald saw the development as reason to abandon the idea of the inevitability of socialism.[24]

As World War II became the dominant subject in the pages of *Politics*, it, too, exacerbated Macdonald's fears of mass society. The journal examined the war not in military or strategic terms, but for its broadest significance. Modern war was treated as an overpowering experience for society. In a much-noted article in the spring of 1945, for example, Macdonald made a case for excluding most of the German public from responsibility for Nazi atrocities. These people were the victims of the modern problem of social organization, he argued, engulfed in institutional actions that spoke for, rather than of, the public. "Modern society has become so tightly organized, so rationalized and routinized that it has the character of a mechanism which grinds on without human consciousness or control," he wrote. The result was that the "individual, be he 'leader' or mass-man, is reduced to powerlessness vis-à-vis the mechanism. More and more, things happen TO people."[25]

Macdonald's pessimism only deepened after the atom-bombings of Hiroshima and Nagasaki. He became the nation's most prominent and fervent critic of the bombings and took the atomic policy as evidence that older social understandings had lost their relevance in the modern bureaucratic world. All simple notions of "Science" and "Progress" representing betterment of the human condition were dashed by these horrors, he wrote, as was "the whole structure of Progressive assumptions on which liberal and socialist theory has been built up."[26]

In 1946, when Macdonald tried to outline a new basis for political action in the postwar world, the impact of these wartime experiences was vivid. He rejected Marxism as an outmoded system. It was too dependent on historical processes, he explained, and therefore too passive in an age when even the possibility of class-based actions had become remote. In its place, Macdonald offered anarchism and pacifism. He advocated that individuals band together to register protests and perform acts of conscience, and that each person become a steward who would cultivate common ideals among his neighbors. Macdonald later praised "anarchist decentralization" as vastly superior to socialist, state-administered collectivism because it would "break up mass society into small communities where individuals can live together as variegated human beings instead of as impersonal units in a mass slum."

In a more personal reflection, he titled one of his articles in the winter of 1946 "Too Big." "The trouble is everything is too damn big," he wrote. Macdonald explained that he passed so many people on the streets of New York City every day that "any response to them as human beings is impossible." A "style of behavior which refuses to recognize the human existence of the others has grown up of necessity. . . . There are so many people that there aren't any people; 7,000 bec[o]mes 0; too big."[27]

Other contributors to *Politics* agreed with Macdonald's concerns and, like him, blamed mass entertainments for encouraging the growth of the mass society. Their criticisms all seem part of a depressing pall that settled over these writers as they tried to preserve some sort of radicalism amid the demise of much of the organized American Left. In the journal's first number in 1944, Melvin Lasky expressed disgust at General Dwight Eisenhower's demand, from the North African theater of operations, to "Give us more movies!" Lasky compared the command to the ancient tradition of buying off popular dissent with "bread and circuses." He criticized the policy, citing Thorstein Veblen's critique of the mechanisms of "distraction" and "submission" involved in the motion picture. "The effective war machine is calculated to absorb liberating efforts of thought or reveries or spontaneity," Lasky wrote. "All private realms are to be liquidated. The inner life is to be hopelessly caught in the mechanics of conformity . . . and the mass is totally coordinated in a dreamless adjustment."[28]

In 1945, a piece entitled "Jazz, Clock and Song of Our Anxiety," praised jazz music as "our only functioning folk art" and explained that it was so because jazz incorporated the "dread feeling of impotence" man encountered in modern America. "Our anxiety . . . is sophisticated," Arthur Steig wrote, describing people as constantly afraid but needing to maintain the appearance of self-confidence "for participation in a Christian, exploitative, vitaminized society." The following year, Dorothy McKenzie, formerly a fiction

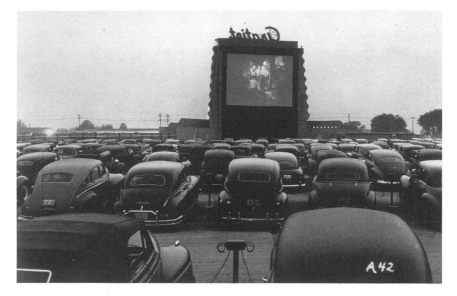

Cars crowded into a drive-in movie provide a quintessential scene from the expanding mass consumer society of the 1950s. Critics like Macdonald believed such crowds and standardized entertainment experiences produced debauched "mass" men and women. (reprinted with permission of the American Automobile Manufacturers Association)

writer for a popular magazine, explained her fears about popular culture and the modern condition: "I thought I detected a frightening tendency in current social and political systems, as in every other field, to remove the citizen from fundamentals, from any possibility of solving his own problems by his own direct action." She asked, "Would popular fiction so affect the national culture that in time life would begin to imitate the fiction formula, coming pre-packaged, with the most stirring and upsetting emotions and the elements of immediate personal will removed?" Already, she wrote, she saw traces of people becoming "more like puppets."[29]

Irving Howe gave the fullest expression to the *Politics* condemnation of mass entertainments in 1948. He explained that mass leisure developments were necessary complements to the exploitative system of industrial work. Modern commercial entertainments must function to break the monotony of work, Howe explained, but not be so attractive that they would hinder workers' return to their jobs. This work-and-prepare-again-for-work cycle, with its "amusement without insight and pleasure without disturbance" produced mass society men and women. The system was "orientated toward a central aspect of industrial society: the depersonalization of the individual." On the one hand, these amusements temporarily diverted workers from their developing "semi-robot status," but, on the other, they fostered "passivity and boredom" because they were designed to offer only a continuous series of novelties to lift people out of routine experience, rather than any truly disturbing ideas that would force an individual response and might undermine the acceptance of this routine.[30]

Besides that by the contributors to his magazine, Macdonald's worries about the uncontrollable scale of modern life, bureaucratic organization, and state control found support in the postwar analyses of fascism. Many of these interpretations carried great weight because they were produced by European emigré intellectuals who had experienced totalitarian systems firsthand. The most important group for influencing the mass culture criticism of Macdonald and his *Politics* colleagues was the "Frankfurt School" of Sociology.

The Institut für Sozialforschung (Institute for Social Research) was founded in Frankfurt, Germany, in 1923 as a center for interdisciplinary studies of society. It followed orthodox Marxist economic inquiry at first, but, under the direction of sociologist Max Horkheimer, by the early 1930s it also merged aesthetic and psychoanalytic concerns in its social analyses. The institute, whose most prominent members included Leo Lowenthal, Friedrich Pollock, Theodor Adorno, Erich Fromm, and Herbert Marcuse, was forced to flee Nazi Germany in 1933 amid growing political and racial persecutions. It moved first to Geneva and then, in 1934, to the United States, where the center was re-formed at Columbia University.[31]

Safely ensconced in Manhattan, the German intellectuals built upon their early philosophical work, creating a system known as Critical Theory. The central tenet of this theory held that all social and cultural aspects of a society were fundamentally related. To approach the truth, any empirical study of a particular aspect of human thought or action would necessarily have to consider all the interrelationships and constraints involved in the society. The theory also required social analysts to take into account the mind's ability to shape as well as reflect reality. This level of complexity in social studies set the Frankfurt School apart from its conventional Marxist forebears, who had typically viewed the world through a lens that enhanced economic concerns above all others, simplifying analyses. The Frankfurt

School approach, in fact, promoted a leap in sophistication for all social science approaches. More innovative for the academic world of the 1930s was that the members of the Frankfurt School shucked the pretense of value-free, disinterested scientific observation of social phenomena. They declared themselves to be social activists as well as analysts. As the historian Martin Jay has paraphrased Horkheimer's explanation of the group's approach, "Critical Theory did not seek truth for its own sake, but sought to effect social change instead."

The potentially revolutionary impact of Critical Theory for empirically oriented American social investigators was severely limited by the language difference. The institute's journal was not published in English until 1940, and only very little of its important theoretical work was translated from German even later in that decade. The Frankfurt School's larger ideas therefore attracted only a small following outside the academy until Herbert Marcuse became important for the New Left in the 1960s.

One part of Critical Theory that did appear in English and attract the attention of American intellectuals, however, was a theory of mass entertainments. Before the institute ceased publication of its journal in 1941 (because of the war and the moves of several members away from New York), it published an issue on mass communications that featured Horkheimer's synopsis (in English) of much of the group's aesthetic theory. Several other translated articles on commercial cultural media also appeared in the early 1940s. Sociologist David Riesman recalled that these pieces were highly exciting for those who had been considering the influence of mass culture in America. Scholars were fascinated by these pathfinding methods and exciting conclusions.[32]

Macdonald was particularly impressed with the Frankfurt School's work. In a 1945 "Popular Culture" column in *Politics*, he quoted Horkheimer, an article by Herta Herzog that appeared in the mass communications issue of the institute journal, and a study by Leo Lowenthal. He also praised the Institute for Social Research for publishing "a great deal of interesting material on Popular Culture." Though Macdonald certainly did not grasp Critical Theory in all its complexity, what he understood was useful. It provided him with both support for his own ideas and some new insights about the value of "difficult" art and the threats that commercial entertainments posed to America.[33]

Critical Theory's view of the difference between mass culture and "art," for example, agreed with Macdonald's distinction established in his *Partisan Review* articles. Both believed that commercial entertainments served to draw off dissent and integrate the people with their existing society by providing comforting messages and usefully distracting amusements.

Horkheimer's 1941 essay, "Art and Mass Culture," offered an historical sketch to show why this was so dangerous. Since John Calvin and the institution of work as man's highest calling, he wrote, life had been split between public and private realms. Labor was a public function and leisure part of the private realm. But from the first, leisure time had been "burdened with a mortgage," a duty to refresh individuals so that they could work successfully. The self-interest of each worker, the simple desire to get ahead, dictated that this segment of his private life be subordinated to business. One of the very few ways people were able to maintain some aspect of private life, according to Horkheimer, was in their family relationships. There, "experiences and images which gave inner direction to the life of every individual" could resist the pressures of economic life. This locus of resistance was slipping away, however, as the demands of work eroded family life. The family was no longer "a kind of second womb, in whose warmth the individual gathered the strength to stand alone outside it." Instead, economic pressures left the family susceptible to outside influences, and the demands of the competitive society were increasingly transmitted directly to children. They were becoming prematurely "tough and shrewd" because the utopian dreams that are a normal part of childhood were being replaced early in life by an adjustment to more limited economic realities. With the leisure part of private life forced to answer to the demands of the public realm, and the private family invaded by the same pressures, Horkheimer believed he was witnessing "the disappearance of the inner life."

The key to preserving this last private, human realm, was art. Horkheimer had no illusions about the role the arts had previously played in society. Long before mass-media entertainments had become important, he wrote, the cultural realm had most often served as an escape from social responsibility: "Men had fled into a private conceptual world and rearranged their thoughts when the time was ripe for rearranging reality. The inner life and the ideal had become conservative factors." But in the twentieth century, even that space for simple refuge from the demands of public life was being extinguished. "Man has lost his power to conceive a world different from that in which he lives." To preserve this breathing space for the imagination, Horkheimer championed "inhospitable works of art" like the prose of Joyce and Pablo Picasso's painting, "Guernica," "works which uncompromisingly express the gulf between the monadic individual and his barbarous surrounding." [34]

This support of the great moderns was similar to the reasoning of Macdonald and the other *Partisan Review* intellectuals in the 1930s and early 1940s. The difficult art of the avant-garde was welcomed for its inherent protest against comfortable and complacent bourgeois life. Although the Frankfurt School did not believe art was capable of completely rising above the social and economic conflicts of capitalist society, they believed it could incorporate the sense that conflicts existed in its forms. Particularly valuable were those productions that produced the least comfortable reactions and most resisted simple accommodation, in effect registering a kind of protest. Art therefore preserved an imaginative sphere for higher sensibilities and visions of a better order. Expressing a sentiment that was consistent among "aesthetic idealists" — those who sought social reform through cultural means — since the late nineteenth century, Horkheimer wrote that art "has preserved the utopia that evaporated from religion." [35]

Mass entertainments deserved condemnation on two grounds in the Frankfurt School argument. First, these transformations of leisure into "supervised routines," in Horkheimer's term, threatened private life. Amusement was becoming too "public" and driven by economic concerns when "the pleasures of the ball park and the movie, the best seller and the radio" were simply passing people's time and restoring them for more work. Second, these entertainments had taken over the position of art in society without taking over its function of surmounting the daily realities. Popular culture was therefore replacing the last outpost where the individual could distance himself from society and was eliminating the private realm of life altogether.[36]

The Frankfurt School's ideas buttressed Macdonald's criticisms of mass entertainments and encouraged his fears about modern society. The best indication of his growing disillusion with American culture, though, is that this dire forecast was actually more optimistic than Macdonald's own view by the late 1940s and 1950s. Critical Theory contained a promise of radical change that he was finding untenable. Its view of mass society maintained that class divisions continued to be strong and relevant and might therefore spur revolutionary change. Macdonald's fears of bureaucratization, by contrast, suggested that classes, like most other social differentiations, were being eclipsed.

He found support for his bleak portrayal of mass society from another German emigré, Hannah Arendt, in her powerful interpretation of totalitarianism. Arendt's 1951 book, *The Origins of Totalitarianism*, provided a detailed explanation of the roots of autocratic state control. She rejected interpretations that attributed the rise of modern despotic regimes to class conflict. Instead, she explained them as the result of the ruthless political organization of helpless citizens. She portrayed these victims as rootless, normless masses open to manipulation. Arendt also equated Nazism and Stalinism as different forms of the same totalitarian impulse, thus encouraging Cold War anti-Communism, and reminded readers that immense danger was inherent in all large modern societies.[37]

Macdonald was simply overwhelmed by Arendt's book. "The theoretical analysis of totalitarianism here impressed me more than any political theory I've read since 1935, when I first read Marx," he wrote. "It gave me the same contradictory sensations of familiarity ("Of course, just what I've been thinking for years.") and shocked discovery ("Can this possibly be true?") that Marx's description of capitalism did." Macdonald believed the manipulability of mass society was the overarching threat of the early postwar era, and he found Arendt's discussion to be its most profound analysis.

The problem with this diagnosis, for Macdonald, was that it came too late to save American society. He believed that modern culture had already left the broad swath of citizens wide open for political exploitation. Not even Arendt's frightening portrayal of totalitarianism could stem the tide. Such a formidable book could not reach "The Man in the Street," he explained, because "our American mass culture has efficiently perverted and suppressed his capacity to think seriously about politics or indeed anything else." The preconditions for totalitarianism in the United States were thus established in part by popular entertainments, in Macdonald's indictment. His mass culture condemnations took on a new and pressing importance in light of Arendt's theme that the aim of fascist regimes was "to shut the masses off from the real world."[38]

Macdonald's eager acceptance of Arendt's theory of mass society and totalitarianism was, in large part, because her ideas were so familiar to his way of thinking. Arendt's explanation of the rise of "mass-man" was in fact the American social scientists' theory of modernization taken to its most fearful extreme. Macdonald and many of his fellow critics had adopted this model, which contended that individuals in "folk" societies had been tightly integrated with their fellows through the bonds of family and community and then set adrift in the rootless, atomistic civilization of modern urban life. This interpretation was their explanation of how the good people were susceptible to the manipulations of entertainment entrepreneurs. Arendt's sociology tied this modernization model to later twentieth-century political developments by suggesting that these detached, disoriented modern individuals desperately wanted to be reintegrated in society. They were therefore easily mobilized by the totalitarians' promise of restructured nations built around firm bonds and associations. She showed how, though a certain social cohesion was of course reestablished by these regimes, it came at the cost of individuals' control over their lives. Finally, Arendt's book reminded Macdonald and his fellow critics that fascists like Adolf Hitler and Benito Mussolini had used the media of mass communications to capture the masses. This was yet more warning for them, then, that the expanding media for entertainment in the United States threatened more exploitation, which might engulf their whole society.

Macdonald's near surrender to the specter of mass society and mass culture was the background from which he wrote the last version of his essay, published in 1960. The changes that he made from 1953 shifted his criticism increasingly to the defense of "high" art, excoriating the "phoney avant-garde," or, as he would now call it, "Midcult." The new focus suggests that he finally found America's cultural problems to be insurmountable.

Macdonald characterized the period of general prosperity after World War II as a new, more "sophisticated" era. By now, the major social challenges of America's past were long completed. The frontier, industry, and immigrants had all been conquered or accommodated, the standard of living had improved across the population, and education had spread (college enrollment had tripled since 1929, he noted). The result was that "money, leisure and knowledge, the prerequisites of culture, are more plentiful and more evenly distributed than ever before." With his political radicalism largely past, Macdonald focused on the fate of avant-garde art in this age of abundant popular culture. The greatest threat was the kind of mass-produced arts that were aimed at the better-off, better-educated postwar citizens. Macdonald described such "Midcult" as having the same features as "Masscult"—"the formula, the built-in reaction, the lack of any standard except popularity"—but said that Midcult "decently covers them with a cultural figleaf." Where Masscult had sought only to please an audience, this new hybrid promised to lend a certain cachet as well because it paid attention to the standards of high culture. It attracted culture-conscious consumers by "watering down" artistic efforts.[39]

Macdonald singled out four literary works, all Pulitzer Prize winners, as typical products of Midcult: Ernest Hemingway's *The Old Man and the Sea*, Thornton Wilder's *Our Town*, Archibald MacLeish's *J.B.*, and Stephen Vincent Benét's *John Brown's Body*. He dissected each, isolating its unmistakable Midcult qualities with descriptions such as "the drone of the pastiche parable, wordy and sentimental"; "the final statement of the midbrow's nostalgia for small-town life, as Norman Rockwell has done it for the lowbrows in his *Post* covers"; "Profound and Soul-Searching, it deals with the Agony of Modern Man"; and "a master of the built-in reaction; it is impossible not to identify the emotion he wants to arouse. . . . One is never puzzled by the unexpected." He went on to explain that all four works were "the products of lapsed avant-gardists who know how to use the modern idiom in the service of the banal." That all four authors were expatriates in the 1920s and had now reentered the fold courting popular success struck him as a profound statement of the overweening power of mass art in the postwar years. The result was that the elite arts he had been championing for a generation were even further removed from the public, and their future apparently even more in doubt. In 1953, Macdonald had written, "There is slowly emerging a tepid, flaccid Middlebrow Culture that threatens to engulf everything in its spreading ooze." In 1960, he believed Midcult was at flood tide, and he conceded that the "tepid ooze" was "spreading everywhere."[40]

At the end of "Masscult and Midcult," Macdonald asked, "What is to be done?" He admitted that he saw little hope for improving the American scene and was resigned to a continued decline in the nation's cultural life. He offered this remarkable précis of his position:

> I see Masscult—and its recent offspring, Midcult—as a reciprocating engine, and who is to say, once it has been set in motion, whether the stroke or the counterstroke is responsible for its continued action? The Lords of *Kitsch* sell culture to the masses. It is debased, trivial culture that avoids

both the deep realities (sex, death, failure, tragedy) and also the simple, spontaneous pleasures, since the realities would be too real and the pleasures too lively to induce . . . "the mood of consent": a narcotized acceptance of the commodities it sells as a substitute for the unsettling and unpredictable (hence unsalable) joy, tragedy, wit, change, originality and beauty of real life. The masses . . . [including the Midcult audience] who have been debauched by several generations of this sort of thing, in turn have come to demand such trivial and comfortable cultural products. Which came first, the chicken or the egg, the mass demand or its satisfaction (and further stimulation), is a question as academic as it is unanswerable. The engine is reciprocating and shows no signs of running down.

Faced with this situation, Macdonald fell back on accepting the idea of two cultures as the best hope for America. Because the entertainment purveyors for so long had treated people as a uniform, passive lump in targeting their product, he believed the people had finally come to act the part. The only recourse, then, was to "let the masses have their Masscult, let the few who care about good writing, painting, music, architecture, philosophy, etc., have their High Culture, and don't fuzz up the distinction with Midcult." Macdonald concluded with a long quotation from the theologian Søren Kierkegaard that condemned the whole concept of a mass public as a misguided, dangerous idea. Kierkegaard called this cumulative description of a large populace a "monstrous abstraction." Such a concept did not refer to any actual association of people with their real connections such as nation, generation, or community. Rather, it artificially reduced their life situations in order to delimit them by some minimal common feature. Such a public, the theologian wrote, "is made up of individuals at the moment when they are nothing." Macdonald cited the thought to conclude, "This is the essence of what I have tried to say."[41]

The deeply pessimistic outlook for American culture presented in "Masscult and Midcult" was a fitting culmination for the Left mass culture criticism of the early twentieth century. It was a sad ending, no doubt, not only for the bleak state it portrayed, but for the uncharacteristic surrender of such a resourceful polemicist as Macdonald. His position does represent, though, the logical last stage of the entertainment condemnations. Particularly because it captures just how tendentious the mass culture criticism had become.

In Macdonald's summary statement, for example, he baldly declared that the content of all the popular arts was "debased." Moreover, he purported to know exactly how all audiences responded to entertainments: in his term, how they allowed themselves to be "debauched." Macdonald had taken his particular aesthetic judgment about the popular arts and his own untested assumption about the public's experience of these forms and from them diagnosed an unprecedented social failure.

The central understandings that had informed the liberal and Left entertainments criticism since the Progressive Era still held sway in Macdonald's arguments in 1960. The inherent "goodness" of the common people was assumed, and consequently so was their agreement with the values and tastes of the critics who believed themselves equally noble. The commercial entertainments were considered to be forces of corruption that did not represent the people's true interests. The people were believed to be highly susceptible to manipulation and exploitation because the modernizing, urbanizing process had progressively severed their communal attachments. And the responsibility of caring intellectuals was taken to include "freeing" the people from this denaturing process so that they might enjoy better, more elevating arts.

These understandings could be so consistent because they were completely endogenous to the beliefs of the Left intellectuals. The premises never had to be tested outside their own assumptions and logic. The masses were cited as the victims of the entertainments, yet their circumstances were evaluated selectively through the critics' eyes. Their own sense of their lives never shaped the critique.

The problem of entertainments had acted as a lightning rod for intellectuals' broader concerns about the social transformations of modern America. Industrialization, and its related surges of migration, immigration, and urban growth had brought great social division and differentiation to American society. These produced a mass, heterogenous public that was largely unknown to society's elites. This new public also encouraged the creation of modern mass entertainments that catered to its tastes and desires. Those who were at odds with the values and practices of the emerging society had created two potent forces to try to contain and control this change: the ideology of "Culture," and the class of critical reformist intellectuals. Both these forces tended to disregard the nature of the people in their determination to "do good" for them. Because both these forces were founded on the belief that the society was being led astray, when this new intelligentsia looked through the reducing lens of "Culture" at the modern entertainments, it could see only corruption.

EPILOGUE: *The Critique under Fire*

Looking back over his critical career shortly before his death in 1982, Dwight Macdonald came to realize the apparent contradiction between his condemnations of popular entertainments and his populist political sympathies. "I've discovered that culturally I'm a snob," he admitted to Diana Trilling. "I'm an intellectual snob." He was quick to add, though, "But politically I've always been very radical and for the people." This stance was, of course, hardly unique to Macdonald. The antinomy between championing the public and denouncing its chosen arts had been at the heart of the American Left's mass culture criticism through the early twentieth century.

Even by 1960, however, when Macdonald published the last installment of his entertainments diatribe, several of the central assumptions behind the critique were increasingly challenged. The source of these revised views was consistent with the original sources of the critique: a reorientation of intellectuals' outlooks rather than any change in the nature of the entertainments. American intellectuals had slowly adjusted to the shape of modernity over the early twentieth century, accepting many of the changes, criticizing and proposing reform for others. But as the entertainments criticism demonstrates, most had consistently doubted the ability of the public to control its new circumstances. It took a new conception of the "common" people that developed toward midcentury to finally weaken the criticism. The revised image of the people credited them with being more resourceful and independent than had been thought. More often now, they were envisioned as active agents trying to shape their own circumstances. This suggestion of a less passive public fundamentally challenged the simple theories of exploitation that had indicted the entertainments. Gradually, this new conception began to change many of the intellectuals' prevailing notions about modernization, the "Culture" ideal, and the assumed consensus of values between Left intellectuals and the broad public. It undermined, in other words, each of the major footings upon which the mass culture critique stood.

Modernization theories were especially subjected to searching challenge. The depiction of a wholly virtuous folk order debauched by the forces of urban-industrial society, an antimodern image created by reformers and social scientists and adopted by most of the mass arts critics, was judged too simplistic. The "folk society" ideal type proved particularly weak. First formally presented by the anthropologist Robert Redfield in 1930, the construct was found in succeeding decades to conflict with empirical evidence of the features of rural and urban communities. Questions were raised, for example, about how "pure" the folk had been in their supposed rustic simplicity. Had they been completely separated from supposed urban characteristics before the encroachment of city life? And what exactly was "urban" about the forces that brought change to agricultural societies? These questions raised the possibility of a different theory of modernization, best suggested in the title of one revisionist discussion, "Urbanization without Breakdown." Newer anthropology work found further fault with the anti-modernists' position, particularly with what one scholar described as the "tendency to view the city as the source of all evil." [1]

The discovery of thriving urban subcultures in America also called the critics' modernization model into doubt. The transition from a tightly knit, ordered, face-to-face, rural society to an anonymous, atomistic, chaotic city order suggested by Redfield and developed in Louis Wirth's ideal types was again shown to overestimate the social change. Studies of life in the metropolis such as William F. Whyte's *Street Corner Society* (1943), Jane Jacobs's *The Death and Life of Great American Cities* (1961), and Herbert Gans's *The Urban Villagers* (1962) described how social integration was maintained and neighborhoods remained cohesive in the modern American city. Wirth's assertion that the moral order that had been provided by primary groups would have to give way to institutional social controls in the new society was largely disproved. These new students of the city discovered thriving subcultures that organized their members' lives through strong systems of norms and customs. [2]

The critics' old modernization model was found to be no more accurate when it was applied to the national culture. The first comprehensive investigation of the integration of America's myriad racial, ethnic, and religious groups, Milton Gordon's *Assimilation in American Life* (1964), revealed complex, overlapping ties that bound the public. Gordon portrayed a network of strong affiliations and associations that not only corrected the belief that the "melting pot" was producing homogenized Americans, but made all notions of a rootless mass seem absurd.

The alarming theories about mass society that had been incorporated in most mass culture denunciations after World War II were also received far more skeptically in later years. Sociologist Daniel Bell, for instance, who generally agreed with the mass society critics' laments about the quality of modern life, nonetheless found their theoretical explanation wanting. Bell's comprehensive evaluation of the theories in 1956 agreed that many of the features of contemporary life seemed to fit the mass society model (increasing social interdependence, declining primary group ties, the extinction of universal faiths and values, and the displacement of traditional leadership elites, for instance). But he found insufficient proof that those features were necessarily produced by a new mass order.

Bell's survey of the most prominent mass society analyses instead revealed their inconsistencies. Definitions of the "mass" varied from author to author, and their descriptions of the kind of social organization mass society supposedly produced were equally discrepant. Bell concluded that the theories did not establish the encroachment of mass society so much as they showed that the critics' particular values had caused them to misperceive the more mundane disorganizing effects produced by democratic, industrial society. An "aristocratic cultural tradition" was being supported by the mass society theorists, and consequently their analyses often seemed to defend privilege. "The theory of the mass society no longer serves as a description of Western society," Bell wrote, "but as an ideology of romantic protest against contemporary society." Edward Shils, another prominent sociologist, also consistently railed against the mass society conception in the latter 1950s and 1960s. He called the theory a "gross distortion" of life in modern liberal-democratic nations. A third scholar, Leon Bramson, discovered bias in the mass society model when he investigated the intellectual assumptions of America's authorities on mass behavior. Bramson showed how the critics' social theories were derived from conservative prejudices in earlier European scholarship, and how this mind-set predisposed them to deride the features of modern liberal societies.[3]

The criticisms of modernization and mass society theories at midcentury weakened the case against popular entertainments. They also encouraged a reconsideration of related models of social "victimization," such as the prevailing theories about the effects of mass communications. From the early decades of the twentieth century, most attacks on popular literature, music, motion pictures, and modern dance styles were based on an implicit assumption that the messages or meanings contained in these forms had direct effects on the public's behavior. The stimulus provided by an entertainment was believed to cause an immediate, direct response. Thus, sexually suggestive literature was cited as causing promiscuity, films depicting robberies were reviled for driving young men into crime, and the emotional freedom of ragtime and jazz was equated with general moral decay. This "hypodermic" theory of the effects of communication media, suggesting the direct injection of ideas into intellectually passive audiences, began to be employed formally in the 1920s. Studies of World War I propaganda, public opinion formation and social psychology, and the new field of consumer marketing research adopted the explanation. The model reached its peak influence in the 1930s in analyzing "fad" behavior, advertising, political leaders' use of radio, and the reactions to Orson Welles's famous "War of the Worlds" broadcast.[4]

By the 1940s, however, this simple theory of media effects had begun to be superseded. Empirical studies of the public's voting behavior, reading practices, and responses to entertainments had discovered that intermediary influences affected the transmission of messages to audiences. The new investigations established the influence of people's social milieu in determining how they received and reacted to communications. They also showed the effects of individuals' unique psychological makeups in how they responded to media suggestion. The most influential theory to arise from this work was the idea that a "two-step flow of communication" operated in the transmitting of messages. Local "opinion leaders" acted as a screen between communicators and the broad audience, according to this view, introducing the influence of personal relationships into people's reactions to the mass media. The new communications theories of the 1940s and 1950s generally did not deny that mass culture forms may have had important influences in American society. But they did present a formidable challenge to the idea of direct and immediate media influences, a particularly important issue amid the enormous expansion of broadcasting and publishing in the postwar years.[5]

The cumulative effect of these major reconsiderations of the impact of modern life was to cause many intellectuals to adopt a more complex portrait of the public. Some began, at least begrudgingly, to acknowledge their substantial differences from the public. This change was particularly jarring for liberal and radical intellectuals because they had often assumed that they spoke "for" the people. This new sense of the people's nature challenged them in particular to reconsider the ideal of "Culture" they had erected for the public.

The notion of a monolithic "American Mind" or "American Culture" rooted in a set of elite arts and writings had remained prominent among intellectuals in the early twentieth century and was further elevated in the atmosphere of superpower rivalry after the Second World War. But challenges to these claims of exclusive value for a particular canon of "high" literary and artistic forms, and for the particular patterns of life associated with them, grew stronger in the succeeding generation. New critics, mainly on the Left, questioned the privileged position of the elite arts, the social consensus this position presumed, and even whether any single cultural standard could be viable for so diverse a nation.

The ideal of "Culture" was not destroyed by any means during this clash. Contemporary debates, both in and out of the academy, over canonical texts and the proper content of the "Western heritage" attest to its life. But for many intellectuals who considered themselves champions of the people, the emerging sense of the differences among the public encouraged a more flexible conception of "culture." The term was now more often defined broadly, in an anthropological sense, acknowledging multiple ways of life. More cultural critics disdained to judge expression as a measure of fixed values.

"Pop" art, "camp," and the "New Sensibility" arose as brief but important intellectual challenges to the older cultural ideal. They specifically denied, for example, the inviolable boundaries between "High Culture" and "Masscult/Midcult" that Macdonald had advocated. The most influential spokesperson of the new outlook, Susan Sontag (interestingly, one of the younger generation of *Partisan Review* writers), declared that its purpose was to break down hierarchical distinctions and overturn the traditional understanding of the serious arts as "moral journalism." Reviewing the development of this new cultural sensibility in 1968, cultural historian John Cawelti noted that "suddenly, in the 1960s, just as it seemed the avant-garde and mass culture had agreed to ignore each other, we find ourselves in the midst of a whole series of artistic events which have crossed over and obfuscated the brow lines." He labeled the phenomenon "Beatles, Batman, and the New Aesthetic."[6]

The enormous growth of the mass entertainments in the decades after World War II, and their sheer familiarity by the latter half of the century, further legitimated popular culture as well. Amid the general prosperity and the unprecedented market for mass arts presented by the "baby boom" generation, a number of mass arts detractors "stopped criticizing," as one historian has put it, "and started explaining." The *Journal of Popular Culture*, founded in 1967, and the Popular Culture Association represented the explainers' claim to academic legitimacy and signaled an important new commitment to the serious study of mass entertainments. Russel Nye's massive 1970 survey of American commercial entertainments, significantly titled *The Unembarrassed Muse*, was a landmark in the new genre. The mounting movement for African Americans' civil rights and social respect in the 1960s also further encouraged mass arts analysis by drawing sympathetic intellectuals to seriously consider blacks' popular cultural expressions.

The result of these revisions and qualifications to intellectuals' sense of mass entertainments has been the undermining of most of the Left's original mass culture critique. Macdonald's condemnations still have numerous supporters, of course. His general message about the mass entertainments' dangers to the public continues to inspire many professional analyses of media effects. Yet today, while Macdonald remains the American writer most commonly cited in popular culture analyses, he is most often invoked as an example of "what went wrong" with mass culture criticism. Contemporary critics of entertainments and defenders of the popular arts now generally agree that the analyses put forth by Macdonald and his fellow critics were misguided.

They have been replaced by a generation of mass culture criticism that clearly shows the changed perception of the people and their plural lives. This work, predominantly the product of newer leftist scholars, generally rejects the idea of a prostrate public. It denies that people are directly manipulated in any simple way by the entertainments, or that these arts are preying upon deluded minds and imposing false needs. Newer critics instead typically posit a far more complicated relationship between entertainments and the heterogenous society. They investigate differences of power in more subtle and nuanced terms of "hegemony" theory and legitimate consumer desires. Another school of mass entertainment analysis has recognized the myriad ways audiences receive and engage these products. Building on new communications theory, researchers have explained how readers and viewers function as "interpretive communities," for example, providing a social context that influences the perceived meanings of popular expressions.[7]

Left intellectuals' condemnation of mass entertainments was rooted, then, almost exclusively within their own internally consistent system of social interpretation. Over the first half of the twentieth century, the criticism grew because of their understandings of modernization and the masses. The intellectuals adopted a particular conception of the mass public that fulfilled their desires to defend others whom they presumed were similarly disserved by the new society. The criticism grew without any sustained examination of the role of the entertainments in the lives of their audiences. The decline of the criticism has begun as critics have discovered their differences with this public, and they face the reality that much of the public in fact competes with them to direct the nation's culture.

The mass culture criticism may therefore serve as a supreme example of just how subjective is our human grasp of meaning. The anthropologist Clifford Geertz has elegantly described man as "an animal suspended in webs of significance he himself has spun." Such webs created by critics over the early half of the twentieth century determined that popular entertainments were a social danger and condemned them before their significance for the nation's public had begun to be understood. Only today, as these perceptions change and intellectual webs are rewoven, can there be any fruitful analysis of the role such popular expression has played in the very different and individual webs of millions of other Americans.[8]

INTRODUCTION

1. The quotations are from Daniel Anderson and appear in Patrick Cooke, "TV or Not TV," *In Health*, December/January 1992, p. 37. The report is D. R. Anderson and P. A. Collins, *The Impact on Children's Education: Television's Influence on Cognitive Development* (Washington, D.C., 1988).

2. Ronald Edsforth, "Popular Culture and Politics in Modern America: An Introduction," in Ronald Edsforth and Larry Bennet, eds., *Popular Culture and Political Change in Modern America* (Albany, N.Y., 1991), p. 3.

3. The stories of Wertham, the Senate committee, and the delinquency crusade are developed in James Gilbert, *A Cycle of Outrage: America's Reaction to the Juvenile Delinquent in the 1950s* (New York, 1986), esp. pp. 91–108, 143–61; Warren Susman, with Edward Griffin, "Did Success Spoil the United States?: Dual Representations in Postwar America," in Lary May, ed., *Recasting America: Culture and Politics in the Age of the Cold War* (Chicago, 1989), pp. 27–28. Edsforth, "Popular Culture and Politics," p. 3. The MLA organizing statement is quoted by Stanley Edgar Hyman, "Ideals, Dangers, and Limitations," in Norman Jacobs, ed., *Culture for the Millions?* (Princeton, 1961), p. 139. Irving Howe, *A Margin of Hope* (San Diego, 1982), p. 179.

4. The earliest use of the phrase "mass culture" I have found in English (*The Oxford English Dictionary* lists a 1939 article) is in Rose Strunsky's translation of Leon Trotsky's *Literature and Revolution* (New York, 1925), p. 193. It appears also in the British critic F. R. Leavis's *Mass Civilization and Minority Culture* (Cambridge, 1930), p. 31; and in these American sources: "Art Is a Weapon!" (Program of the Workers Cultural Federation) *New Masses* 7 (August 1931): 12; F. Cudworth Flint, review of *Fiction and the Reading Public*, by Q. D. Leavis (1932), *Symposium* 4 (1933): 502; Joshua Kunitz, "Literary Wars in the U.S.S.R.," *New Masses* 11 (12 June 1934): 16.

5. Patrick Brantlinger, *Bread and Circuses: Theories of Mass Culture as Social Decay* (Ithaca, N.Y., 1983), pp. 17–52.

6. John Higham, "The Reorientation of American Culture in the 1890s," in John Weiss, ed., *The Origins of Modern Consciousness* (Detroit, 1965), pp. 25–48; Lewis Perry, *Intellectual Life in America* (New York, 1984), pp. 312–13.

7. John Kasson, *Amusing the Million: Coney Island at the Turn of the Century* (New York, 1978); Kathy Peiss, *Cheap Amusements: Working Women and Leisure in Turn-of-the-Century New York* (Philadelphia, 1986); Robert Sklar, *Movie-Made America* (New York, 1975), pp. 3–157; Lary May, *Screening Out the Past: The Birth of Mass Culture and the Motion Picture Industry* (New York, 1980); Lewis A.

Erenberg, *Steppin' Out: New York Nightlife and the Transformation of American Culture, 1890–1930* (Chicago, 1981); Neil Leonard, *Jazz and the White Americans* (Chicago, 1962); Macdonald Smith Moore, *Yankee Blues: Musical Culture and American Identity* (Bloomington, Ind., 1985); Albert F. McLean, Jr., *American Vaudeville as Ritual* (Lexington, Ky., 1965), esp. pp. 66–90; Gunther Barth, *City People: The Rise of Modern City Culture in Nineteenth-Century America* (New York, 1980), pp. 192–228; Roy Rosenzweig, *Eight Hours for What We Will: Workers and Leisure in an Industrial City, 1870–1920* (Cambridge, 1983), esp. pp. 191–221; Francis G. Couvares, "The Triumph of Commerce: Class Culture and Mass Culture in Pittsburgh," in Michael H. Frisch and Daniel J. Walkowitz, eds., *Working-Class America* (Urbana, Ill., 1983), pp. 123–52; Michael Rogin, " 'The Sword Became a Flashing Vision': D. W. Griffith's *The Birth of a Nation*," *Representations* 9 (Winter 1985): 150–95, and "The Great Mother Domesticated: Sexual Difference and Sexual Indifference in D. W. Griffith's *Intolerance*," *Critical Inquiry* 15 (Spring 1989): 510–55. A book that does not focus on entertainments but is nevertheless essential to understanding these issues of cultural change is Roland Marchand, *Advertising the American Dream: Making Way for Modernity, 1920–1940* (Berkeley, 1985).

8. Richard Pells, *The Liberal Mind in a Conservative Age: American Intellectuals in the 1940s and 1950s* (New York, 1985), pp. 216–32; Gilbert, *A Cycle of Outrage*; Andrew Ross, *No Respect: Intellectuals and Popular Culture* (New York, 1989); Herbert Gans, *Popular Culture and High Culture* (New York, 1976), pp. 19–64; Christopher Brookeman, *American Culture and Society since the 1930s* (New York, 1984); Charles C. Alexander, *Holding the Line: The Eisenhower Era, 1952–1961* (Bloomington, Ind., 1975), pp. 137–43; Serge Guilbaut, *How New York Stole the Idea of Modern Art: Abstract Expressionism, Freedom, and the Cold War* (Chicago, 1983), pp. 33–38; T. J. Jackson Lears, "A Matter of Taste: Corporate Cultural Hegemony in a Mass Consumption Society," in May, ed., *Recasting America*, pp. 38–57; Neil Jumonville, "The New York Intellectuals and Mass Culture Criticism," *Journal of American Culture* 12 (Spring 1989): 87–95; Daniel Bell, *The Cultural Contradictions of Capitalism* (New York, 1976), pp. 44–45; Thomas M. Kando, *Leisure and Popular Culture in Transition* (St. Louis, 1975), pp. 49–62. Lazarsfeld's judgment, originally published in 1948, is quoted in Paul F. Lazarsfeld, "Mass Culture Today," in Jacobs, ed., *Culture for the Millions?*, p. xiv.

9. Lawrence Levine, *Highbrow/Lowbrow: The Emergence of Cultural Hierarchy in America* (Cambridge, Mass., 1988); Paul Dimaggio, "Cultural Entrepreneurship in Nineteenth-Century Boston: The Creation of an Organizational Base for High Culture in America," and "Cultural Entrepreneurship in Nineteenth-Century Boston, Part II: The Classification and Framing of American Art," *Media, Culture and Society* 4 (1982): 33–50, 303–22. John G. Cawelti, "With the Benefit of Hindsight: Popular Culture Criticism," *Critical Studies in Mass*

Communication 2 (1985): 363–79, also develops the continuities in the criticism. The idea of a consistent, rather than episodic, mass culture critique stems from James Gilbert's discussion in *Cycle of Outrage*, p. 4. Daniel Horowitz takes this longer perspective on intellectuals' responses to the emerging consumer culture in *The Morality of Spending: Attitudes toward the Consumer Society in America, 1875–1940* (Baltimore, 1985).

10. George Lipsitz, "Popular Culture: This Ain't No Sideshow," in George Lipsitz, *Time Passages: Collective Memory and American Popular Culture* (Minneapolis, 1990), pp. 3–20; John Fiske, *Understanding Popular Culture* (Boston, 1989); Dennis Davis and Thomas F. N. Puckett, "Mass Entertainment and Community: Toward a Culture-Centered Paradigm for Mass Communication Research," Michael Real, "The Challenge of a Culture-Centered Paradigm: Metatheory and Reconciliation in Media Research," and Lana F. Rakow, "Some Good News–Bad News about a Culture-Centered Paradigm," all in *Communication Yearbook* 15 (1992): 3–57; Winfried Fluck, "Popular Culture as a Mode of Socialization: A Theory about the Social Functions of Popular Culture Forms," *Journal of Popular Culture* 21 (Winter 1987): 31–46. See also the literature discussed in the Epilogue.

CHAPTER ONE

1. Cornelia Comer, "Vanishing Lady," *Atlantic*, December 1911, p. 727; Henry F. May, *The End of American Innocence: A Study of the First Years of Our Own Time, 1912–1917* (New York, 1959). For the growing sense of despair among the cultural elite in the Gilded Age, see Ellery Sedgewick III, "The American Genteel Tradition in the Early Twentieth Century," *American Studies* (Spring 1984): 50, 53; John Sproat, *The "Best Men": Liberal Reformers in the Gilded Age* (New York, 1968); Stow Persons, *The Decline of American Gentility* (New York, 1973); Martin Green, *The Problem of Boston* (New York, 1966).

2. Thomas L. Haskell, *The Emergence of Professional Social Science: The American Social Science Association and the Nineteenth-Century Crisis of Authority* (Urbana, Ill., 1977); Lawrence R. Veysey, *The Emergence of the American University* (Chicago, 1965); John Higham, "The Matrix of Specialization," and Lawrence Veysey, "The Plural Organized Worlds of the Humanities," in Alexandra Oleson and Andrew Voss, eds., *The Organization of Knowledge in Modern America 1860–1920* (Baltimore, 1979); Morton White, *Social Thought in America: The Revolt against Formalism* (Boston, 1957); T. J. Jackson Lears, *No Place of Grace: Antimodernism and the Transformation of American Culture 1880–1920* (New York, 1981).

3. The saloon figures are cited in Jon M. Kingsdale, "The 'Poor Man's Club': Social Functions of the Urban Working-Class Saloon," *American Quarterly* 25

(1973): 472–89. For newspaper figures, see Edwin Emery, *The Press and America* (Englewood Cliffs, N.J., 1962), p. 345; cited in Garth S. Jowett, "The Emergence of Mass Society: The Standardization of American Culture, 1830–1920," *Prospects* 7 (1982): 214; Michael Schudson, *Discovering the News* (New York, 1978). For periodical figures, see John Tebbel and Mary Ellen Zuckerman, *The Magazine in America, 1741–1990* (New York, 1991), p. 68. For vaudeville and dance hall statistics, see Alan Havig, "The Commercial Amusement Audience in Early Twentieth-Century American Cities," *Journal of American Culture* 5 (Spring 1982): 1–19.

4. Robert Sklar, *Movie-Made America* (New York, 1975); Russell Lynes, *The Lively Audience* (New York, 1985); Lewis Erenberg, *Steppin' Out: New York Nightlife and the Transformation of American Culture, 1890–1930* (Chicago, 1981).

5. May, *End of American Innocence*, pp. 52–80.

6. Rollin Lynde Hartt, *The People at Play* (1909; reprint, New York, 1975), pp. 110, 174, 172, 183, 92–93, 96, 107, vii, 15, 3, 4, 16, 6, 8, 31, 65. For Hartt's background, see *Who's Who in America*, vol. 11 (1920–21), s.v. "Hartt, Rollin Lynde."

7. "A Careful Study of Diversions," *New York Times*, 10 July 1909; *Nation* 88 (24 June 1909): 628; "The Amusements of the Masses," *Dial* 47 (1 July 1909): 23; American Library Association, *Booklist* 5 (January 1909): 168; "Humors of American Life," *American Review of Reviews* 40 (August 1909): 255.

8. Hartt, *People at Play*, pp. 174, 175, 184–85.

9. Frederick Winsor, "Boys and the Theater," *Atlantic Monthly* 107 (March 1911): 354, 351; Samuel Hopkins Adams, "The Indecent Stage," *American Magazine* 68 (May 1909): 41, 46.

10. R. A. Scott-James, "Popularity in Literature," *North American Review* 197 (May 1913): 683; "Fiction as a Pleasant Poison," *Dial* 54 (1 February 1913): 86; "Magazines Made to Sell," *Dial* 62 (11 January 1917): 13. See also "The Theatrical Uplift," *Dial* 47 (1 October 1909): 219; Winsor, "Boys and the Theatre," p. 351. The 1913 *Dial* editorial did not completely endorse the minister but took a more moderate stance toward novels, judging some valuable, some execrable, and most unwelcome but not any worse influences than "many forms of diversion or sensationalism."

11. "Laxative Literature," *Dial* 58 (10 June 1915): 451; Owen Wister, "Quack-Novels and Democracy," *Atlantic Monthly* 115 (June 1915): 724, 725, 722. See also Lorin Deland's definition of "people of Bad Taste" in "A Plea for the Theatrical Manager," *Atlantic Monthly* 102 (October 1908): 493. For the criticism of appeals to the "primitive" in popular music, see Horatio Parker, "Our Taste in Music," *Yale Review* 7 (July 1918): 783; and the criticisms investigated in Frank Rossiter, "The Genteel Tradition in American Music," *Journal of American Culture* 4 (Winter 1981): 107–15.

12. Brander Matthews, "Are the Movies a Menace to the Drama?," *North American Review* 205 (March 1917): 450; Henry Wysham Lanier, "The Educational

Future of the Moving Picture," *American Review of Reviews* 50 (December 1914): 726; "Moving Pictures Ad Nauseam," *American Review of Reviews* 38 (December 1908): 744, 745. Claudy's article appeared in *Photo-Era* in October 1908. Another 1917 article presented arguments for both sides of the question of whether motion pictures were a "desirable amusement" and listed under the charge of lowering the public taste: "(a) Appeal is to the lower side of nature. (b) Spectators become accustomed to the sensational." See "Motion Pictures: A Brief for Debate," *Independent* 89 (5 March 1917): 427.

13. Glenn C. Altschuler, *Race, Ethnicity, and Class in American Social Thought* (Arlington Heights, Ill., 1982), pp. 40–75.

14. Hartt, *People at Play*, pp. 30, 96, 93–94.

15. Lewis Perry, *Intellectual Life in America* (New York, 1984), pp. 37–38.

16. Schudson, *Discovering the News*, pp. 3–11, 88–120; S. Elizabeth Bird, *For Enquiring Minds* (Knoxville, 1992), pp. 7–38. William R. Taylor, *In Pursuit of Gotham* (New York, 1992), pp. 69–91; Winfried Fluck, "Popular Culture as a Mode of Socialization: A Theory about the Social Functions of Popular Culture Forms," *Journal of Popular Culture* 21 (Winter 1987): 31–46.

17. Clifford Geertz, "Art as a Cultural System," *Modern Language Notes* 91 (1976): 1475–76, 1497. Elliott J. Gorn, "The Wicked World: The *National Police Gazette* and Gilded-Age America," *Media Studies Journal* 6 (Winter 1992): 1–15; Anthony Comstock, *Traps for the Young* (New York, 1883), quoted in ibid., p. 1; Bird, *Enquiring Minds*. For the problems with such scientific or empirical analyses of popular culture, see Ien Ang, *Watching Dallas* (New York, 1985), esp. pp. 13–50.

18. For the details of these criticisms, see Paul R. Gorman, "The Development of an American Mass Culture Critique, 1910–1960" (Ph.D. diss., University of California, Berkeley, 1990), chap. 2.

19. Charles H. A. Wager, "Democracy and Literature," *Atlantic Monthly* 116 (October 1915): 480; Deland, "Plea for the Theatrical Manager," p. 497; "Theatrical Uplift," p. 220. See also William Phelps, "Condition and Tendencies of the Drama," *Yale Review* (October 1911): 89. A 1908 review of a book on popular ballads commended the author for not overvaluing the forms or setting them up "as rivals to the poetry of art." A *Nation* review of the work had previously praised its "full recognition of the limitations of popular literature." See George Lyman Kittredge, "The Popular Ballad," *Atlantic Monthly* 101 (February 1908): 278; and the review of Francis B. Gummere, *The Popular Ballad* (Boston, 1907), in the *Nation* 85 (8 August 1907): 122. For an overview of the intellectuals' devotion to standards of "high" culture, see Perry, *Intellectual Life in America*, and the similar developments in Britain in Raymond Williams, *Culture and Society, 1780–1950* (New York, 1958).

20. My sense of these developments comes largely from Roger Stein, *John Ruskin and Aesthetic Thought in America* (Cambridge, Mass., 1967), and Neil Harris,

The Artist in American Society (Chicago, 1966). Joseph Ellis, *After the Revolution* (New York, 1979), is also suggestive. A fine short summary is Helen Horowitz, *Culture and the City* (Lexington, Ky., 1976), pp. 1–26.

21. Early indications of this use of the arts as a standard and a device for steering social behavior came from members of the Federalist Party, as this American gentry went into decline after Thomas Jefferson became president in 1800. The Federalist John Kirkland, for example, combined a republican fear of luxury with an idea of reform through expressive culture in the *Monthly Anthology* in 1807. He contended, "We are becoming familiar with wealth. Out of wealth grows luxury. If those enjoyments that flow from literature and taste are not emulated, we shall be exposed to that ennervating and debasing luxury, the object of which is sensual indulgence, its immediate effect, vice, and its ultimate issue, public degradation and ruin." Quoted in Ellis, *After the Revolution*, pp. 214–15. See also Henry May, *The Enlightenment in America* (New York, 1976), pp. 350–56.

22. This account is based on Murray Krieger's lecture, "The Precious Object: Fetish as Aesthetic," in his *Arts on the Level: The Fall of the Elite Object* (Knoxville, 1981), pp. 3–24. Paul Dimaggio contends that ambiguity is the key to "the ideology of connoisseurship" and the framing of a high culture realm. See his "Cultural Entrepreneurship in Nineteenth-Century Boston, Part II: The Classification and Framing of American Art," *Media, Culture and Society* 4 (1982): esp. 317–18; and Alan Gowans, *Learning to See: Historical Perspective on Modern Popular/Commercial Arts* (Bowling Green, Ohio, 1981), esp. pp. 18–19.

23. Lawrence W. Levine, *Highbrow/Lowbrow: The Emergence of Cultural Hierarchy in America* (Cambridge, Mass., 1988), pp. 171–242.

24. Ibid., pp. 177, 206–7, 215, 218, 227. Paul Dimaggio writes that in Boston, the Brahmins' desire for "exclusivity" as a status group overcame their need, as a social class, for establishing the hegemony of their values. Dimaggio, "Cultural Entrepreneurship in Nineteenth-Century Boston: The Creation of an Organizational Base for High Culture in America," *Media, Culture and Society* 4 (1982): 48, and "Cultural Entrepreneurship, Part II," pp. 306–19. Helen Horowitz, in *Culture and the City*, sees the late nineteenth-century cultural philanthropy efforts as, on the contrary, increasingly democratic. This interpretation is questioned in Kenneth Kusmer's review essay, "The Social History of Cultural Institutions: The Upper-Class Connection," *Journal of Interdisciplinary History* 12 (Summer 1979): 137–46.

25. Hartt, *People at Play*, pp. 112, 111, 40; Deland, "Plea for the Theatrical Manager," p. 497.

CHAPTER TWO

1. Rheta Childe Dorr, *What Eight Million Women Want* (Boston, 1910), pp. 208–10, 226, 201–5. The number in the title referred to Dorr's estimate of "modern women" in the United States. She focused on the dance halls because foremost among "the things women want" were the "objects which tend to conserve the future mothers of children." See pp. 322, 320–21.

2. Frederic C. Howe, "What to Do with the Motion-Picture Show: Shall It Be Censored?," *Outlook* 107 (20 June 1914): 412.

3. The difference between the dance hall and dance academy was that halls offered only public dances while academies offered dance instruction as well.

4. For attendance figures, see the following surveys: Francis R. North, *A Recreation Survey of the City of Waltham, Massachusetts* (Waltham, Mass., 1913); Michael M. Davis, *The Exploitation of Pleasure; A Study of Commercial Recreations in New York City* (New York, 1912); *Public Recreation. Transactions of the Commonwealth Club of California*, vol. 8 (San Francisco, June 1913), pp. 181–309; Rowland Haynes, *Recreation Survey, Detroit, Michigan* (Detroit, 1913); "Recreation Survey of Kansas City, Mo.," *Second Annual Report of the Recreation Department of the Board of Public Welfare* (Kansas City, 1912), pp. 3–68; Juvenile Protective Association, *Recreation Survey of Cincinnati* (Cincinnati, 1913). The statistics of these surveys are tabulated and discussed in Alan Havig, "The Commercial Amusement Audience in Early Twentieth-Century American Cities," *Journal of American Culture* 5 (Spring 1982): 1–19. The dance hall references are in "Dancing Academies: Some Possibilities," *Charities and the Commons* 21 (27 February 1909): 1018; Davis, *Exploitation of Pleasure*, pp. 16, 13–14, 15. My discussion of the dance hall problem and reform efforts in this chapter is particularly informed by Kathy Peiss, *Cheap Amusements: Working Women and Leisure in Turn-of-the-Century New York* (Philadelphia, 1986), esp. pp. 163–84.

5. Dorr, *What Women Want*, p. 228.

6. Mary Kingsbury Simkhovitch, *The City Worker's World in America* (New York, 1917), p. 110; Louise deKoven Bowen, "Our Most Popular Recreation Controlled by the Liquor Interests: A Study of Public Dance Halls" (1912), in *Speeches, Addresses, and Letters of Louise deKoven Bowen* (Ann Arbor, Mich., 1937), p. 242; "Municipal Dance-Halls," *Outlook* 101 (24 August 1912): 902. Criticisms of liquor's involvement in dance halls and academies include "Dancing Academies," p. 1018; Davis, *Exploitation of Pleasure*, p. 14; Belle Linder Israels, "The Way of the Girl," *Survey* 22 (3 July 1909): 490, 494.

7. Israels, "Way of the Girl," p. 495; Bowen, "Our Most Popular Recreation," p. 243; "The Cleveland Experiment," *Outlook* 101 (24 August 1912): 903; "Municipal Dance-Halls," *Outlook* 101 (24 August 1912): 902; John Collier, "Leisure Time: The Last Problem of Conservation," *Playground* 6 (June 1912): 99. See also Davis, *Exploitation of Pleasure*, p. 14; "Commercial Recreation Trans-

formed," *Playground* 11 (May 1917): 207; Julia Schoenfeld, "Commercial Recreation Legislation," *Playground* 7 (March 1914): 461.

8. Louise Bowen, "Five and Ten Cent Theaters," in *Speeches, Addresses, and Letters of Louise deKoven Bowen* (Ann Arbor, Mich., 1937), p. 141; John Collier, "Motion Picture," *Proceedings of the Child Conference for Research and Welfare* (New York, 1910), pp. 110–11.

9. Quoted in Collier, "Motion Picture," p. 110; Bowen, "Five and Ten Cent Theaters," p. 139; J. W. G., "Responsibility of the Moving Picture Show for Crime," *Journal of the American Institute of Criminal Law and Criminology* 1 (January 1911): 788. The case was originally treated in the *New Jersey Law Journal*. For similar worries about influences on children, see Rowland Haynes, "Value and Limitations of Moving Picture Legislation," *Playground* 9 (November 1915): 312.

10. Belle Israels, "Dance Problem," *Playground* 4 (October 1910): 243; Bowen, "Our Most Popular Recreation," p. 241; Jane Addams, "Some Reflections on the Failure of the Modern City to Provide Recreation for Young Girls," *Charities and the Commons* 21 (5 December 1908): 366; Jane Addams, "Public Recreation and Social Morality," *Charities and the Commons* 18 (3 August 1907): 494. This was later incorporated in her *The Spirit of Youth and the City Streets* (New York, 1909). On the criticism of dance hall proprietors, see also Robert Weyeneth, "Moral Spaces: Reforming the Landscape of Leisure in Urban America, 1850–1920" (Ph.D. diss., University of California, Berkeley, 1984), p. 134; Davis, *Exploitation of Pleasure*, pp. 16–17.

11. Addams, "Failure of the Modern City," pp. 367, 365–66; Collier, "Leisure Time," p. 101; "The Morals of the Movies," *Survey* 35 (4 March 1916): 662.

12. "Morals of the Movies," p. 662.

13. Israels, "Dance Problem," pp. 249, 244, 248. The plan was described in "Dancing Academies," pp. 1018–19. A similar program in Cleveland is mentioned in "Municipal Dance-Halls," *Outlook* 101 (24 August 1912): 902–3. See also Bowen, "Our Most Popular Recreation," pp. 245–46. On dance hall "substitution," and other regulation efforts, see Elizabeth I. Perry, " 'The General Motherhood of the Commonwealth': Dance Hall Reform in the Progressive Era," *American Quarterly* 37 (Winter 1985): 719–33. An exception to practice of regulation rather than prohibition was the temporary closing of public dance halls in Fort Worth, Texas. This was cited, and labeled "extreme," in Buffalo City Planning Association, *Recreation Survey of Buffalo* (Buffalo, 1925), p. 91.

14. Charles Matthew Feldman, *The National Board of Censorship (Review) of Motion Pictures 1909–1922* (New York, 1977), pp. 20–86; Robert Fisher, "Film Censorship and Progressive Reform: The National Board of Censorship of Motion Pictures, 1909–1922," *Journal of Popular Film* 4 (1975): 143–56; Garth Jowett, *Film: The Democratic Art* (Boston, 1976), pp. 111–13, 126–30.

15. On Victorian standards for women and amusement, see Lewis Erenberg, *Steppin' Out: New York Nightlife and the Transformation of American Culture, 1890–*

1930 (Chicago, 1981), pp. 6–25; and Elaine May, *Great Expectations* (Chicago, 1980), pp. 29–33.

16. Don S. Kirschner, "The Ambiguous Legacy: Social Justice and Social Control in the Progressive Era," *Historical Reflections* 2 (Summer 1975): 69–88; "'Movie' Manners and Morals," *Outlook* 113 (26 July 1916): 694–95. The continuity of the progressives' behavioral standards with those of nineteenth-century moralists is developed in Daniel Horowitz, *The Morality of Spending: Attitudes toward the Consumer Society in America, 1875–1940* (Baltimore, 1985), pp. 50–66.

17. While reformers and social workers condemned work routines for their ill effects on laborers, they were generally not willing to criticize the economic system as a whole. Nor, despite these often harsh conditions, were they prepared to dispense with the ideal of work as a force for order in society. This ambivalence about industrialism fundamentally shaped their reforms. See Richard L. McCormick, *The Party Period and Public Policy: American Politics from the Age of Jackson to the Progressive Era* (New York, 1986), pp. 263–88.

18. Mary E. McDowell, "The Right to Leisure," *Playground* 4 (January 1911): 330, 328. See also George F. Kenngott, *The Record of a City* (New York, 1912), p. 202.

19. Howard S. Braucher, "Play and Social Progress," *Annals of the American Academy of Political and Social Science* 35 (January–June 1910): 326, 328.

20. Kenngott, *Record of a City*, p. 202.

21. Addams, *Spirit of Youth*, pp. 27, 18–19; Davis, *Exploitation of Pleasure*, pp. 33, 36.

22. Frederic C. Howe, "Leisure," *Survey* 31 (3 January 1914): 415; Bowen, "Our Most Popular Recreation," p. 241; Addams, *Spirit of Youth*, pp. 91–92. See also Davis, *Exploitation of Pleasure*, pp. 3–4.

23. Intellectuals' "scientific" readings of the popular arts were discussed in Chapter 1.

24. On the "victim" ideology, see David J. Rothman, "The State as Parent: Social Policy in the Progressive Era," in Willard Gaylin et al., eds., *Doing Good: The Limits of Benevolence* (New York, 1981), pp. 69–95; Robert Westbrook, "Lewis Hine and the Ethics of Progressive Camerawork," *Tikkun* 2 (April/May 1987): 24–29.

25. This interpretation is informed by Peiss, *Cheap Amusements*, pp. 88–114.

26. David Glassberg, "Restoring a 'Forgotten Childhood': American Play and the Progressive Era's Elizabethan Past," *American Quarterly* 32 (Fall 1980): 351–68. On progressives' values, see Jean B. Quandt, *From the Small Town to the Great Community* (New Brunswick, N.J., 1970).

27. Addams, *Spirit of Youth*, pp. 99, 13.

28. Clarence E. Rainwater, *The Play Movement in the United States* (Chicago, 1922), p. 11. The historiography of the play movement, as with so many reform efforts, has divided along interpretive lines judging the activities as either "benevolence," or attempts at "social control." Studies suggesting benevolence are Rainwater, *Play Movement*, and Allen Davis, *Spearheads for Reform* (New York, 1967).

Interpretations stressing "social control" are Lawrence Finfer, "Leisure as Social Work in the Urban Community: The Progressive Recreation Movement, 1890–1920" (Ph.D. diss., Michigan State University, 1974); Paul Boyer, *Urban Masses and Moral Order in America, 1820–1920* (Cambridge, Mass., 1978); Dominick Cavallo, *Muscles and Morals: Organized Playgrounds and Urban Reform, 1880–1920* (Philadelphia, 1981). Also, a number of recent studies have found a significant working-class involvement in controlling public recreation programs. See Stephen Hardy, *How Boston Played: Sport, Recreation, and Community, 1865–1915* (Boston, 1982); Francis Couvares, "The Triumph of Commerce: Class Culture and Mass Culture in Pittsburgh," in Michael H. Frisch and Daniel J. Walkowitz, eds., *Working-Class America* (Urbana, Ill., 1983); and Roy Rosenzweig, *Eight Hours for What We Will: Workers and Leisure in an Industrial City, 1870–1920* (Cambridge, 1983). These approaches are discussed in Stephen Hardy and Alan G. Ingham, "Games, Structures, and Agency: Historians of the American Play Movement," *Journal of Social History* 17 (Winter 1983): 285–301.

29. Glassberg, "Restoring a 'Forgotten Childhood,'" pp. 351–68; J. M. Golby and A. W. Purdue, *The Civilization of the Crowd* (New York, 1985), pp. 17–40.

CHAPTER THREE

1. Frederick J. Hoffman, Charles Allen, and Carolyn T. Ulrich, *The Little Magazine* (Princeton, 1946). I have chosen not to consider *The Masses* in this chapter because the themes of its occasional criticism of popular culture were most fully developed the Left journals considered in Chapter 5.

2. Ibid., pp. 86–92; G. A. Janssens, "The *Dial* and the *Seven Arts*," *Papers on Language and Literature* 41 (Fall 1968): 442–58.

3. Editorial, *Seven Arts* 1 (November 1916): 52–53. The 1917 editorial appeared in *Seven Arts* 2 (May 1917): vii; quoted in Dickran Tashjian, *Skyscraper Primitives: Dada and the American Avant-Garde 1910–1925* (Middletown, Conn., 1975), p. 247.

4. Van Wyck Brooks, *The Wine of the Puritans* (London, 1908), quoted in James Hoopes, *Van Wyck Brooks, in Search of American Culture* (Amherst, Mass., 1977), p. 60. Brooks's theory is discussed in Hoopes, *Van Wyck Brooks*, pp. 59–68. On the anti-American atmosphere at Harvard, see Hoopes's discussion of the university years in Brooks's memoir, *Scenes and Portraits* (New York, 1954), pp. 102–12, and Henry May, *The End of American Innocence: A Study of the First Years of Our Own Time, 1912–1917* (New York, 1959), pp. 56–62.

5. Van Wyck Brooks, *America's Coming-of-Age* (New York, 1915), p. 118; Hoopes, *Van Wyck Brooks*, pp. 99–101. For the development of the "Highbrow" and "Lowbrow" terms, see Lawrence Levine, *Highbrow/Lowbrow: The Emergence of Cultural Hierarchy in America* (Cambridge, Mass., 1988), pp. 221–23.

6. Brooks, *Coming-of-Age*, pp. 16–17.

7. Paul L. Rosenfeld, "The American Composer," *Seven Arts* 1 (November 1916): 90–93. An indication of Brooks's influence was that at the inception of the *Seven Arts*, Waldo Frank wrote to him that *America's Coming-of-Age* served as the editors' critical inspiration. See Hoopes, *Van Wyck Brooks*, p. 110.

8. James Oppenheim, Editorial, *Seven Arts* 1 (December 1916): 153–54.

9. Ernest Bloch, "Man and Music," trans. Waldo Frank, *Seven Arts* 1 (March 1917): 495, 502, 501, 495. On the persistence of aesthetic idealism among the cultural radicals, see James Hoopes, "The Culture of Progressivism: Croly, Lippman, Brooks, Bourne, and the Idea of American Artistic Decadence," *Clio* 7 (Fall 1977): 91–111; and Wilfred McClay, "Two Versions of the Genteel Tradition: Santayana and Brooks," *New England Quarterly* 55 (September 1982): esp. 381.

10. Harold Stearns, "A Poor Thing, But Our Own," *Seven Arts* 1 (March 1917): 520, 515–19.

11. Randolph S. Bourne, "The Heart of the People," *New Republic* 3 (3 July 1915): 233, reprinted in Bourne, *War and the Intellectuals, Collected Essays 1915–1919*, ed. Carl Resek (New York, 1964), pp. 171–74. Quotations appear on pp. 173–74, 171, 173.

12. Randolph S. Bourne, "Trans-National America," *Atlantic Monthly* 118 (July 1916): 86–97, reprinted in Bourne, *War and the Intellectuals*, pp. 107–23. Quotations appear on pp. 114, 113.

13. Frontispiece, *Little Review* 3 (August 1916); Anderson further explained the "Life for Art's sake" theme in the August 1916 issue, writing, "Life takes care of itself, rolls on from the first push, then falls over the edge. Art uses up all the life it can get—and remains forever." See Anderson, "A Real Magazine," p. 1.

14. Margaret C. Anderson, "What the Public Doesn't Want," *Little Review* 4 (August 1917): 22, 20; Ezra Pound, Editorial, *Little Review* 4 (May 1917): 6; Pound, "Cooperation," *Little Review* 5 (July 1918): 54–55. The cover slogan was Pound's suggestion, according to a comment by Jane Heap. See Mary Widney, "The Public Taste," *Little Review* 7 (July–August 1920): 23. Pound, in his earlier position as foreign editor of *Poetry* magazine, had denounced the notion that poetry was "made to entertain." It was merely flattery for "the mob," Pound wrote, "to tell them that their importance is so great that the solace of lonely men, and the lordliest of arts, was created for their amusement." See Pound, "This Constant Preaching to the Mob," *Poetry* 8 (June 1916): 144–45.

15. Israel Solon, "The Writer and His Job," *Little Review* 5 (June 1918): 34, 32, 34.

16. Jane Heap, "The 'Art Season,'" *Little Review* 8 (Spring 1922): 59; Heap reply to Widney, "Public Taste," *Little Review* 7 (July–August 1920): 23; Heap reply in "The Reader Critic," *Little Review* 5 (July 1918): 58. Ezra Pound had similarly objected to *Poetry* magazine's use of Walt Whitman's phrase, "To have great poetry, we must first have great audiences," as its motto. See his exchange with Harriet Monroe, "The Audience," *Poetry* 5 (October 1914): 29–32.

17. R. J. Coady, "American Art," *Soil* 1 (January 1917): 55, 56; Coady, "American Art," pp. 3–4. The title of the magazine apparently came from Coady's expression in the December 1916 issue that American art "has grown out of the soil and through the race and will continue to grow." Later he wrote, "Art does not drop from the clouds; on the contrary, I think, it begins with planting potatoes." See Coady, "The Indeps," *Soil* 1 (July 1917): 202.

18. Editor's Note, *Soil* 1 (December 1916): 42. Appearing in *Soil's* first number were Nicholas Carter, "The Pursuit of the Lucky Clew"; Adam Hull Shirk, "The Dime Novel as Literature"; J.B., "Bert Williams"; Charles Chaplin, "Making Fun"; Robert Coady, "Censoring the Motion Picture"; and J. P. McGowan, "The Motion Picture."

19. The word "Dada" means a variety of things in different languages ("yes, yes" in Rumanian and "rocking horse" in French, for instance). But Tristan Tzara, a leader of the movement, insisted that these references were all nonsense, intentionally foolish. "DADA MEANS NOTHING." Tashjian, *Skyscraper Primitives*, pp. 12, 9.

20. Will Bray [Matthew Josephson], "Apollinaire: Or Let Us Be Troubadours," *Secession* 1 (Spring 1922): 11. This pen name is attributed to Josephson in David Shi, *Matthew Josephson: Bourgeois Bohemian* (New Haven, Conn., 1981), p. 295.

21. Matthew Josephson, "The Great American Billposter," *Broom* 3 (November 1922): 305, 309; Matthew Josephson, "Made in America," *Broom* 2 (June 1922): 269, 266, 270. The *Little Review* had adopted a similar aesthetic by 1923.

22. The prewar efforts at social activism through cultural criticism were also continued by Van Wyck Brooks in the 1920s. He tried to maintain the *Seven Arts* tradition in his position as literary editor of a new magazine, the *Freeman*.

23. On the combined radicalisms, see James Burkhart Gilbert, *Writers and Partisans* (New York, 1968), pp. 8–47; Daniel Aaron, *Writers on the Left* (New York, 1977).

24. Comment, *Dial* 70 (January 1921): 122–23. Because these two are generally considered the most important cultural journals of the late 1910s and 1920s, the relationship between the *Dial* and the *Seven Arts* has been a source of scholarly contention. There were certain obvious continuities between them. For instance, Paul Rosenfeld joined the *Dial* as music editor after the demise of the *Seven Arts*, Randolph Bourne was slated to become the political editor of the *Dial* until his death in the flu epidemic of 1918, and Van Wyck Brooks was recognized with the *Dial's* annual award for excellence in American letters in 1924. But in the most important matters of editorial posture and critical policy, the break between the two journals was far more apparent. For the debate over the magazines' relationship, see William Wasserstrom, *The Time of the "Dial"* (Syracuse, N.Y., 1963); Nicholas Joost, *Scofield Thayer and the "Dial"* (Carbondale, Ill., 1964); and G. A. M. Janssens, *The American Literary Review: A Critical History 1920–1950* (The Hague, 1968), pp. 32–89. Joost's and Janssens's interpretations of the discontinuities between the reviews is supported by Lewis

Mumford, "On the *Dial*," *New York Review of Books* 2 (20 February 1964): 3–5.

25. Comment, *Dial* 73 (August 1922): 240; W. C. Blum [James Sibley Watson], "American Letter," *Dial* 70 (May 1921): 565, 563, 564, 566; Comment, *Dial* 75 (September 1923): 311–12.

26. Comment, *Dial* 74 (April 1923): 417; Comment, *Dial* 75 (December 1923): 615; Blum [Watson], "American Letter," p. 563; W. C. Blum [Watson], "American Letter," *Dial* 71 (September 1921): 347; T. S. Eliot, "London Letter," *Dial* 73 (June 1922): 94–96; Scofield Thayer, "Gladiators, Brown Skins, et Cetera," *Dial* 71 (August 1921): 245–49; Edmund Wilson, Jr., "The Theatre," *Dial* 74 (April 1923): 421–22, and "The Theatre," *Dial* 75 (September 1923): 309.

27. Scofield Thayer, Comment, *Dial* 70 (April 1921): 488, 489.

28. Comment, *Dial* 74 (April 1923): 418, 419, 417; Blum, "American Letter," *Dial* (May 1921), p. 563; Thayer, "Gladiators," p. 248.

29. Edmund Wilson, Jr., review of *The Seven Lively Arts*, by Gilbert Seldes, *Dial* 77 (September 1924), reprinted in Wilson, *The Shores of Light* (New York, 1952), p. 164. On Seldes's reputation, see also Reuel Denney, "The Discovery of Popular Culture," in Robert E. Spiller and Eric Larrabee, eds., *American Perspectives* (Cambridge, Mass., 1961), p. 167; and Paul Buhle, "Introduction: The 1960s Meet the 1980s," in Buhle, ed., *Popular Culture in America* (Minneapolis, 1987), p. xvi.

30. Gilbert Seldes, *The Seven Lively Arts* (1924; reprint, New York, 1957), p. 13.

31. Ibid., pp. 104, 103, 31, 181–82, 194, 35–37, 207, 264, 98, 99. Seldes partially recanted his slighting of the black jazz artists in the notes he appended to the 1957 edition of the book.

CHAPTER FOUR

1. Ernest W. Burgess, introduction to *The Taxi-Dance Hall: A Sociological Study in Commercialized Recreation and City Life*, by Paul G. Cressey (Chicago, 1932), p. xiii. (Emphasis in original.) On intellectuals' concern with "civilization" in the 1920s, see Warren Susman, *Culture as History* (New York, 1984), pp. 105–21.

2. C. Wright Mills, "The Professional Ideology of Social Pathologists," *American Journal of Sociology* 49 (September 1943), reprinted in Irving Louis Horowitz, ed., *Power, Politics, and People: The Collected Essays of C. Wright Mills* (New York, 1963), p. 525.

3. Paul Boyer et al., *The Enduring Vision* (Lexington, Mass., 1993), pp. 812, 814, 877–78.

4. Maurice R. Davie, *Problems of City Life: A Study in Urban Sociology* (New York, 1932), pp. 585–86; Nels Anderson and Eduard Lindeman, *Urban Sociology* (New York, 1928), p. 170; Arthur Evans Wood, *Community Problems* (New York, 1928), pp. 405, 406. See also Stuart Alfred Queen and Delbert Martin Mann,

Social Pathology (New York, 1925), pp. 645–48; and Edward Alsworth Ross, *The Outlines of Sociology* (New York, 1933), p. 334. Ross's book was a condensation of his 1920 text, *Principles of Sociology* (New York, 1920).

5. Henry B. Chamberlain, "Recreation and Crime," *New York Times*, 28 May 1922, quoted in Wood, *Community Problems*, p. 280; Queen and Mann, *Social Pathology*, pp. 646–47.

6. Wood, *Community Problems*, p. 279; Queen and Mann, *Social Pathology*, p. 647; Davie, *Problems of City Life*, p. 571. Wood also wrote that, under modern industrial conditions, the worker "becomes a machine" and "the human being is found to be shut in by the material framework of civilization." He explained that improving leisure was crucial because it was futile to hope for change in industry: "Even Mahatma Gandhi drives a Ford!" See pp. 285–86.

7. Wood, *Community Problems*, p. 407; Davie, *Problems of City Life*, p. 624.

8. Wood, *Community Problems*, p. 409; Davie, *Problems of City Life*, p. 624.

9. Nels Anderson and Eduard Lindeman's introduction to *Urban Sociology* disparages the "protester," who is "Never willing to accept the city as he finds it. . . . Science does not need these objectives; the search for facts is its own reward." *Urban Sociology*, p. xxvii; James F. Short, *The Social Fabric of the Metropolis* (Chicago, 1971), pp. xviii–xx.

10. Queen and Mann, *Social Pathology*, p. 646; Anderson and Lindeman, *Urban Sociology*, pp. 164–65; Davie, *Problems of City Life*, p. 579; Ross, *Outlines of Sociology*, p. 334.

11. Davie, *Problems of City Life*, pp. 581–82, 579–80.

12. Ordway Tead, *Instincts in Industry: A Study of Working-Class Psychology* (Boston, 1918), p. 174; Davie, *Problems of City Life*, pp. 604–5; Wood, *Community Problems*, pp. 283–84, 405–6; Robert A. Woods, *The Neighborhood in Nation Building* (Boston, 1923), p. 124, quoted in Wood, *Community Problems*, p. 283.

13. Garth Jowett, *Film: The Democratic Art* (Boston, 1976), pp. 220, 225. (Emphasis in original.)

14. Maria Ward Lambin, "Report of the Public Dance Hall Committee of the San Francisco Center of the California Civic League of Women Voters" (1924), quoted in Wood, *Community Problems*, p. 421; Wood, *Community Problems*, pp. 414, 415. For discussion of Lambin's report and another she conducted of New York City dance facilities, see Wood, *Community Problems*, pp. 416–21.

15. LeRoy E. Bowman and Maria Ward Lambin, "Evidences of Social Relations as Seen in the Types of New York City Dance Halls," *Journal of Social Forces* 3 (January 1925): 290; Wood, *Community Problems*, p. 418; Davie, *Problems of City Life*, pp. 597, 599.

16. Elon H. Moore, "Public Dance Halls in a Small City," *Sociology and Social Research* 14 (January–February 1930): 256, 263, 258–60.

17. Alfred H. Lloyd, "Ages of Leisure," *American Journal of Sociology* 28 (September 1922): 176. An indication of the growing interest in the issue is Rolf Meyer-

sohn's "A Comprehensive Bibliography on Leisure, 1900–1958," in Eric Larrabee and Rolf Meyersohn, eds., *Mass Leisure* (Glencoe, Ill., 1958), pp. 389–419. This purports to list, by decade, all works on leisure written in English. There are 49 citations in the 1910s, 200 in the 1920s, and more than 400 in the 1930s.

18. Clarence E. Rainwater, "Socialized Leisure," *Journal of Applied Sociology* 7 (May–June 1923): 256; Weaver Pangburn, "The Worker's Leisure and His Individuality," *American Journal of Sociology* 27 (January 1922): 434. On modern work, see Rainwater, "Socialized Leisure," p. 255, and Lloyd, "Ages of Leisure," pp. 168, 171; Joseph K. Hartt, "The Place of Leisure in Life," *Annals of the American Academy of Political and Social Science* 118 (March 1925): 114.

19. George B. Cutten, *Threat of Leisure* (New Haven, Conn., 1926), pp. 75, 7, 12, 66, 67–68, 70, 69, 110, 96, 72, 71, 70.

20. Margaret M. Caffrey, *Ruth Benedict* (Austin, 1989), pp. 120–37.

21. Stuart Chase, *Mexico: A Study of Two Americas* (New York, 1931); Richard Pells, *Radical Visions and American Dreams* (New York, 1973), pp. 101–2; Margaret Mead, *Coming of Age in Samoa* (New York, 1928); Ruth Benedict, *Patterns of Culture* (Boston, 1934); Caffrey, *Ruth Benedict*, pp. 145–46, 206, 210–13; Robert Redfield, *Tepoztlan: A Mexican Village* (Chicago, 1930); Reuel Denney, "The Discovery of Popular Culture," in Robert E. Spiller and Eric Larrabee, eds., *American Perspectives* (Cambridge, Mass., 1961), p. 170; Susman, *Culture as History*, pp. 155–56; George E. Marcus and Michael J. Fischer, *Anthropology as Cultural Critique* (Chicago, 1986), pp. 158–59, 130. The chapters of comparison between American and Samoan child-rearing practices in Mead's book were added at the request of her publishers. The book became a best-seller. See Marcus and Fischer, *Anthropology as Cultural Critique*, p. 158.

22. Marcus and Fischer, *Anthropology as Cultural Critique*, p. 129. This new moral critique of modern society is discussed in Daniel Horowitz, *The Morality of Spending: Attitudes toward the Consumer Society in America, 1875–1940* (Baltimore, 1985), pp. 134–65.

23. Robert S. Lynd and Helen Merrell Lynd, *Middletown: A Study in American Culture* (New York, 1929), pp. 21, 5.

24. Ibid., pp. 271–73, 278, 283, 285, 287, 309–10, 267–68, 251–63.

25. On the "Chicago School" see Fred H. Mathews, *Quest for an American Sociology* (Montreal, 1977); Short, *Social Fabric of the Metropolis*; Robert E. L. Faris, *Chicago Sociology, 1920–1932* (Chicago, 1967). On Robert Lynd's relation to this sociology, see Richard Wightman Fox, "Epitaph for Middletown," in Richard Wightman Fox and T. J. Jackson Lears, eds., *The Culture of Consumption* (New York, 1983), p. 123.

26. The liberalism of the Chicago School is discussed in Dennis Smith, *The Chicago School: A Liberal Critique of Capitalism* (London, 1988).

27. Louis Wirth, "Urbanism as a Way of Life," *American Journal of Sociology* 44 (July 1938): 1–2, 5, 7. Although the general patterns suggested in the city cul-

ture analysis were not new—drawing from the models of Ferdinand Tönnies, Émile Durkheim, Max Weber, and Charles Horton Cooley, for example—the Chicago scholars, with their ethnographic fieldwork, presented their findings as theoretical breakthroughs.

28. Robert Park, "The City: Suggestions for the Investigation of Human Behavior in the Urban Environment," *American Journal of Sociology* 20 (March 1915), quoted in Morton White and Lucia White, *The Intellectual versus the City* (Cambridge, Mass., 1962), pp. 166–67; Andy Lees, *Cities Perceived* (New York, 1985), p. 301. For the titles of the studies, see Cressey, *Taxi-Dance Hall*, flyleaf; and Lees, *Cities Perceived*, p. 300.

29. Wirth, "Urbanism as a Way of Life," p. 22; Robert Park, "Community Organization and the Romantic Temper," *Journal of Social Forces* 3 (May 1925): 675; Daniel J. Czitrom, *Media and the American Mind* (Chapel Hill, N.C., 1982), pp. 118–19; White and White, *The Intellectual versus the City*, pp. 165–66.

30. Burgess, introduction to Cressey, *Taxi-Dance Hall*, pp. xiii–xv.

31. Cressey, *Taxi-Dance Hall*, pp. 282, 177, 262, 287.

32. On the development of social theory models, and the assumptions inherent in ideal-type methods, see Thomas Bender, *Community and Social Change in America* (Baltimore, 1978), pp. 15–43.

33. The "de-folked" term is from George M. Foster, "What Is Folk Culture?," *American Anthropologist* 55 (April–June 1953): 162.

34. Bender, *Community and Social Change in America*, p. 25.

CHAPTER FIVE

1. Louis Adamic, "What the Proletariat Reads," *Saturday Review of Literature* 11 (1 December 1934): 321; Myra Page, "Dope—for the Workers," *Daily Worker*, 17 January 1931, p. 4. The *Daily Worker*'s circulation, Page estimated optimistically, approached 200,000.

2. Robert Forsythe [Kyle Crichton], "A Kind Word for Hollywood," *New Masses* 12 (3 July 1934): 44; Harry Alan Potamkin, *The Eyes of the Movie* (New York, 1934), reprinted in Lewis Jacobs, ed., *The Compound Cinema: The Film Writings of Harry Alan Potamkin* (New York, 1977), pp. 243–69; quotation appears on p. 251.

3. Pauline Zutringer, "Machine Art Is Bourgeois," *New Masses* 4 (February 1929): 31; Paul Peters, "Building a New Theatre," *Student Review* 3 (Summer 1934): 19, and Ben Blake, "Red Theatres at Work," *Student Review* 2 (April 1933): 6; Ashley Pettis, "Two Worlds of Music," *New Masses* 8 (February 1933): 12.

4. A concise explanation of the Soviet developments is in Eric Homberger, "Proletarian Literature and the John Reed Clubs 1929–1935," *American Studies* 13 (1979): 221–44; Edward J. Brown, *The Proletarian Episode in Russian Literature*,

1928–1932 (1950; reprint, New York, 1971). For the debate over Soviet influence in American Communism, see Theodore Draper's review essays, "American Communism Revisited," *New York Review of Books*, 9 May 1985, pp. 32–40, and "The Popular Front Revisited," *New York Review of Books*, 30 May 1985, pp. 44–50; Gary Gerstle, "Mission from Moscow: American Communism in the 1930s," *Reviews in American History* 12 (December 1984): 559–66.

5. Irwin Granich [Michael Gold], "Towards Proletarian Art," *Liberator* 4 (February 1921): 21–23. On Gold's early career, see Daniel Aaron, *Writers on the Left* (New York, 1977), pp. 84–86; James Gilbert, *Writers and Partisans: A History of Literary Radicalism in America* (New York, 1968), pp. 78–79. Aaron explains the pen name on p. 409, n. 33.

6. Michael Gold, "Two Critics in a Bar-Room," *Liberator* 4 (September 1921): 30.

7. Raymond Williams, *Marxism and Culture* (Oxford, 1977), esp. pp. 108–14. The "alternative" culture model is applied in Roy Rosenzweig, *Eight Hours for What We Will: Workers and Leisure in an Industrial City, 1870–1920* (Cambridge, 1983), esp. p. 223. In the latter 1920s and 1930s, there were occasional complaints from within the Party about the narrowness of Gold's kind of approach to culture. Robert Wolf wrote in the *New Masses* that "the Communist movement in this country has no more use for a great artist than a regimental bugler has for a symphonic orchestral score," while Henry George Weiss criticized the magazine's poetry for not being understandable ("people say it 'don't mean anything' ") like that of Industrial Workers of the World bard Joe Hill. Wolf, "Literature and Revolution," *New Masses* 4 (January 1929): 19; Weiss, "Give Us Poems for Workers," *New Masses* 5 (July 1929): 22, and "Poetry and Revolution," *New Masses* 5 (October 1929): 9. See also Ralph Cheyney, "On New Program for Writers," *New Masses* 5 (February 1930): 21; J. P. Neets, "Let Us Master Our Art!," *New Masses* 6 (July 1930): 23.

8. Michael Gold, "Thoughts of a Great Thinker," *Liberator* 5 (March 1922): 24. For the Soviet line, see S. Frederick Starr, *Red and Hot: The Fate of Jazz in the Soviet Union* (New York, 1983).

9. Robin E. Dunbar, "Mammonart and Communist Art," *Daily Worker*, 23 May 1925, Special Magazine Supplement; Robert Minor, "Art as a Weapon in the Class Struggle," *Daily Worker*, 22 September 1925, p. 5; Homberger, "Proletarian Literature and John Reed Clubs," pp. 228–29.

10. Robert Wolf, "What There Isn't and Why Not," *New Masses* 3 (February 1928): 18; Theodore Draper, *American Communism and Soviet Russia* (1960; reprint, New York, 1977), pp. 190–91.

11. Homberger, "Proletarian Literature and John Reed Clubs," pp. 229–30, 232–33; Helen A. Harrison, "John Reed Club Artists and the New Deal: Radical Responses to Roosevelt's 'Peaceful Revolution,' " *Prospects* 5 (1980): 242–43. John Reed was a radical journalist of the World War I era who, for many, epitomized the revolutionary spirit. He wrote *Ten Days That Shook the World* (New York,

1919), the classic account of the Soviet revolution. By 1934, there were thirty John Reed Clubs in the United States. The description of the militant Soviet cultural line is quoted in Katerina Clark, "Utopian Anthropology as a Context for Stalinist Literature," in Robert C. Tucker, ed., *Stalinism: Essays in Historical Interpretation* (New York, 1977), p. 183.

12. Before the Third Period, even sporadic criticisms of mass amusements, such as an article about the origins of motion pictures that described contemporary films as instruments of class domination, did not appear in a context suggesting a blanket condemnation of commercial forms. Next to the movie article, and flanked by stories about a construction worker drowned in cement, employers' obliviousness to the dangers of iron workers throwing red-hot rivets, and the demands of the Stage Hands' Union for a new wage scale, was a picture of Dorothy Sands, captioned: "This charmer is creating quite a hit with her impersonations in the 'Grand Street Follies' at the Booth Theatre." See the *Daily Worker*, 3 August 1928, p. 4.

13. Statement, *Experimental Cinema* 1 (February 1931); Lewis Jacobs, "The New Cinema, a Preface to Film Form," *Experimental Cinema* 1 (February 1930): 13; Frederick Hoffman, Charles Allen, and Carolyn Ulrich, *The Little Magazine* (Princeton, 1946), p. 385. Jacobs's feelings about the movies' popular subject matter and its typical treatment were clear in the 1930 piece: "In America the cinema has become a parasitic medium conditioned for sex nomads and daydreamers. Its plastics are projected upon the most melodramatic aspects of behavior; a fetish is made of the cinema's fact recording powers, and its celluloid marionettes are deified. Sociologically, the American film is superficial; its environments are entombed in sentimental applications, and the conventions of its relations (psychological as well as cineplastic) are an imposition."

14. Lewis Jacobs, "Eisenstein," *Experimental Cinema* 1 (February 1931): 4.

15. For Potamkin's background and reputation as a film critic, see Lewis Jacobs's introduction to Jacobs, ed., *Compound Cinema*, esp. p. xxv; V. F. Calverton, *The Liberation of American Literature* (New York, 1932); David Platt, "The Screen," *New Masses* 10 (27 February 1934): 30. The fervor of Potamkin's newfound militancy is indicated by his experience as an American delegate to the 1930 world conference on proletarian culture. He had to be reprimanded by the organization's general secretary for his "feverish radicalism" after insisting, against a looser Soviet line, that there must be a pure revolutionary, proletarian base for cultural efforts, to the exclusion even of those bourgeois figures most sympathetic to the leftist efforts. See Homberger, "Proletarian Literature and the John Reed Clubs," p. 239.

16. Harry Alan Potamkin, *The Eyes of the Movie*, in Jacobs, ed., *Compound Cinema*, pp. 244, 243; and "Holy Hollywood," in Samuel D. Schmalhausen, ed., *Behold America* (New York, 1931), reprinted in Jacobs, ed., *Compound Cinema*, pp. 239, 238–39, 232.

17. Philip Sterling, "Songs of War," *New Masses* 7 (December 1931): 18-20.

18. Michael Gold, "Toward an American Revolutionary Culture," *New Masses* 7 (July 1931): 12. Gold's article was also concerned with indicting the popular news purveyors who were the chief Red-baiters of the era: "The people want news—they read newspapers—it is a normal taste—but the capitalists who own newspapers have fastened the habit of cheap crime and sports news upon the people. Mass degradation pays—it forms a habit—the slaves demand their daily dope—it is given to them by the Hearst and Scripps coke peddlers—by the tabloids." The addiction metaphor continued to be prevalent in mass culture criticism through the postwar decades and is still frequently used.

19. Homberger, "Proletarian Literature and the John Reed Clubs," pp. 231, 243-44; Harrison, "John Reed Club Artists and the New Deal," pp. 248-49; Clark, "Utopian Anthropology," pp. 184-85; Irving Howe and Lewis Coser, *The American Communist Party* (New York, 1957), pp. 319-25.

20. Earl Browder, "Communism and Literature," in Henry Hart, ed., *American Writers' Congress* (New York, 1935), pp. 68-69.

21. Donald Ogden Stewart, "The Horrible Example," and "The Second Writers' Congress," both in Henry Hart, ed., *The Writer in a Changing World* (New York, 1937), pp. 119, 256; Lawrence H. Schwartz, *Marxism and Culture: The CPUSA and Aesthetics in the 1930s* (Port Washington, N.Y., 1980), p. 62.

22. Hope Hale, quoted in Donald Ogden Stewart, *Fighting Words* (New York, 1940), pp. 46, 43, 44.

23. Stewart, *Fighting Words*, pp. 79-80, 88.

24. The "sellout" thesis was advanced, beginning very early in the Popular Front period, by Marxist critics of the Communist Party. Its most vociferous partisans, the "New York Intellectuals," are discussed in Chapter 6.

25. On advertising, see Roland Marchand, *Advertising the American Dream* (Berkeley, 1985), esp. pp. 52-63. The spread of motion pictures and nightlife are treated in Lary May, "Making the American Way: Moderne Theatres, Audiences, and the Film Industry 1929-1945," *Prospects* 12 (1987): 89-124; and Lewis A. Erenberg, "From New York to Middletown: Repeal and the Legitimization of Nightlife in the Great Depression," *American Quarterly* 38 (Winter 1986): 761-78. May expressly makes the case for this era as the beginning of a nationwide mass culture on pp. 107-11. The change in the 1930s is best understood when compared to the studies of earlier eras by each of these authors: Lary May, *Screening Out the Past: The Birth of Mass Culture and the Motion Picture Industry* (New York, 1980), and Lewis A. Erenberg, *Steppin' Out: New York Nightlife and the Transformation of American Culture, 1890-1930* (Chicago, 1981). The radio statistics are cited in Alice Goldfarb Marquis, "Radio Grows Up," *American Heritage* 34 (August-September 1983): 70; "Size of the Radio Industry in the United States," in Wilbur Schramm, ed., *Mass Communications*, 2d ed. (Urbana, Ill., 1960), p. 196; William C. Ackerman, "The Dimensions of American Broadcast-

ing," *Public Opinion Quarterly* 9 (Spring 1945): 1–18; Leo Lowenthal, "Biographies in Popular Magazines," in Paul Lazarsfeld and Frank Stanton, eds., *Radio Research 1942–1943* (New York, 1944), pp. 507–48.

26. Malcolm Cowley, *Exile's Return* (New York, 1934), esp. pp. 3–9, and the lists of writers' birthdates, pp. 311–16. For the comparison of the Stearns volumes, see Charles C. Alexander, *Here the Country Lies* (Bloomington, Ind., 1980), p. 224.

27. Charles Seeger, "A Program for Proletarian Composers," *Daily Worker*, 16 January 1934, p. 5, quoted in Richard A. Reuss, "The Roots of American Left-Wing Interest in Folksong," *Labor History* 12 (Spring 1971): 270. Reuss's article is also the best source on the development of the political songbooks. The Collective was made up mainly of younger composers such as Henry Cowell and Elie Siegmeister, though Aaron Copland was also affiliated with the group. See Reuss, "Roots of Left-Wing Interest," p. 269, and "Folk Music and Social Conscience: The Musical Odyssey of Charles Seeger," *Western Folklore* 38 (October 1979): 221–38; David K. Dunaway, "Unsung Songs of Protest: The Composers Collective of New York," *New York Folklore* 5 (Summer 1979): 1–19, and "Charles Seeger and Carl Sands: The Composers' Collective Years," *Ethnomusicology* 24 (May 1980): 159–68. Seeger wrote under the name "Carl Sands."

28. Worker's Music League, *Workers Song Book* (New York, 1934); Composers Collective, *Songs of the People* (New York, 1937); Reuss, "Roots of Left-Wing Interest," pp. 271–73. The battle for proletarian purity in the Third Period produced odd situations. Reuss notes that when the Workers Music League produced its own *Red Song Book* in 1932 (when the Collective was still being organized), containing a number of popular-tune strike songs, a review in the organization's own journal panned them for their lack of musical sophistication. See Reuss, "Roots of Left-Wing Interest," pp. 270–71. Marc Blitzstein, who wrote the musical "The Cradle Will Rock," was one member of the Collective who embraced popular music. Seeger also made a remarkable switch to adopt the folk genre by the mid-1930s. He became assistant director of the folk and social music program of the Works Progress Administration's Federal Music Project. His son Pete, of course, became a central figure in American folk music. See Dunaway, "Unsung Songs of Protest," pp. 9, 13; Reuss, "Musical Odyssey of Charles Seeger," p. 234.

29. L. E. Swift [Elie Siegmeister], "The Auvilles' Songs," *New Masses* 13 (5 February 1935): 28. Reuss, "Roots of Left-Wing Interest," p. 276.

30. Michael Gold, "Change the World!," *Daily Worker*, 2 January 1936, p. 5; Carl Sands, "Songs by Auvilles Mark Step Ahead in Workers' Music," *Daily Worker*, 15 January 1935, p. 5; Reuss, "Roots of Left-Wing Interest," pp. 276–77.

31. For the particular developments of the Left's folk music sensibilities, see R. Serge Denisoff, "The Proletarian Renascence: The Folkness of the Ideological Folk," *Journal of American Folklore* 82 (January–March 1969): 51–65. The

Almanac Singers, an ever-changing group of folk singers, kept up the criticism of popular commercial music in the 1940s, writing in 1941, for instance, that "people know inwardly that these 'hits' are no part of their working, slaving, worrying, and no solution to their troubles." Almanac Singers, "Songs of Work, Trouble, Hope," *People's World*, 28 October 1941, p. 5, quoted in Denisoff, "Proletarian Renascence," p. 53.

32. John Lomax and Alan Lomax suggested the increased interest in folk forms in *American Ballads and Folk Songs* (New York, 1934), esp. pp. xxv–xxvi; "Fiddling to Henry Ford," *Literary Digest* 88 (2 January 1926): 33–34, 36, 38; Alexander, *Here the Country Lies*, pp. 207–10.

33. Robert W. Gordon, "Report of the Archive of American Folk Song" (10 May 1932), reprinted in Debora G. Kodish, " 'A National Project with Many Workers,' Robert Winslow Gordon and the Archive of American Folk Song," *Quarterly Journal of the Library of Congress* 35 (October 1978): 232; Joan Shelley Rubin, *Constance Rourke and American Culture* (Chapel Hill, N.C., 1980); Samuel I. Bellman, *Constance M. Rourke* (Boston, 1981). On the interplay between commercial forms and "folk" music, see also Norman Cohen, "Tin Pan Alley's Contribution to Folk Music," *Western Folklore* 29 (January 1970): 9–20. Rourke, it should be noted, was not wholly uncritical about the effects of mass media upon communication. She did, however, see great potential for technology in popularizing the arts.

34. Thomas H. Uzzell, "The Love Pulps," *Scribner's* 103 (April 1938): 36–41; Harland Manchester, "True Stories," *Scribner's* 104 (August 1938): 25–29, 60; Merle Curti, "Dime Novels and the American Tradition," *Yale Review* 26 (June 1937): 761–78; Charles Seeger, "Music in America," *Magazine of Art* 31 (July 1938): 409–11, 435–36; Sigmund Spaeth, "Dixie, Harlem, and Tin Pan Alley," *Scribner's* 99 (January 1936): 23–26. The general greater willingness to accept the entertainments as legitimate expressions of America is discussed in Alexander, *Here the Country Lies*, pp. 179, 230–31.

35. On the Kharkov resolution, see "International Chronicle: America," *Literature of the World Revolution* 3 (1931): 152. On the Communist Party's policies toward blacks, see Mark I. Solomon, *Red and Black: Communism and Afro-Americans, 1929–1935* (New York, 1988); Draper, *American Communism and Soviet Russia*, pp. 315–56; Howe and Coser, *The American Communist Party*, pp. 204–16.

36. Starr, *Red and Hot*, pp. 82–96. Gorky's article, "The Music of the Gross," appeared in *Pravda*, 18 April 1928.

37. Michael Gold, "Notes of the Month," *New Masses* 5 (February 1930): 3. The Workers Cultural Federation piece is "Art Is a Weapon!," *New Masses* 7 (August 1931): 12. The notion of the "pure" victim that has been applied to African Americans is skillfully rebuffed in Lawrence W. Levine, *Black Culture and Black Consciousness* (Oxford, 1977).

38. Charles Edward Smith, "Class Content of Jazz Music," *Daily Worker*, 21 October 1933, quoted in Starr, *Red and Hot*, p. 99. On the doctrine of the "two jazzes," see Starr, *Red and Hot*, pp. 96–99.

39. Another of the Communists' approaches to the problem of separating blacks and jazz was to ignore popular music while heralding expressly militant black protest songs. The *New Masses* presented an article concerning African Americans almost every month in the early 1930s, but wrote nothing directly addressing their popular music as a cultural expression. A succinct overview of the literature on early jazz is in Russell Lynes, *The Lively Audience: A Social History of Visual and Performing Arts in America, 1890–1950* (New York, 1985), pp. 103–15.

40. "The Communist Party," *Fortune*, 10 September 1934, p. 73. On the 1930 concert, see Mark Naison, *Communists in Harlem during the Depression* (Urbana, Ill., 1983), pp. 36–37. The *New Masses* ad appeared in vol. 4, March 1929, p. 31.

CHAPTER SIX

1. Studies of the New York Intellectuals have become numerous, especially in recent years. The most useful general portraits are in James Gilbert, *Writers and Partisans: A History of Literary Radicalism in America* (New York, 1968); Alan M. Wald, *The New York Intellectuals: The Rise and Decline of the Anti-Stalinist Left from the 1930s to the 1980s* (Chapel Hill, N.C., 1987); Terry A. Cooney, *The Rise of the New York Intellectuals: "Partisan Review" and Its Circle* (Madison, Wis., 1986); Alexander Bloom, *Prodigal Sons: The New York Intellectuals and Their World* (New York, 1986). Other useful accounts are in Irving Howe, "The New York Intellectuals: A Chronicle and a Critique," *Commentary*, October 1968, pp. 29–51; S. A. Longstaff, "The New York Family," *Queen's Quarterly* 83 (Winter 1976): 556–73; Grant Webster, "New York Intellectuals: The Bourgeois Avant-Garde," in his *The Republic of Letters: A History of Postwar American Literary Opinion* (Baltimore, 1979), pp. 209–92; and Norman Mailer's critical but suggestive interpretation, "Up the Family Tree," *Partisan Review* 35 (Spring 1968): 234–52. A number of the New Yorkers have written interesting memoirs as well. Alfred Kazin's *Starting Out in the Thirties* (Boston, 1965), Irving Howe's *A Margin of Hope* (San Diego, 1982), and Dwight Macdonald's *Memoirs of a Revolutionist* (New York, 1957) are especially helpful. The Communist Party's proletarian culture program was discussed in Chapter 5.

2. Wallace Phelps [William Phillips] and Philip Rahv, "Problems and Perspectives in Revolutionary Literature," *Partisan Review* 1 (June–July 1934): 3–10.

3. Cooney, *New York Intellectuals*, pp. 15, 39–41; Bloom, *Prodigal Sons*, pp. 26, 74.

4. All of the books about the New York Intellectuals treat the Jewish roots of most, their problems of assimilation, and the appeals of modernism. The most useful on cosmopolitanism is Cooney, *New York Intellectuals*, pp. 67–94;

David A. Hollinger, "Ethnic Diversity, Cosmopolitanism and the Emergence of the American Liberal Intelligentsia," *American Quarterly* 28 (1975): 133–51. The growth of intellectual status in the United States is traced in Burton Bledstein, *The Culture of Professionalism* (New York, 1976).

5. William Phillips, "How *Partisan Review* Began," *Commentary*, December 1976, p. 42; Alan Lelchuk, "Philip Rahv: The Last Years," in Arthur Edelstein, ed., *Images and Ideas in American Culture: The Functions of Criticism: Essays in Memory of Philip Rahv* (Hanover, N.H., 1979), p. 204, quoted in Cooney, *New York Intellectuals*, p. 41.

6. Howe, *Margin of Hope*, p. 9.

7. On the attractions of Communism for the *Partisan Review* group, see Cooney, *New York Intellectuals*, pp. 38–66; Bloom, *Prodigal Sons*, pp. 43–67.

8. Phillips, "How *Partisan Review* Began," p. 43. Irving Howe, though he remained a socialist, was intimately familiar with the philosophy of those who considered themselves to compose the most advanced segments of the Left, and has aptly described the *Partisan Review* ethos. "Modernist writers we admired on principle," he wrote. "It seemed only right that we of one vanguard should tip our hats to the giants of another." Howe, *Margin of Hope*, p. 57.

9. Granville Hicks, "Our Magazines and Their Functions," *New Masses* 12 (18 December 1934), reprinted in Jack Alan Robbins, ed., *Granville Hicks in the "New Masses"* (Port Washington, N.Y., 1974), pp. 263–66. Many political favors were repaid with appointments to the first *Partisan Review* editorial board, but within the first few issues it became apparent that Rahv and Phillips directed the magazine. See Cooney, *New York Intellectuals*, p. 39. Hicks was certainly not the only one, in the 1930s or afterward, disturbed by the New Yorkers' brashness. Accounts of the groups' activities frequently mention their penchant for polemic and their often irritating ambition. The reputation they earned among fellow Communists may be partly suggested by the nickname Rahv and Phillips acquired, "the Bobbsey Twins of Leftist Literature," and one writer's intimation of an authoritarian streak in the New York intelligentsia, describing them as having a "leanin' toward Lenin." See Jack Conroy and Curt Johnson, eds., *Writers in Revolt: The Anvil Anthology* (New York, 1973), p. xviii.

10. Wallace Phelps [William Phillips], "Sensibility and Modern Poetry," *Dynamo* 1 (Summer 1934): 25.

11. Philip Rahv, "How the Waste Land Became a Flower Garden," *Partisan Review* 1 (September–October 1934): 42, 40–41.

12. Wallace Phelps [William Phillips] and Philip Rahv, "Criticism," *Partisan Review* 2 (April–May 1935): 16–25; quotations appear on pp. 17, 18. In an earlier editorial, they similarly noted that revolutionary literature seemed to be divided between the "intellectual" and the "popular" and encouraged writers to bring these strata together by trying to "raise the cultural level of the masses," to the superior sensibility. See Editorial Statement, *Partisan Review* 1 (February–

March 1934): 2. The problem of the misfit between revolutionary modern forms and the apparently antimodern proletariat was left to be solved by the revolution itself. They explained that "great literature grows out of the highest level of a contemporary culture," and that as long as American education was in the hands of capitalists, "the values of such literature will come into conflict with the mental habits of untrained readers." The radical movement, and then the overthrow of capitalism and a new system of intellectual training, they trusted to bring the masses to see the light.

13. Gilbert, *Writers and Partisans*, pp. 158, 168. Cooney, *New York Intellectuals*, pp. 100–102; Bloom, *Prodigal Sons*, pp. 71–72. The three new editors of the revived magazine were contemporaries at Yale: Frederick Dupee, Dwight Macdonald, and George L. K. Morris.

14. In the fall of 1940, a few months after Trotsky was murdered, Macdonald praised him for showing that "intellects, too, could make history." See Dwight Macdonald, "Politics Past," in Macdonald, *Memoirs of a Revolutionist: Essays in Political Criticism* (New York, 1957), p. 15; Macdonald, "Trotsky Is Dead," *Partisan Review* 7 (September–October 1940): 344–45. The relationship between Trotsky and those at *Partisan Review*, especially Macdonald, is discussed in Bloom, *Prodigal Sons*, pp. 107–13.

15. Leon Trotsky, *Literature and Revolution*, trans. Rose Strunsky (New York, 1925), p. 225. For a discussion of Trotsky's cultural views and their reception in the Soviet Union, see Isaac Deutscher, *The Prophet Unarmed — Trotsky: 1921–1927* (1959; reprint, New York 1980), pp. 164–200. An example of Trotsky-style interpretation of bourgeois literature is Philip Rahv, "Dostoevsky and Politics: Notes on 'The Possessed,'" *Partisan Review* 5 (July 1938): 25–36. Criticism of the Soviet regime for Trotsky thus was based to a significant degree on cultural evaluation as well, encouraging the New York Intellectuals' approach. In 1937, both in a book and in a piece written for *Partisan Review*, Trotsky insisted that the arts had to be kept separate from political control, labeling Stalin's program in the arts an historic failure, an "epoch of mediocrities, laureates, and toadies." See Leon Trotsky, *The Revolution Betrayed* (London, 1937), p. 173, quoted in Bloom, *Prodigal Sons*, p. 110; and Trotsky, "Art and Politics," *Partisan Review* 5 (August–September 1938): 3–10.

16. William Phillips and Philip Rahv, "Literature in a Political Decade," in Horace Gregory, ed., *New Letters in America* (New York, 1937), pp. 170–80; quotations appear on pp. 177, 171, 172, 175, 176.

17. Dwight Macdonald, "Laugh and Lie Down," *Partisan Review* 4 (December 1937), pp. 50, 44.

18. Dwight Macdonald, "The Soviet Cinema: 1930–1938," *Partisan Review* 5 (July 1938): 37. (Emphasis in original.)

19. Dwight Macdonald, "The Soviet Cinema: 1930–1938, Part II," *Partisan Review* 5 (August–September 1938): 36, 45–46.

20. The visitor's comment was quoted in a Moscow journal, Macdonald explained. The journal agreed with her evaluation and added, "They have long since been replaced by others of a much higher artistic value."

21. Dwight Macdonald, "Soviet Society and Its Cinema," *Partisan Review* 6 (Winter 1939): 80–95. Macdonald's view was drawn from the theory of Kurt London, in his *The Seven Soviet Arts* (New York, 1938), which argued that the high arts in Russia and throughout the West had for centuries been separated from the masses by social barriers; thus when the masses now came in contact with art in the twentieth century, neither old forms nor new forms had any a priori appeal for them.

22. Quoted in John O'Brian, ed., *Clement Greenberg: The Collected Essays and Criticism* (Chicago, 1986), 1:xxii; Wald, *New York Intellectuals*, p. 207.

23. Clement Greenberg, "Avant-Garde and Kitsch," *Partisan Review* 6 (Fall 1939): 34–49.

CHAPTER SEVEN

1. Suggestions of Macdonald's centrality in mass culture criticism appear from his contemporaries in Edward Shils, "Daydreams and Nightmares: Reflections on the Criticism of Mass Culture," *Sewanee Review* 65 (1957): 588–89; T. S. Eliot, *Notes towards a Definition of Culture* (1949; reprint, New York, 1968), p. 9; D. W. Brogan, "The Problem of High Culture and Mass Culture," *Diogenes* 5 (1954): 1; Harold Rosenberg, "Pop Culture and Kitsch Criticism," *Dissent* 5 (Winter 1958): 16; and in retrospective interpretations in John Cawelti, untitled review, *American Quarterly* 20 (1968): 254; Joan Shelley Rubin, " 'Information, Please!': Culture and Expertise in the Interwar Period," *American Quarterly* 35 (Winter 1983): 501; James Gilbert, *A Cycle of Outrage: America's Reaction to the Juvenile Delinquent in the 1950s* (New York, 1986), p. 119; Charles C. Alexander, *Holding the Line: The Eisenhower Era, 1952–1961* (Bloomington, Ind., 1975), p. 142; Christopher Brookeman, *American Culture and Society since the 1930s* (New York, 1984), p. 46. Examples of direct criticism of Macdonald from newer critics are in Christopher Lasch, "Mass Culture Reconsidered," *democracy* 1 (October 1981): 9–10; Tania Modleski, introduction to Modleski, ed., *Studies in Entertainment, Critical Approaches to Mass Culture* (Bloomington, Ind., 1986), pp. ix–x, xix; and Donald Lazere, "Introduction: Entertainment as Social Control," in Lazere, ed., *American Media and Mass Culture* (Berkeley, 1987), p. 2. Critics' objections to the larger approach he typified are in Paul Buhle, "Introduction: The 1960s Meet the 1980s," in Buhle, ed., *Popular Culture in America* (Minneapolis, 1987), p. xv; and Juan Flores, "Reinstating Popular Culture: Responses to Christopher Lasch," *Social Text* 4 (1985): 116–17. The origins of the

"mass culture" phrase, which did not involve Macdonald, were examined in the Introduction.

2. Diana Trilling, "An Interview with Dwight Macdonald," in William Phillips, ed., *Partisan Review: The Fiftieth Anniversary Edition* (New York, 1984), p. 327. This interview provides several fascinating insights to Macdonald. It was conducted in the spring of 1979 and his recollections were, of course, dependent upon his memory. I have quoted from the transcript when Macdonald's statements are supported by contemporary evidence of his thinking.

3. Dwight Macdonald, "Politics Past," in Macdonald, *Memoirs of a Revolutionist: Essays in Political Criticism* (New York, 1957), p. 7; Stephen Whitfield, *A Critical American: The Politics of Dwight Macdonald* (Hamden, Conn., 1984), p. 6. See also James B. Gilbert, *Writers and Partisans: A History of Literary Radicalism in America* (New York, 1968), p. 169; and Alexander Bloom, *Prodigal Sons: The New York Intellectuals and Their World* (New York, 1986), p. 72. The Hedonists' bywords, expressed on their stationery, were "CYNICISM, ESTHETICISM, CRITICISM, PESSIMISM."

4. Dwight Macdonald, "The Teaching of English at Yale," *Yale Lit.* (1927), described in Macdonald, *Discriminations: Essays and Afterthoughts, 1938-1974* (New York, 1974), p. 174, n. 1; Macdonald, *Memoirs of a Revolutionist*, p. 7; Macdonald later recalled Phelps as being "the god of all those athletes." See Trilling, "Interview with Dwight Macdonald," p. 318. The discussion of Phelps is in Rubin, "Culture and Expertise in the Interwar Period," *American Quarterly* 35 (Winter 1983): 502-10. Macdonald later recalled that he "despised" his classmates at Exeter and Yale: "They were just ordinary guys and I was quite a bright fellow. I just had the biggest contempt for them." Trilling, "Interview with Macdonald," p. 317.

5. Trilling, "Interview with Macdonald," p. 317. On Mencken and the larger antibourgeois criticism of the 1920s, see Frederick J. Hoffman, *The Twenties*, rev. ed. (New York, 1962), pp. 344-415; George H. Douglas, *H. L. Mencken, Critic of American Life* (Hamden, Conn., 1978).

6. Macdonald, "Politics Past," pp. 7-8; Trilling, "Interview with Macdonald," p. 314; Whitfield, *A Critical American*, pp. 6-7.

7. Dwight Macdonald, review of Eliot, *For Lancelot Andrewes*, *Miscellany* 1 (December 1929): 39, 38. Gilbert, *Writers and Partisans*, p. 169. The *Miscellany* was published with Frederick Dupee and George L. K. Morris, later fellow *Partisan Review* editors.

8. Macdonald, "Robinson Jeffers," *Miscellany* 1 (July 1930): 1.

9. Macdonald, "Our Elizabethan Movies," *Miscellany* 1 (December 1929): 29, 33, 27, 28. Macdonald did not offer a blanket praise for the medium, however. Comparing films to Elizabethan theater, which also turned out hundreds of productions a year, he saw the same "complete chaos of good, bad, and mediocre." In many of the most impressive pictures, in fact, brilliant technique

overcame "slight philosophical content." But, as Macdonald explained, "That nine out of ten movies are cheap, banal, drearily shallow means nothing except that, as everyone knows, nine out of ten attempts at artistic creation are failures. The tenth film justifies the rest."

10. Macdonald, "Eisenstein, Pudovkin and Others," *Miscellany* 1 (March 1931): 21, 19.

11. "The Communist Party," *Fortune* 10 (September 1934): 69–74, 154–56, 159–60, 162. Macdonald explains he was the author of the article in Trilling, "Interview with Macdonald," p. 316; Gilbert, *Writers and Partisans*, p. 172.

12. Macdonald, *Memoirs of a Revolutionist*, pp. 9–12, 17; Trilling, "Interview with Macdonald," pp. 314–17; "The Communist Party," *Fortune* 10 (September 1934): 156, 160; Whitfield, *Critical American*, p. 11.

13. Macdonald, "Politics Past," p. 9. See also Whitfield, *Critical American*, p. 9.

14. Macdonald, "Politics Past," p. 25; Trilling, "Interview with Macdonald," p. 313; Whitfield, *Critical American*, pp. 11–13.

15. Richard Pells, *The Liberal Mind in a Conservative Age* (New York, 1985), pp. 174–81; Whitfield, *Critical American*, pp. 43–53. Contributors to *Politics* between 1944 and 1949 included Bruno Bettelheim, Albert Camus, Simone Weil, George Orwell, C. Wright Mills, Richard Hofstadter, Oscar Handlin, Milton Mayer, Paul Goodman, Irving Kristol, James Agee, Nathan Glazer, Daniel Bell, and Marshall McLuhan.

16. Dwight Macdonald, "A Theory of Popular Culture," *Politics* 1 (February 1944): 20–23. Macdonald added, in a note on p. 21, "The success of *Reader's Digest* illustrates the law: here is a magazine which in a few years has attracted an enormous circulation simply by reducing to even lower terms the already superficial formula of commercial periodicals. Where *Harpers* treats in six pages a theme requiring twelve, *Reader's Digest* cuts the six pages to two, making it three times as 'readable' and three times as superficial."

17. Ibid., pp. 22–23.

18. Ibid., p. 21.

19. Ibid., pp. 20–23; Dwight Macdonald, "A Theory of Mass Culture," *Diogenes* 3 (Summer 1953): 1–17, reprinted in Bernard Rosenberg and David Manning White, eds., *Mass Culture* (Glencoe, Ill., 1957), pp. 59–73; Dwight Macdonald, "Masscult and Midcult," *Partisan Review* (Spring, Summer, 1960), reprinted in Dwight Macdonald, *Against the American Grain* (New York, 1962), pp. 3–75.

20. Macdonald, "Popular Culture," p. 20; Macdonald, "Mass Culture," p. 59.

21. Macdonald, "Mass Culture," pp. 61, 62.

22. Ibid., p. 69. (Emphasis in original.) Macdonald's ideas about "masses" and their inability to have "culture" can be traced virtually verbatim to a response to his "Theory of Popular Culture" by a *Politics* writer identified only as "European." See "Notes on Mass Culture," *Politics* 3 (November 1946): 353–56.

23. Macdonald, "Mass Culture," pp. 69, 70.

24. Macdonald, "Future of Democratic Values," *Partisan Review* 10 (July–August 1943): 330–31, 332.

25. Dwight Macdonald, "The Responsibility of Peoples," *Politics* 2 (March 1945): 86–87. A good discussion of this piece and of Macdonald's philosophy in this era is in Robert Cummings, "Resistance and Victimization: Dwight Macdonald in the 1940s," *New Politics* 1 (Summer 1986): 213–32; Whitfield, *Critical American*, pp. 58–63.

26. Dwight Macdonald, "The Bomb," *Politics* 2 (September 1945): 260, quoted in Paul Boyer, *By the Bomb's Early Light* (New York, 1985), p. 234. Boyer provides an overview of Macdonald's criticisms of the bombings, pp. 233–37; Whitfield, *Critical American*, pp. 63–64; Pells, *Liberal Mind*, pp. 45–46.

27. Dwight Macdonald, "Too Big," *Politics* 3 (December 1946): 391; Dwight Macdonald, "The Root Is Man," *Politics* 3 (April 1946): 104–8. See also Cummings, "Macdonald in the 1940s," *New Politics* 1 (Summer 1986): 224–26; Boyer, *Bomb's Early Light*, pp. 235–37; Whitfield, *Critical American*, pp. 65–72. The support for "anarchist decentralization" is in Macdonald, "Why I Am No Longer a Socialist," *Liberation* 3 (May 1958): 7.

28. Melvin Lasky, " 'The Breadline and the Movies,' " *Politics* 1 (February 1944): 10. Veblen's piece under this title appeared as an editorial in the *Dial*, 14 June 1919.

29. Dorothy McKenzie, "The Time the Lady Writer Imagined Me," *Politics* 3 (August 1946): 243; Arthur Steig, "Jazz, Clock and Song of Our Anxiety," *Politics* 2 (August 1945): 246–47.

30. Irving Howe, "Notes on Mass Culture," *Politics* 5 (Spring 1948): 120–23, reprinted in Rosenberg and White, eds., *Mass Culture*, pp. 496–503; quotations from p. 497.

31. For the history of the institute, see Martin Jay, *The Dialectical Imagination* (Boston, 1973), and his article, "The Frankfurt School in Exile," *Perspectives in American History* 6 (1972): 339–85; Anthony Heilbut, *Exiled in Paradise* (New York, 1983), pp. 84–91.

32. Jay, "Frankfurt School," pp. 367, 344, 355–56, 358, 366–67.

33. Dwight Macdonald, "Field Notes," *Politics* 2 (April 1945): 112–13. He also cited Erich Fromm's *Escape from Freedom* in "The Future of Democratic Values," *Partisan Review* 10 (July–August 1943): 328. In "A Theory of Mass Culture" in 1953, he repeated these references, with paraphrases of Horkheimer and Lowenthal, and added a section praising Adorno's "brilliant essay" on popular music (the essay had appeared in the 1941 mass communications issue). He wrote of Adorno and Lowenthal again in "Masscult and Midcult" in 1960. Jay suggests the Frankfurt School influenced Macdonald in "Frankfurt School in Exile," p. 367.

34. Max Horkheimer, "Art and Mass Culture," *Zeitschrift für Sozialforschung* 9 (1941): 294, 292–93, 293–94.

35. Ibid., p. 292; Jay, *Dialectical Imagination*, pp. 179–80; Stanley Aronowitz,

"Enzensberger on Mass Culture: A Review Essay," *Minnesota Review* (Fall 1976): 95. For overviews of Critical Theory's mass society and culture criticism, see also Patrick Brantlinger, *Bread and Circuses: Theories of Mass Culture as Social Decay* (Ithaca, N.Y., 1983), pp. 222–48; H. Stuart Hughes, *The Sea Change: The Migration of Social Thought 1930–1965* (New York, 1975), pp. 134–88; Oscar Negt, "Mass Media: Tools of Domination or Instruments of Liberation? Aspects of the Frankfurt School's Communications Analysis," in Kathleen Woodward, ed., *The Myths of Information: Technology and Postindustrial Culture* (Madison, Wis., 1980), pp. 65–87.

36. Horkheimer, "Art and Mass Culture," p. 303.
37. On Arendt's book and its influence, see Pells, *Liberal Mind*, pp. 85–96; Heilbut, *Exiled in Paradise*, pp. 407–14.
38. Hannah Arendt, *The Origins of Totalitarianism* (New York, 1951); Dwight Macdonald, "A New Theory of Totalitarianism," *New Leader* 34 (14 May 1951): 17–19. Macdonald's political outlook in 1951 was captured in his praise for Arendt for recognizing "our society is rotting and that, if the Nazi-Soviet totalitarians are the extreme expression of this rot, their liberal-progressive opponents are also infected, and that a fundamentally new way of thinking (and, above all, feeling) is necessary if we are to escape destruction" (p. 17).
39. Macdonald, "Masscult and Midcult," pp. 36–37.
40. Macdonald, "Theory of Mass Culture," pp. 63–64, 51, 40, 41–47; Macdonald, "Masscult and Midcult," p. 54.
41. Macdonald, "Masscult and Midcult," pp. 75, 71–72, 73. On the question of whether those who have been conceived as masses had become automata, see Macdonald's disagreements with Raymond Williams's *The Long Revolution* in his review, "Looking Backward," *Encounter* (June 1961), reprinted in *Against the American Grain*, pp. 229–39.

EPILOGUE

1. Oscar Lewis, "Urbanization without Breakdown: A Case Study," *Scientific Monthly* 75 (July 1952): 31–41. Robert Redfield, *Tepoztlan: A Mexican Village* (Chicago, 1930), and "The Folk Society," *American Journal of Sociology* 52 (January 1947): 293–308. The strongest challenge to Redfield was Oscar Lewis's reevaluation of the village in *Life in a Mexican Village, Tepoztlan Restudied* (Urbana, Ill., 1951). The revision was extended in Horace Miner, "The Folk-Urban Continuum," *American Sociological Review* 17 (October 1952): 529–37; George M. Foster, "What Is Folk Culture?," *American Anthropologist* 55 (April–June 1953): 159–73; and briefly summarized in Noel P. Gist and Sylvia F. Fava, *Urban Society*, 6th ed. (New York, 1974), pp. 33–34. The interwar social science approaches to modernization were treated in Chapter 4.

2. William A. Schwab, *Urban Sociology* (Reading, Mass., 1982), pp. 22–23; Peter Saunders, *Social Theory and the Urban Question*, 2d ed. (New York, 1986), pp. 104–5. The reference is to Louis Wirth's "Urbanism as a Way of Life," discussed in Chapter 4. Wirth's model had acknowledged the possibility of such surviving "social worlds" in the modernizing process, but proof of their existence nonetheless was interpreted as a blow to his urbanization theory. A more comprehensive summary of the literature rebutting Wirth's hypothesis is in Thomas Bender, *Community and Social Change in America* (Baltimore, 1978), pp. 25–27.

3. Leon Bramson, *The Political Context of Sociology* (Princeton, 1961); Daniel Bell, "The Theory of Mass Society: A Critique," *Commentary*, July 1956, pp. 75–83; quotations appear on pp. 83, 78; Edward Shils, "Daydreams and Nightmares: Reflections on the Criticism of Mass Culture," *Sewanee Review* (1957): 587–608, "Mass Society and Its Culture" *Daedalus* 89 (Spring 1960): 288–314, and "The Theory of Mass Society," *Diogenes* 39 (1962): 45–66; the quotation appears in this last article, p. 47. The comprehensive review of mass society theory, William Kornhauser's *The Politics of Mass Society* (Glencoe, Ill., 1959), suggested modern society was very susceptible to, but not characterized by, mass properties. See also Harold Wilensky, "Mass Society and Mass Culture: Interdependence or Independence?," *American Sociological Review* 29 (April 1964): esp. 177.

4. Michael R. Real, "Media Theory: Contributions to an Understanding of American Mass Communication," *American Quarterly* 32 (1980): 241–42; Daniel J. Czitrom, *Media and the American Mind* (Chapel Hill, N.C., 1982), pp. 122–26; Roger L. Brown, "Approaches to the Historical Development of Mass Media Studies," in Jeremy Tunstall, ed., *Media Sociology* (London, 1970), pp. 45–47; Melvin L. DeFleur and Sandra Ball-Rokeach, *Theories of Mass Communication*, 3d ed. (New York, 1975), pp. 153–61. The director of the Payne Fund studies of motion pictures in the early 1930s went so far as to translate the hypodermic theory into an equation that multiplied the content and suspected influence of the movies by the frequency of audience attendance to arrive at a measure of the medium's total social impact. See Garth Jowett, *Film: The Democratic Art* (Boston, 1976), esp. pp. 220–21.

5. Todd Gitlin, "Media Sociology: The Dominant Paradigm," *Theory and Society* 6 (1978): 205–53; Real, "Media Theory," p. 242; Czitrom, *Media and the American Mind*, pp. 122–46. Gitlin's article, a thorough critique of the postwar theories of media effects, indicates the continuing debate.

6. John G. Cawelti, "Beatles, Batman, and the New Aesthetic," *Midway* 9 (Autumn 1968): 49–70; Susan Sontag, "One Culture and the New Sensibility" (1965), reprinted in Sontag, *Against Interpretation* (New York, 1966), pp. 293–304. A secondary treatment is Andrew Ross, *No Respect: Intellectuals and Popular Culture* (New York, 1989), pp. 135–70. Irving Howe delivered a blistering rebuke of the "new sensibility" for the older *Partisan Review* intellectuals in "The New York Intellectuals," *Commentary*, October 1968, p. 47. On the relative flexibility

of contemporary cultural categories, see Lawrence Levine, *Highbrow/Lowbrow: The Emergence of Cultural Hierarchy in America* (Cambridge, Mass., 1988), pp. 243–48.

7. For overviews of the newer criticism, see Donald Lazere, ed., *American Media and Mass Culture* (Berkeley, 1987); Tania Modleski, ed., *Studies in Entertainment: Critical Approaches to Mass Culture* (Bloomington, Ind., 1986). Janice Radway is the leading American advocate of the audience reception approach. See her articles "Reading Is Not Eating: Mass-Produced Literature and the Theoretical, Methodological, and Political Consequences of a Metaphor," *Book Research Quarterly* 2 (Fall 1986): 7–29; and "Identifying Ideological Seams: Mass Culture, Analytic Method, and Political Practice," *Communication* 9 (1986): 93–123; and her book *Reading the Romance: Women, Patriarchy, and Popular Literature* (Chapel Hill, N.C., 1984). The "interpretive communities" concept is from Stanley Fish, *Is There a Text in This Class?: The Authority of Interpretive Communities* (Cambridge, Mass., 1980). British work is most theoretically advanced in appreciating the dynamics of popular culture reception, particularly the Marxian-Gramscian approach of Stuart Hall and the scholars around the Birmingham Centre for Contemporary Cultural Studies. A central statement is Hall's "Culture, the Media, and the 'Ideological Effect,'" in James Curran et al., eds., *Mass Communication and Society* (London, 1977), pp. 315–48. A useful overview and bibliography of recent approaches to mass culture analysis is in Chandra Mukerji and Michael Schudson, "Popular Culture," *Annual Review of Sociology* 12 (1986): 47–66.

8. Clifford Geertz, "Thick Description: Toward an Interpretive Theory of Culture," in Geertz, *The Interpretation of Cultures: Selected Essays* (New York, 1973), p. 5.

SELECT BIBLIOGRAPHY

NEWSPAPERS AND PERIODICALS

American Magazine, 1909–12
American Review of Reviews, 1908–15
Atlantic Monthly, 1900–1918
Broom, 1922
Charities and the Commons, 1905–9
Commentary, 1948–60
Daily Worker, 1925–39
Dial, 1905–18, 1921–24
Experimental Cinema, 1930–31
Liberator, 1921–22
Little Review, 1916–22
Miscellany, 1929–31
New Masses, 1928–38
North American Review, 1900–1918
Outlook, 1905–16
Partisan Review, 1934–60
Playground, 1912–17
Politics, 1944–49
Seven Arts, 1916–17
Soil, 1916–17
Student Review, 1933–34
Survey, 1909–17
Yale Review, 1911–20

BOOKS, ARTICLES, AND THESES

Aaron, Daniel. *Writers on the Left*. Rev. ed. New York, 1977.
Ackerman, William. "The Dimensions of American Broadcasting." *Public Opinion Quarterly* 9 (Spring 1945): 1–18.
Addams, Jane. *The Spirit of Youth and the City Streets*. New York, 1909.
Alexander, Charles C. *Here the Country Lies*. Bloomington, Ind., 1980.
———. *Holding the Line: The Eisenhower Era, 1952–1961*. Bloomington, Ind., 1975.
Altschuler, Glenn C. *Race, Ethnicity, and Class in American Social Thought*. Arlington Heights, Ill., 1982.

Anderson, D. R., and P. A. Collins. *The Impact on Children's Education: Television's Influence on Cognitive Development.* Washington, D.C., 1988.

Anderson, Nels, and Eduard Lindeman. *Urban Sociology.* New York, 1928.

Ang, Ien. *Watching Dallas: Soap Opera and the Melodramatic Imagination.* Translated by Della Couling. New York, 1985.

Arendt, Hannah. *The Origins of Totalitarianism.* New York, 1951.

Barth, Gunther. *City People: The Rise of Modern City Culture in Nineteenth-Century America.* New York, 1980.

Baughman, James L. *The Republic of Mass Culture: Journalism, Filmmaking and Broadcasting in America since 1941.* Baltimore, 1992.

Bell, Daniel. *The Cultural Contradictions of Capitalism.* New York, 1976.

———. "The Theory of Mass Society: A Critique." *Commentary,* July 1956, pp. 75–83.

Bellman, Samuel I. *Constance M. Rourke.* Boston, 1981.

Bender, Thomas. *Community and Social Change in America.* Baltimore, 1978.

Bird, S. Elizabeth. *For Enquiring Minds: A Cultural Study of Supermarket Tabloids.* Knoxville, 1992.

Bledstein, Burton. *The Culture of Professionalism.* New York, 1976.

Bloom, Alexander. *Prodigal Sons: The New York Intellectuals and Their World.* New York, 1986.

Bowen, Le Roy E., and Mari W. Lambin. "Evidences of Social Relations as Seen in Types of New York City Dance Halls." *Journal of Social Forces* 3 (January 1925): 286–91.

Boyer, Paul. *By the Bomb's Early Light: American Thought and Culture at the Dawn of the Atomic Age.* New York, 1985.

———. *Urban Masses and Moral Order in Urban America, 1820–1920.* Cambridge, Mass., 1978.

Boyer, Paul, et al. *The Enduring Vision.* Lexington, Mass., 1993.

Bramson, Leon. *The Political Context of Sociology.* Princeton, 1961.

Brantlinger, Patrick. *Bread and Circuses: Theories of Mass Culture as Social Decay.* Ithaca, N.Y., 1983.

Brookeman, Christopher. *American Culture and Society since the 1930s.* New York, 1984.

Buhle, Paul, ed. *Popular Culture in America.* Minneapolis, 1987.

Caffrey, Margaret M. *Ruth Benedict.* Austin, 1989.

Cavallo, Dominick. *Muscles and Morals: Organized Playgrounds and Urban Reform, 1880–1920.* Philadelphia, 1981.

Cawelti, John G. *Adventure, Mystery, and Romance: Formula Stories as Art and Popular Culture.* Chicago, 1976.

———. "Beatles, Batman, and the New Aesthetic." *Midway* 9 (Autumn 1968): 49–70.

———. "With the Benefit of Hindsight: Popular Culture Criticism." *Critical Studies in Mass Communication* 2 (1985): 363–79.

Cohen, Norman. "Tin Pan Alley's Contribution to Folk Music." *Western Folklore* 29 (January 1970): 9–20.

Cooke, Patrick. "TV Or Not TV." *In Health* 5 (December/January 1992): 33–43.

Cooney, Terry A. *The Rise of the New York Intellectuals: "Partisan Review" and Its Circle.* Madison, Wis., 1986.

Couvares, Francis G. "The Triumph of Commerce: Class Culture and Mass Culture in Pittsburgh." In *Working-Class America*, edited by Michael H. Frisch and Daniel J. Walkowitz, 123–52. Urbana, Ill., 1983.

Cowley, Malcolm. *Exile's Return.* New York, 1934.

Cressey, Paul G. *The Taxi-Dance Hall: A Sociological Study in Commercialized Recreation and City Life.* Chicago, 1932.

Czitrom, Daniel. *Media and the American Mind.* Chapel Hill, N.C., 1982.

Davie, Maurice R. *Problems of City Life: A Study in Urban Sociology.* New York, 1932.

Davis, Dennis, and Thomas F. N. Puckett. "Mass Entertainment and Community: Toward a Culture-Centered Paradigm for Mass Communication Research." *Communication Yearbook* 15 (1992): 3–34.

Denisoff, R. Serge. "The Proletarian Renascence: The Folkness of the Ideological Folk." *Journal of American Folklore* 82 (January–March 1969): 51–65.

Deutscher, Isaac. *The Prophet Unarmed — Trotsky: 1921–1927.* New York, 1959.

Diggins, John P. *The Rise and Fall of the American Left.* New York, 1992.

———. *Up from Communism.* New York, 1975.

Dimaggio, Paul. "Cultural Entrepreneurship in Nineteenth-Century Boston: The Creation of an Organizational Base for High Culture in America," and "Cultural Entrepreneurship in Nineteenth-Century Boston, Part II: The Classification and Framing of American Art." *Media, Culture, and Society* 4 (1982): 33–50, 303–22.

Dorr, Rheta Childe. *What Eight Million Women Want.* Boston, 1910.

Draper, Theodore. "American Communism Revisited." *New York Review of Books,* 9 May 1985, pp. 32–40.

———. "The Popular Front Revisited." *New York Review of Books,* 30 May 1985, pp. 44–50.

Edsforth, Ronald. "Popular Culture and Politics in Modern America: An Introduction." In *Popular Culture and Political Change in Modern America*, edited by Ronald Edsforth and Larry Bennet, 1–15. Albany, N.Y., 1991.

Ellis, Joseph. *After the Revolution: Profiles of Early American Culture.* New York, 1979.

Erenberg, Lewis. "From New York to Middletown: Repeal and the Legitimization of Night Life in the Great Depression." *American Quarterly* 38 (Winter 1986): 761–78.

————. *Steppin' Out: New York Nightlife and the Transformation of American Culture, 1890–1930*. Chicago, 1981.

Faris, Robert E. L. *Chicago Sociology, 1920–1932*. Chicago, 1967.

Finfer, Lawrence. "Leisure as Social Work in the Urban Community: The Progressive Recreation Movement, 1890–1920." Ph.D. diss., Michigan State University, 1974.

Fish, Stanley. *Is There a Text in This Class?: The Authority of Interpretive Communities*. Cambridge, Mass., 1980.

Fisher, Robert. "Film Censorship and Progressive Reform: The National Board of Censorship of Motion Pictures, 1909–1922." *Journal of Popular Film* 4 (1975): 143–56.

Fiske, John. *Reading The Popular*. Boston, 1989.

————. *Understanding Popular Culture*. Boston, 1989.

Fluck, Winfried. "Popular Culture as a Mode of Socialization: A Theory about the Social Functions of Popular Culture Forms." *Journal of Popular Culture* 21 (Winter 1987): 31–46.

Fox, Richard Wightman, and T. J. Jackson Lears, eds. *The Culture of Consumption*. New York, 1983.

Gans, Herbert. *Popular Culture and High Culture*. New York, 1974.

Geertz, Clifford. "Art as a Cultural System." *Modern Language Notes* 91 (1976): 1473–99.

————. *The Interpretation of Cultures: Selected Essays*. New York, 1973.

Gerstle, Gary. "Mission from Moscow: American Communism in the 1930s." *Reviews in American History* 12 (December 1984): 559–66.

Gilbert, James B. *A Cycle of Outrage: America's Reaction to the Juvenile Delinquent in the 1950s*. New York, 1986.

————. *Writers and Partisans: A History of Literary Radicalism in America*. New York, 1968.

Gitlin, Todd. "Media Sociology: The Dominant Paradigm." *Theory and Society* 6 (1978): 205–53.

Glassberg, David. "Restoring a 'Forgotten Childhood': American Play and the Progressive Era's Elizabethan Past." *American Quarterly* 32 (Fall 1980): 351–68.

Golby, J. M., and A. W. Purdue. *The Civilization of the Crowd: Popular Culture in England 1750–1900*. New York, 1985.

Gorman, Paul R. "The Development of an American Mass Culture Critique, 1910–1960." Ph.D. diss., University of California, Berkeley, 1990.

Gorn, Elliott. "The Wicked World: The *National Police Gazette* and Gilded-Age America." *Media Studies Journal* 6 (Winter 1992): 1–15.

Gowans, Alan. *Learning to See: Historical Perspective on Modern Popular/Commercial Arts*. Bowling Green, Ohio, 1981.

Green, Martin. *The Problem of Boston: Some Readings in Cultural History*. New York, 1966.

Guilbaut, Serge. *How New York Stole the Idea of Modern Art: Abstract Expressionism, Freedom, and the Cold War.* Chicago, 1983.

Hardy, Stephen, and Alan G. Ingham. "Games, Structures, and Agency: Historians of the American Play Movement." *Journal of Social History* 17 (Winter 1983): 285–301.

Harris, Neil. *The Artist in American Society.* Chicago, 1966.

Harrison, Helen A. "John Reed Club Artists and the New Deal: Radical Responses to Roosevelt's 'Peaceful Revolution.'" *Prospects* 5 (1980): 241–68.

Hartt, Rollin Lynde. *The People at Play.* 1909. Reprint. New York, 1975.

Haskell, Thomas L. *The Emergence of Professional Social Science: The American Social Science Association and the Nineteenth-Century Crisis of Authority.* Urbana, Ill., 1977.

Havig, Alan. "The Commercial Amusement Audience in Early Twentieth-Century American Cities." *Journal of American Culture* 5 (Spring 1982): 1–19.

Heilbut, Anthony. *Exiled in Paradise.* New York, 1983.

Higham, John. "A Matrix of Specialization." In *The Organization of Knowledge in Modern America, 1869–1920,* edited by Alexandra Oleson and Andrew Voss, 3–18. Baltimore, 1979.

——. "The Reorientation of American Culture in the 1890s." In *The Origins of Modern Consciousness,* edited by John Weiss, 25–48. Detroit, 1965.

Hoffman, Frederick J. *The Twenties.* Rev. ed. New York, 1962.

Hoffman, Frederick J., Charles Allen, and Carolyn T. Ulrich. *The Little Magazine.* Princeton, 1946.

Hollinger, David A. "Ethnic Diversity, Cosmopolitanism and the Emergence of the American Liberal Intelligentsia." *American Quarterly* 28 (1975): 133–51.

Homberger, Eric. "Proletarian Literature and the John Reed Clubs, 1929–1935." *American Studies* 13 (1979): 221–44.

Hoopes, James. "The Culture of Progressivism: Croly, Lippman, Brooks, Bourne, and the Idea of American Artistic Decadence." *Clio* 7 (Fall 1977): 91–111.

——. *Van Wyck Brooks, in Search of American Culture.* Amherst, Mass., 1977.

Horowitz, Daniel. *The Morality of Spending: Attitudes toward the Consumer Society in America, 1875–1940.* Baltimore, 1985.

Horowitz, Helen L. *Culture and the City.* Lexington, Ky., 1976.

Howe, Irving. *Decline of the New.* New York, 1970.

——. *A Margin of Hope.* New York, 1982.

——. "The New York Intellectuals: A Chronicle and a Critique." *Commentary,* October 1968, pp. 29–51.

Howe, Irving, and Lewis Coser. *The American Communist Party.* New York, 1957.

Hughes, H. Stuart. *Consciousness and Society: The Reorientation of European Social Thought.* New York, 1958.

———. *The Sea Change: The Migration of Social Thought 1930–1965*. New York, 1975.

Hyman, Stanley Edgar. "Ideals, Dangers, and Limitations." In *Culture for the Millions?*, edited by Norman Jacobs, 124–41. Princeton, 1961.

Jacobs, Norman, ed. *Culture for the Millions?* Princeton, 1961.

Janssens, G. A. *The American Literary Review: A Critical History 1920–1950*. The Hague, 1968.

———. "The *Dial* and the *Seven Arts*." *Papers on Language and Literature* 41 (Fall 1968): 442–58.

Jay, Martin. *The Dialectical Imagination*. Boston, 1973.

———. "The Frankfurt School in Exile." *Perspectives in American History* 6 (1972): 339–85.

Joost, Nicholas. *Scofield Thayer and the "Dial."* Carbondale, Ill., 1964.

Jowett, Garth S. *Film: The Democratic Art*. Boston, 1976.

Jumonville, Neil. "The New York Intellectuals and Mass Culture Criticism." *Journal of American Culture* 12 (Spring 1989): 87–95.

Kando, Thomas M. *Leisure and Popular Culture in Transition*. St. Louis, 1975.

Kasson, John. *Amusing the Million: Coney Island at the Turn of the Century*. New York, 1978.

Kazin, Alfred. *Starting Out in the Thirties*. Boston, 1965.

Kirschner, Don S. "The Ambiguous Legacy: Social Justice and Social Control in the Progressive Era." *Historical Reflections* 2 (Summer 1975): 69–88.

Kornhauser, William. *The Politics of Mass Society*. Glencoe, Ill., 1959.

Krieger, Murray. *Arts on the Level: The Fall of the Elite Object*. Knoxville, 1981.

Kusmer, Kenneth. "The Social History of Cultural Institutions: The Upper-Class Connection." *Journal of Interdisciplinary History* 12 (Summer 1979): 137–46.

Lazarsfeld, Paul. "Mass Culture Today." In *Culture for the Millions?*, edited by Norman Jacobs, ix–xxv. Princeton, 1961.

Lazere, Donald, ed. *American Media and Mass Culture*. Berkeley, 1987.

Lears, T. J. Jackson. "A Matter of Taste: Corporate Cultural Hegemony in a Mass Consumption Society." In *Recasting America: Culture and Politics in the Age of the Cold War*, edited by Lary May, 38–57. Chicago, 1989.

———. *No Place of Grace: Antimodernism and the Transformation of American Culture, 1880–1920*. New York, 1981.

Leavis, F. R. *Mass Civilization and Minority Culture*. Cambridge, 1930.

Leonard, Neil. *Jazz and the White Americans*. Chicago, 1962.

Levine, Lawrence. *Black Culture and Black Consciousness: Afro-American Folk Thought from Slavery to Freedom*. New York, 1977.

———. *Highbrow/Lowbrow: The Emergence of Cultural Hierarchy in America*. Cambridge, Mass., 1988.

Lipsitz, George. *Time Passages: Collective Memory and American Popular Culture*. Minneapolis, 1990.

Longstaff, S. A. "The New York Family." *Queen's Quarterly* 83 (Winter 1976): 556–73.

Lowenthal, Leo. "Biographies in Popular Magazines." In *Radio Research 1942–1943*, edited by Paul Lazarsfeld and Frank Stanton, 507–48. New York, 1944.

Lynd, Robert S., and Helen M. Lynd. *Middletown: A Study in American Culture.* New York, 1929.

Lynes, Russell. *The Lively Audience.* New York, 1985.

———. *The Tastemakers.* New York, 1955.

McCormick, Richard L. *The Party Period and Public Policy: American Politics from the Age of Jackson to the Progressive Era.* New York, 1986.

Macdonald, Dwight. *Against the American Grain.* New York, 1962.

———. *Discriminations: Essays and Afterthoughts, 1938–1974.* New York, 1974.

———. *Memoirs of a Revolutionist: Essays in Political Criticism.* New York, 1957.

McLean, Albert F., Jr. *American Vaudeville as Ritual.* Lexington, Ky., 1965.

Mailer, Norman. "Up the Family Tree." *Partisan Review* 35 (Spring 1968): 234–53.

Mann, Delbert M., and Stuart A. Queen. *Social Pathology.* New York, 1925.

Marchand, Roland. *Advertising the American Dream: Making Way for Modernity, 1920–1940.* Berkeley, 1985.

Marcus, George E., and Michael J. Fischer. *Anthropology as Cultural Critique.* Chicago, 1986.

Mathews, Fred H. *Quest for an American Sociology.* Montreal, 1977.

May, Elaine T. *Great Expectations.* Chicago, 1980.

May, Henry F. *The End of American Innocence: A Study of the First Years of Our Own Time, 1912–1917.* New York, 1959.

———. *The Enlightenment in America.* New York, 1976.

May, Lary. "Making the American Way: Moderne Theatres, Audiences, and the Film Industry, 1929–1945." *Prospects* 12 (1987): 89–124.

———. *Screening Out the Past: The Birth of Mass Culture and the Motion Picture Industry.* New York, 1980.

———, ed. *Recasting America: Culture and Politics in the Age of the Cold War.* Chicago, 1989.

Mills, C. Wright. *Power, Politics, and People: The Collected Essays of C. Wright Mills.* Edited by Irving Louis Horowitz. New York, 1963.

Modleski, Tania, ed. *Studies in Entertainment, Critical Approaches to Mass Culture.* Bloomington, Ind., 1986.

Moore, Elon H. "Public Dance Halls in a Small City." *Sociology and Social Research* 14 (January–February 1930): 256–63.

Moore, Macdonald Smith. *Yankee Blues: Musical Culture and American Identity.* Bloomington, Ind., 1985.

Mukerji, Chandra, and Michael Schudson. "Popular Culture." *Annual Review of Sociology* 12 (1986): 47–66.

Mumford, Lewis. "On the Dial." *New York Review of Books* 2 (20 February 1964): 3–5.

Naison, Mark. *Communists in Harlem during the Depression.* Urbana, Ill., 1983.

Nash, George H. *The Conservative Intellectual Movement in America.* New York, 1976.

Oleson, Alexandra, and Andrew Voss, eds. *The Organization of Knowledge in Modern America, 1869–1920.* Baltimore, 1979.

Park, Robert E. "Community Organization and the Romantic Temper." *Journal of Social Forces* 3 (May 1925): 673–77.

Peiss, Kathy. *Cheap Amusements: Working Women and Leisure in Turn-of-the-Century New York.* Philadelphia, 1986.

Pells, Richard. *The Liberal Mind in a Conservative Age: American Intellectuals in the 1940s and 1950s.* New York, 1985.

———. *Radical Visions and American Dreams.* Middletown, Conn., 1973.

Perry, Elizabeth I. " 'The General Motherhood of the Commonwealth': Dance Hall Reform in the Progressive Era." *American Quarterly* 37 (Winter 1985): 719–33.

Perry, Lewis. *Intellectual Life in America.* New York, 1984.

Persons, Stow. *American Minds: A History of Ideas.* New York, 1958.

———. *The Decline of American Gentility.* New York, 1973.

Quandt, Jean B. *From the Small Town to the Great Community: The Social Thought of Progressive Intellectuals.* New Brunswick, N.J., 1970.

Radway, Janice. *Reading the Romance: Women, Patriarchy, and Popular Literature.* Chapel Hill, N.C., 1984.

Rakow, Lana F. "Some Good News–Bad News about a Culture-Centered Paradigm." *Communication Yearbook* 15 (1992): 47–57.

Real, Michael. "The Challenge of a Culture-Centered Paradigm: Metatheory and Reconciliation in Media Research." *Communication Yearbook* 15 (1992): 35–46.

———. "Media Theory: Contributions to an Understanding of American Mass Communication." *American Quarterly* 32 (1980): 239–58.

Rogin, Michael. " 'The Sword Became a Flashing Vision': D. W. Griffith's *The Birth of a Nation.*" *Representations* 9 (Winter 1985): 150–95.

———. "The Great Mother Domesticated: Sexual Difference and Sexual Indifference in D. W. Griffith's *Intolerance.*" *Inquiry* 15 (Spring 1989): 510–55.

Rosenberg, Bernard, and David Manning White. *Mass Culture: The Popular Arts in America.* Glencoe, Ill., 1957.

Rosenzweig, Roy. *Eight Hours for What We Will: Workers and Leisure in an Industrial City, 1870–1920.* Cambridge, 1983.

Ross, Andrew. *No Respect: Intellectuals and Popular Culture.* New York, 1989.

Ross, Edward A. *The Outlines of Sociology.* Rev. ed. New York, 1933.

Rossiter, Frank. "The Genteel Tradition in American Music." *Journal of American Culture* 4 (Winter 1981): 107–15.

Rothman, David J. "The State as Parent: Social Policy in the Progressive Era." In *Doing Good: The Limits of Benevolence.* Updated edition, edited by Willard Gaylin et al., 69–95. New York, 1981.

Rubin, Joan Shelley. *Constance Rourke and American Culture.* Chapel Hill, N.C., 1980.

———. *The Making of Middlebrow Culture.* Chapel Hill, N.C., 1992.

Schudson, Michael. *Discovering the News: A Social History of American Newspapers.* New York, 1978.

Schwartz, Lawrence H. *Marxism and Culture: The CPUSA and Aesthetics in the 1930s.* Port Washington, N.Y., 1980.

Sedgewick, Ellery, III. "The American Genteel Tradition in the Early Twentieth Century." *American Studies* 25 (Spring 1984): 49–67.

Seldes, Gilbert. *The Seven Lively Arts.* New York, 1924.

Shi, David. *Matthew Josephson: Bourgeois Bohemian.* New Haven, Conn., 1981.

Shils, Edward. "Daydreams and Nightmares: Reflections on the Criticism of Mass Culture." *Sewanee Review* (1957): 587–608.

———. "Mass Society and Its Culture." *Daedalus* 89 (Spring 1960): 288–314.

———. "The Order of Learning in the United States." In *The Organization of Knowledge in Modern America, 1869–1920,* edited by Alexandra Oleson and Andrew Voss, 19–47. Baltimore, 1979.

———. "The Theory of Mass Society." *Diogenes* 39 (1962): 45–66.

Short, James F. *The Social Fabric of the Metropolis.* Chicago, 1971.

Simkhovitch, Mary Kingsbury. *The City Worker's World in America.* New York, 1917.

Sklar, Robert. *Movie-Made America: A Cultural History of American Movies.* New York, 1975.

Smith, Dennis. *The Chicago School: A Liberal Critique of Capitalism.* London, 1988.

Solomon, Mark I. *Red and Black: Communism and Afro-Americans, 1929–1935.* New York, 1988.

Sproat, John. *The "Best Men": Liberal Reformers in the Gilded Age.* New York, 1968.

Starr, S. Frederick. *Red and Hot: The Fate of Jazz in the Soviet Union.* New York, 1983.

Stein, Roger. *John Ruskin and Aesthetic Thought in America.* Cambridge, Mass., 1967.

Susman, Warren. *Culture as History.* New York, 1984.

Susman, Warren, with Edward Griffin. "Did Success Spoil the United States?: Dual Representations in Postwar America." In *Recasting America: Culture and Politics in the Age of the Cold War,* edited by Lary May, 19–37. Chicago, 1989.

Tashjian, Dickran. *Skyscraper Primitives: Dada and the American Avant-Garde, 1910–1925.* Middletown, Conn., 1975.

Taylor, William R. *In Pursuit of Gotham.* New York, 1992.

Tead, Ordway. *Instincts in Industry: A Study of Working-Class Psychology.* Boston, 1918.

Tebbel, John, and Mary Ellen Zuckerman. *The Magazine in America, 1741–1990.* New York, 1991.

Trotsky, Leon. *Literature and Revolution.* Translated by Rose Strunsky. New York, 1925.

Veysey, Lawrence R. *The Emergence of the American University.* Chicago, 1965.

———. "The Plural Organized World of the Humanities." In *The Organization of Knowledge in Modern America, 1869–1920,* edited by Alexandra Oleson and Andrew Voss, 51–106. Baltimore, 1979.

Wald, Alan. *The New York Intellectuals: The Rise and Decline of the Anti-Stalinist Left from the 1930s to the 1980s.* Chapel Hill, N.C., 1987.

Wasserstrom, William. *The Time of the "Dial."* Syracuse, N.Y., 1963.

Webster, Grant. *The Republic of Letters: A History of Postwar Literary Opinion.* Baltimore, 1979.

Westbrook, Robert. "Lewis Hine and the Ethics of Progressive Camerawork." *Tikkun* 2 (April/May 1987): 24–29.

Weyeneth, Robert Richardi. "Moral Spaces: Reforming the Landscape of Leisure in Urban America, 1850–1920." Ph.D. diss., University of California, Berkeley, 1984.

White, Morton. *Social Thought in America: The Revolt against Formalism.* Boston, 1957.

White, Morton, and Lucia White. *The Intellectual versus the City.* Cambridge, Mass., 1962.

Whitfield, Stephen. *A Critical American: The Politics of Dwight Macdonald.* Hamden, Conn., 1984.

Wilensky, Harold. "Mass Society and Mass Culture: Interdependence or Independence?" *American Sociological Review* 29 (April 1964): 173–97.

Williams, Raymond. *Culture and Society, 1780–1950.* New York, 1958.

———. *Marxism and Culture.* Oxford, 1977.

Wilson, Edmund. *The Shores of Light.* New York, 1952.

Wirth, Louis. "Urbanism as a Way of Life." *American Journal of Sociology* 44 (July 1938): 1–24.

Wood, Arthur Evans. *Community Problems.* New York, 1928.

INDEX

Adamic, Louis, 109
Adams, Samuel Hopkins, 20
Addams, Jane, 40, 46, 47, 50–51
African American music, 16, 80–81
American Magazine, 20
American Review of Reviews, 21–22
Anderson, Margaret, 65, 67
Anderson, Nels: *Urban Sociology*, 85, 89
Anthropology: development of, 96–100; ethnographic paradigm of, 98–99
Apollinaire, Guillaume, 71
Arendt, Hannah: and Dwight Macdonald, 180–81; *Origins of Totalitarianism*, 180–81
Arts: acceptance of, in early America, 28–29; as collectible objects, 29–31; as reform tools, 29–32
Atlantic Monthly, 16, 17, 20, 21
Atomic bombings, 173
Automobiles, 89–90
Auville, Ray and Linda, 129–30

Babbitt, Irving, 56
Bell, Daniel, 188
Benedict, Ruth, 97–98; *Patterns of Culture*, 98
Boas, Franz, 97
Booklist (American Library Association): review of *The People at Play*, 19
Bourgeois outlook, 22–23
Bourne, Randolph, 8, 55; on popular culture, 62–64; on cultural pluralism, 62–65; mass culture criticism of, 62–65; views criticized, 64–65

Bowen, Louise, 37, 38, 40
Bramson, Leon, 188
Brantlinger, Patrick, 4
Braucher, Howard, 45
"Bread and Circuses," 4
Brooks, Van Wyck, 55, 76; *Wine of the Puritans*, 56; on popular culture, 56, 57–58; *America's Coming of Age*, 57–58; views criticized, 60, 73
Broom, 54, 70, 71, 72, 75
Browder, Earl, 124
Burgess, Ernest, 83–84 101, 103, 105

Cawelti, John, 190
Chaplin, Charlie, 77–78
Chase, Stuart: *Mexico: A Study of Two Americas*, 98, 105
Chicago School sociologists, 101–6
Claudy, C. H., 21
Coady, Robert J., 68–70, 204 (n. 17)
Collier, John, 40, 86–87 94
Comer, Cornelia, 15
Commerce: and mass culture, 40–41, 135
Commercialized recreation, 84, 95, 102, 103
Communism, American: mass culture criticism of, 8, 108–36; mass culture criticism of, three periods, 111–36; Soviet influence, 112; mass culture criticism of, moralism in, 115–16; nature of membership, 1920s, 116; mass culture criticism of, intellectual bias, 116–17; mass culture criticism of, and victimization theory, 120–22; mass culture criticism of, views criticized, 120–23, 134–36;

mass culture criticism of, and progressives' criticisms, 122–23; folk culture program of, 128–32; mass culture criticism of, in Popular Front era, 130; mass culture criticism of, and critical tradition, 132, 135; mass culture criticism of, on jazz, 133–35; proletarian culture movement, 138–39; and Dwight Macdonald, 164–65

Composers Collective, 129, 212 (n. 28); *Songs of the People*, 129; *Workers Song Book*, 129

Comstock, Anthony, 26

Conservative intellectuals: mass culture criticism of, 7, 13–33; social problems of, in early twentieth century, 14–15; class and ethnic prejudices of, 22; WASP backgrounds of, 22; bourgeois outlook of, 22–23; and cultural hierarchy, 28–33; assumption of universal aesthetic standards, 31–33; modernists on, 54–55

Cooley, Charles Horton, 90

Cressey, Paul: *The Taxi-Dance Hall*, 103

Critical Theory (Frankfurt School): defined, 176–78; and Dwight Macdonald, 177–80

Cultural hierarchy, 28–33; establishment of, 6; and popular arts, 28; and cultural philanthropists, 30–31; in Gilded Age, 30–32; and modernists, 54, 60–61; anthropological model, 97; and sociological theory, 101; opposition to, 190

Cultural journals, 16–17

Curti, Merle, 131–32

Cutten, George Barton: *The Threat of Leisure*, 95–96

Dadaism: defined, 70; in America, 70–71; on popular culture, 71; on popular culture, views criticized, 71

Daily Worker, 116, 117, 130, 134; in Third Period, 117–18; changing cultural policy, 124

Dance halls: progressive intellectuals on, 35–38, 41–42; social problems in, 92; substitute versions of, 92

Davie, Maurice: *Problems of City Life*, 85, 86, 87, 89, 90, 92

Deland Lorin, 32

Dial (Chicago), 16, 20, 21, 204–5 (n. 24); review of *The People at Play*, 19

Dial (New York), 54, 72–76; aesthetic theory of, 72–76; mass culture criticism of, 74–76

Dickens, Charles, 171

Dimaggio, Paul, 6, 198 (n. 24)

Dorr, Rhetta Childe, 35, 43, 44, 49

Dunbar, Robin, 116

Dupee, Frederick, 165

Edsforth, Ronald, 2

Eisenstein, Sergei, 119

Eliot, T. S., 73, 161–62

Elitism: of modernists, 66–68; of New York Intellectuals, 157

England, Elizabethan, 50–51

Ethnography, 97–101

Experimental Cinema, 118–19

Fascism, 176

Fischer, Michael, 98–99

Folk culture: presumed death of, 50–51, 91–94; survival in modern era, 106, 132; American intellectuals on, in 1930s, 130–32

Folk music, 128–30, 212–13 (n. 31)

Formalism, 73–75

Fortune, 135, 161, 165

Frank, Waldo, 55

Frankfurt School: history of, 176; and Dwight Macdonald, 176–80, 221 (n. 33); mass culture criticism of, 179

Gans, Herbert: *The Urban Villagers*, 187

Geertz, Clifford, 26, 192

Genteel intellectuals. *See* Conservative intellectuals

Gold, Michael: background, 112–13; call for proletarian literature, 113; mass culture criticism of, and Van Wyck Brooks's criticism, 113–14; mass culture criticism of, 113–15, 121–22, 211 (n. 18); mass culture criticism of, and progressives' criticism, 114–15; mass culture criticism of, views criticized, 114–15; *New Masses* criticism, 117; on folk music, 129–30; on white patronization of jazz, 134; criticized by New York intellectuals, 139, 147

Gordon, Milton: *Assimilation in American Life*, 187

Gordon, Robert W., 131

Gorky, Maxim, 133

Gorn, Elliott, 27

Great Depression. *See* Communism, American; New York Intellectuals

Greenberg, Clement: creates new mass culture criticism, 150, 153–56; "Avant-Garde and Kitsch," 152–56; view of public's cultural capacity, 154

"Gresham's Law of Culture," 168

Hale, Hope, 125

Hall, Stuart, 223 (n. 7)

Hartt, Rollin Lynde, 17–23, 32, 44; on popular culture audiences, 23; *The People at Play*, 32–33

Heap, Jane, 67–68

Hearst, William Randolph, 24

Herriman, George. *See* "Krazy Kat"

Herzog, Herta, 177

Hicks, Granville, 139, 147

"Highbrow/Lowbrow" argument, 57–58

Horkheimer, Max, 176, 177; "Art and Mass Culture," 178–79

Horowitz, Helen, 198 (n. 24)

Howe, Frederic, 47

Howe, Irving, 175–76

Immigrants: Jewish, in motion picture industry, 15; Jewish, in popular music industry, 16; conservatives on, 22

Industrial work, 45, 86–87

Intellectuals: bias against television, 1; Left and liberal, optimism of, 4–5; as distinct group, 6; as "democratic clerisy," 10; paternalism, 10; and social diversity, 10–11, 52; and turn-of-the-century problems, 15; scientific worldview, 23–26; optimism of, before World War I, 71–72; new views of entertainments, 126–28; and view of public, 186; Left and liberal, and differences with public, 189–90. *See also* Communism, American; Conservative intellectuals; Macdonald, Dwight; Modernist intellectuals; New York Intellectuals; Progressive intellectuals; Social scientists

Israels, Belle, 38, 40, 41–42

Jacobs, Jane: *The Death and Life of Great American Cities*, 187

Jacobs, Lewis, 118–20, 210 (n. 13)

Jazz, 80–81; Gilbert Seldes on, 80–81;
  Communists on, 133–35
Jeffers, Robinson, 161–62
John Reed Club, 117, 123, 138, 209–10
  (n. 11)
Josephson, Matthew, 70–71
Journal of Popular Culture, 191
Juvenile delinquency, 86

Kant, Immanuel, 29–30
Kierkegaard, Soren, 183
"Krazy Kat" (Herriman), 77–78
Krieger, Murray, 29

Lasky, Melvin, 174
Lazarsfeld, Paul, 6
League of American Writers, 124–26
Leisure, 94–96, 206–7 (n. 17)
Levine, Lawrence, 6, 30
Lindeman, Eduard: *Urban Sociology*,
  85, 89
"Little magazines," 54. See also *Broom*;
  Dial; *Little Review*; *Miscellany*;
  Modernism; *Secession*; *Seven Arts*;
  Soil
Little Review, 54, 65–68, 69, 75 "Lost
  Generation," 127–28
Lowenthal, Leo, 177
Lynd, Robert and Helen: *Middletown*,
  98–100; mass culture criticism of,
  99–100, 105

Macdonald, Dwight: mass culture
  criticism of, 8–9, 148, 158–85; mass
  culture criticism of, exhaustion of
  critique, 9, 183–84; mass culture
  criticism of, shifting of blame,
  150–52; early life, 159; mass culture
  criticism of, and earlier criticisms,
  159; mass culture criticism of, on
  William Lyon Phelps, 159–60; mass
  culture criticism of, and conservative criticism, 160–61, 167–68;
  social-aesthetic theory of, 161–62;
  mass culture criticism of, and progressives' criticism, 162–63; and
  Soviet aesthetic line, 163; mass culture criticism of, and intellectual
  elitism, 163–64; mass culture criticism of, championing of public,
  164; and *Partisan Review*, 165, 166;
  "Theory of Popular Culture," 166–
  70; mass culture criticism of, on
  folk and mass arts, 167; mass culture criticism of, social science criticisms, 167; mass culture criticism
  of, on threat to elite arts, 167–68;
  mass culture criticism of, and modernists' criticism, 167–68, 169–70;
  mass culture criticism of, views criticized, 169–70, 184–85, 191; mass
  culture criticism of, evolution of
  views, 170; "Masscult and Midcult," 170, 181–83; "Theory of Mass
  Culture," 170–81; shifting political
  philosophy, after World War II,
  173–74; mass culture criticism of,
  on mass society, 174–76; mass culture criticism of, and Left mass culture criticism, 183–85
McDowell, Mary, 45
McKenzie, Dorothy, 174–75
Marcus, George, 98–99
Mass culture: origin of phrase, 2;
  defined, 7
Mass culture criticism: defined, 1–2, 7;
  ancient origins of, 4; historiography
  of, 5–7; media of, 7; charges of
  immorality and sensationalism, 7,
  20–23, 37–39, 43, 59–60; and modernization models, 8, 104–7; as ideology, 9–10; and intellectuals' self-
  interest, 9–10; view of public in, 10;
  debut of modern version, 34; and

women, 43; environmental theory, 45–47, 96; charges of damaging families, 47; and social diversity, 51–52; and mass men and women, 62–65; charges of pathology, 84; psychological interpretation, 87; and urban life, 87, 88; ethnographic paradigm in, 98–104; criticism of, 186–92. *See also* Bourne, Randolph; Brooks, Van Wyck; Communism, American; Conservative intellectuals; *Dial* (New York); Frankfurt School; Gold, Michael; Greenberg, Clement; Hartt, Rollin Lynde; Macdonald, Dwight; Modernist intellectuals; Modernization theory; New York Intellectuals; Progressive intellectuals; Seldes, Gilbert; Social scientists

Mass entertainments. *See* Popular culture

Mass society theory: and Randolph Bourne, 62–65; and Dwight Macdonald, 171–75; criticism of, 187–88. *See also* Arendt, Hannah; Bell, Daniel; Bramson, Leon; Shils, Edward

May, Henry, 14

Mead, Margaret: *Coming of Age in Samoa*, 97

Media effects, 189

Mencken, H. L., 76

Mills, C. Wright, 84, 166

Minor, Robert, 115

Miscellany, 161–62

Modernism: defined, 54; media of, 54; and New York Intellectuals, 140–57; and Dwight Macdonald, 168, 179; and Frankfurt School, 179

Modernist intellectuals, 53–81; mass culture criticism of, 8, 75–76, 81–82; mass culture criticism of, and conservatives, 68; mass culture criticism of, views criticized, 75–76

Modernization theory, 180–81; and mass culture critique, 8, 104–7; and mass entertainments, 89, 96, 104; and social scientists, 89, 96, 104–6; criticism of, 105–6, 186–87; and New York Intellectuals, 149–50; view of public in, 149–50; and Dwight Macdonald, 167

Modern Language Association, 2

Moore, Elon, 93

Motion pictures: progressives on, 38–39; Gilbert Seldes on, 81; sociologists on, 91; Communists on, 109–10, 118–21; and intellectuals, 162–63; Dwight Macdonald on, 162–63, 218–19 (n. 9)

Myth orientation. *See* Popular culture

Nation: review of *The People at Play*, 19

National Board of Censorship of Motion Pictures, 42

National Police Gazette, 24, 26

New Masses, 110, 117, 120, 121, 123, 129; and early *Partisan Review*, 142

Newspapers, 24–27

New York Intellectuals: mass culture criticism of, 2, 8, 137–57; and Communist Party, 138–39; mass culture criticism of, social sources, 138–39; on proletarian arts, 138–39; composition of group, 138–40; and Marxism, 139, 141–42; intellectualism of, 140; and European Modernism, 140–41, 215 (n. 8); evolution of *Partisan Review*, 142–50; and literary criticism, 144–45; mass culture criticism of, view of public, 144–45; collapse of first *Partisan Review*, 145;

and new *Partisan Review*, 145–46; on "Lost Generation" intellectuals, 147; aesthetic views of, 147–48; and popular culture, 148–50; mass culture criticism of, views criticized, 149, 152; mass culture criticism of, and conservative criticisms, 150, 157; mass culture criticism of, new argument introduced, 156–57

New Yorker, 148

New York Times: review of *The People at Play*, 19; as information newspaper, 25, 26

New York World, 24

North American Review, 16, 21, 22

Oppenheim, James, 55, 59–60

Ortega y Gasset, Jose, 169

Our Movie-Made Children, 91

Outlook, 37, 38, 43

Pangburn, Weaver, 94

Park, Robert, 100–102

Partisan Review. *See* New York Intellectuals

Paternalism, 48–49, 65

Patten, Simon, 94

Payne Fund studies, 91

"Penny Press," 24

Phelps, William Lyon, 159

Phillips, William, 165; aesthetic standards of, 138–39, 142–45; family background of, 139–40. *See also* New York Intellectuals

Plato: *Phaedrus*, 23

Playground, 45

Play Movement, 51, 201–2 (n. 28)

Politics, 166

Popular culture: recent interpretations, 2, 9, 190–92; historiography of, 5–7; defined, 7; author's interpretation of, 11; expansion of, in

early twentieth century, 15, 36; science orientation, 24–26; myth-orientation, 24–27; multiple readings of, 26–27; reform plans for, 41–42, 50–51; scientific reading, of progressives, 48–49; scientific reading, of modernists, 58–62; expansion of, between World Wars, 84; in Popular Front era, 123–28; expansion of, in 1930s, 126–27. *See also* Automobiles; Dance halls; Jazz, "Krazy Kat"; Motion pictures; Newspapers; "Penny Press"; Sports; Tabloid magazines; Theater, "Tin Pan Alley"

Potamkin, Harry Alan: *The Eyes of the Movie*, 109–10, 120; film criticism of, 119–21, 123–24, 210 (n. 15)

Pound, Ezra, 66–67, 203 (n. 14)

Progressive intellectuals: mass culture criticism of, 8, 34–52, 76; mass culture criticism of, and conservatives, 39, 44–52; mass culture criticism of, three new ideas, 39–42; class and ethnic prejudices, 43, 51–52; and conservatives, 43–44; and universal values, 51–52

Proletarian culture movement, 111–113; and mass culture criticism, 111–23; influence, in early 1930s, 118; intellectual bias in, 118–20

Proletarian Literature in the United States, 123

Radicals, cultural. *See* Modernist intellectuals

Radicals, political. *See* Communism, American

Radway, Janice, 223 (n. 7)

Rahv, Philip, 165; aesthetic standards of, 138–39, 142–45; family background of, 140; and mass culture,

143; and modernism, 143–44. *See also* New York Intellectuals
Rainwater, Clarence, 95
Reader's Digest, 219 (n. 16)
Recreation surveys, 36, 85–86
Redfield, Robert, 98, 187
Reformers. *See* Progressive intellectuals
Riesman, David, 177
Rosenfeld, Paul, 59–60
Rourke, Constance, 131
Ruskin, John, 29

Santayana, George, 73
Saturday Evening Post, 113–14, 115
Science orientation. *See* Popular culture
Scott-James, R. A., 21
Scribner's, 132
Secession, 70, 71, 72, 75
Seeger, Charles, 129, 132
Seldes, Gilbert: on popular culture criticisms, 7; mass culture criticism of, 8, 80–81; and popular culture, 76–82
Seven Arts, 55–65, 70, 71, 73, 74, 75; aesthetic views of, 55–56, 118; intellectualist bias in, 70
Seven Lively Arts, The, 76–81; views criticized, 78–80
Shils, Edward, 188
Simkhovitch, Mary, 37
Social sciences, 96–104
Social scientists: mass culture criticism of, 8, 83–107; appreciation of audiences' cultural demands, 66; mass culture criticism of, and progressives, 87–88. *See also* Anthropology; Ethnography; Sociologists
Sociologists: professional role of, 88–89; recreation ideal of, 89–94. *See also* Social scientists

Sociology, 84, 101
Soil, 68–70, 71, 75
Solon, Israel, 67
Sontag, Susan, 190
Sports, 75
Stearns, Harold: on *Seven Arts*, 61–62; and *America Now*, 128; and *Civilization in the United States*, 128
Steig, Arthur, 174
Sterling, Philip, 121
Stewart, Donald Ogden, 124–25
Student Review, 110
Survey, 40

Tabloid magazines, 108, 109, 125, 127, 132
Tashjian, Dickran, 69
Taxi-Dance Hall, 103–4
Taylor, William R., 25
Tead, Ordway: *Social Pathology*, 86, 89–90
Thayer, Scofield, 73
Theater, 110
"Tin Pan Alley," 121
Trotsky, Leon: and Soviet cultural line, 112; *Literature and Revolution*, 146; and New York Intellectuals, 146; cultural theory of, 146, 216 (n. 15); and Dwight Macdonald, 165

Urban life, 45–46, 187
U.S. Department of Education, 1
U.S. Senate Subcommittee to Investigate Juvenile Delinquency, 2
U.S.S.R.: cultural direction in, 112; Third Period cultural line in, 117; changing cultural line in, 123–28, 150–51; and African Americans, 133; motion pictures in, 150–51

Victim ideology: and mass culture criticism, 8, 35, 47–50; and Communists, 114–15; and African Americans, 134–36; and New York Intellectuals, 145; and Dwight Macdonald, 152, 165–66; criticism of, 188–89

Watson, James Sibley, 73, 74–75
Wendell, Barrett, 56
Wertham, Frederick: *The Seduction of the Innocent*, 2
Whiteman, Paul, 81

Whitman, Walt, 55, 59, 69, 70
Whyte, William F.: *Street Corner Society*, 187
Wilson, Edmund, 73, 76
Winsor, Frederick, 20
Wirth, Louis, 187; "Urbanism as a Way of Life," 101–2, 104–5
Wister, Owen, 21
Wood, Arthur Evans: *Community Problems*, 85, 86, 87, 90, 92